Wittenwiler's *Ring* and the Anonymous Scots Poem
Colkelbie Sow

Fig. 1

FIG. 2

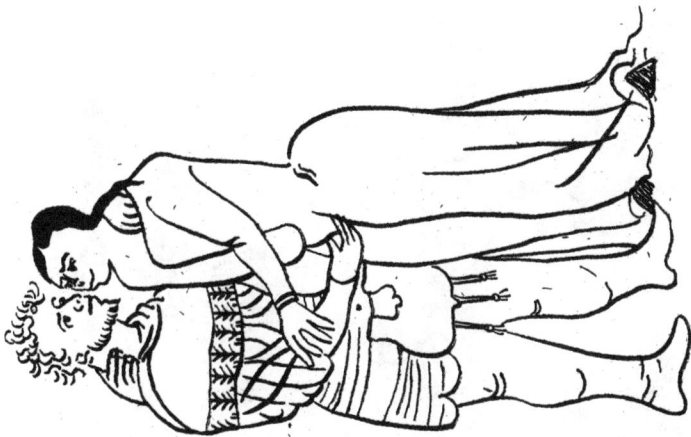

FIG. 4

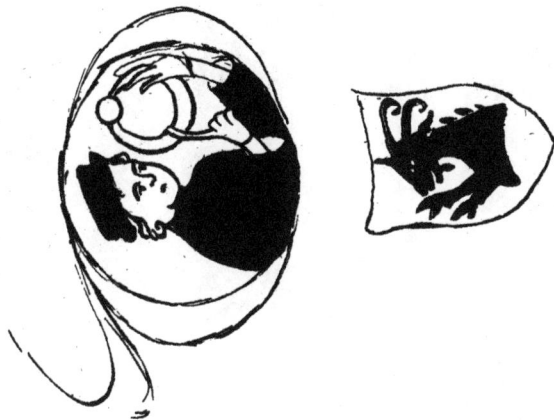

FIG. 3

FIG. 5

Wittenwiler's *Ring* and the Anonymous Scots Poem *Colkelbie Sow*

Two Comic-Didactic Works from the Fifteenth Century

TRANSLATED BY GEORGE FENWICK JONES

UNC Studies in the Germanic Languages and Literatures
Number 18

Suggested citation: Jones, George Fenwick. *Wittenwiler's Ring and the
Anonymous Scots Poem Colkelbie Sow: Two Comic-Didactic Works from
the Fifteenth Century*. Chapel Hill: University of North Carolina Press,
1956. DOI: https://doi.org/10.5149/9781469657615_Jones

Library of Congress Cataloging-in-Publication Data
Names: Jones, George Fenwick.
Title: Wittenwiler's Ring and the Anonymous Scots Poem Colkelbie
    Sow : Two comic-didactic works from the fifteenth century / by
    George Fenwick Jones.
Other titles: University of North Carolina Studies in the Germanic
    Languages and Literatures ; no. 18.
Description: Chapel Hill : University of North Carolina Press, [1956]
    Series: University of North Carolina Studies in the Germanic
    Languages and Literatures.
Identifiers: LCCN 56058739 | ISBN 978-0-8078-8018-0 (pbk)
    | ISBN 978-1-4696-5761-5 (ebook)
Subjects: Colkelbie sow. | Ring.
Classification: LCC PD25 .N6 NO. 18

TABLE OF CONTENTS

WITTENWILER'S *RING*

PART ONE — THE COURTSHIP

PART TWO — THE WEDDING

PART THREE — THE CONFLICT

"COLKELBIE SOW"

FOREWORD TO THE *RING* TRANSLATION

(What is said here of the *Ring* translation largely holds for that
of "Colkelbie Sow," which is included in this volume because of
certain affinities between the two poems. These affinities are
discussed in the exposition following the latter work.)

In speaking of the history of the Swiss Confederacy, Edward
Gibbon said that he would like to study it, "but the materials of
this history are inaccessible to me, fast locked in the obscurity
of an old barbarous German dialect, of which I am totally ig-
norant, and which I cannot resolve to learn for this sole and
peculiar purpose." Similarly Wittenwiler's *Ring* is inaccessible
to many people, being locked in the obscurity of this same old
barbarous German dialect. This is regrettable, since the *Ring*
is a work of considerable value; and it is the purpose of this
translation to unlock it for a larger public.

Goethe once said that translators are like panders who show
us half veiled beauties and thereby arouse in us an irresistible
desire for the original; and it is hoped that this translation will
serve the same purpose. Perhaps a twentieth-century reader
will question whether the *Ring* is really a thing of beauty; but
he can certainly not deny that it is a document of immense
cultural value, for it would be difficult to find any work that
better summarizes the knowledge, tastes, and ideals of its age.
As a true child of the fifteenth century, Wittenwiler loved en-
cyclopaedic knowledge; and consequently his work abounds in
information of every sort and is a treasure trove for students
of medieval literature, history, theology, sociology, law, medi-
cine, warfare, and folklore. Like the theater-director in Goethe's
Faust, he seems to have believed that if you present enough you
are bound to have something for everybody.

Among literary genres alone the *Ring* includes an aubade,
a rondeau, a madrigal, country-dances, a yodel, a Mailehen,
proverbs, farces, a peasant-tournament, a peasant-wedding, a
mock-confession, love-letters, religious allegory, an ars amandi,
a memento mori, and a Totenklage. There are also references
to popular German heroic epics, courtly Arthurian romances,
saints' legends, biblical stories, beast epics, and fables. In addi-
tion, the *Ring* quotes generously from classic and patristic Latin
writers.

The *Ring*'s value lies not only in the abundance of its subject
matter. Because of the ingenuousness of most late-medieval

writers we can often see the true motivation for what they wrote, whereas this is largely concealed from us in contemporary works. Wittenwiler clearly expresses his intent in his preface; and his work is so long and all-embracing that many of his passages, obscure in themselves, are clarified by parallels elsewhere in the text, especially when the latter paraphrase extant Latin writings.

Like many other works of its time, the *Ring* has many passages that strike us today as being in exceedingly poor taste. After first trying to disguise or delete such indelicate passages, I finally decided that any bowdlerization would detract too much from the poem. Recent editions of Chaucer and Rabelais have passages as vulgar as those in the *Ring*, and some current novels have even worse. Therefore, instead of falsifying my matter, I shall warn the gentle reader to proceed no further if he is easily offended. As Chaucer says in warning his reader against his vulgar Miller's tale, "Blameth nat me if that ye chese amys."

The translator is aware of how much the *Ring* loses in a prose translation, for the original owes much of its merriment to Wittenwiler's spirited use of rime and meter, which carry the reader along in a more relaxed and less critical frame of mind. However, twentieth-century readers have no palate for such long-winded versification. Besides that, all attempts at rime are a compromise with the matter; and in the case of the *Ring* the subject matter is clearly more important than the form. To use Wittenwiler's own words, "Wise matter wants no rime" (v. 3520). As we shall see, most of his matter is wise, regardless of its comical disguise.

My translation is based on a photostatic copy of the only known *Ring* manuscript, that in the Landesarchiv in Meiningen, Germany. However, in order that it may serve as a key to the standard edition by Edmund Wiessner, I have followed his verse enumeration and have accepted most of his emendations, declining only those which I find unacceptable or unnecessary. Since the manuscript has no punctuation, I have followed English usage and my own interpretation; and therefore this translation differs considerably from Wiessner's edition in both punctuation and syntax. Typical points in which I deviate from Wiessner and other scholars are summarized in Appendix I.

In many respects Wittenwiler's syntax is closely related to English, in some instances even closer than to modern German. As a result, it has been possible to translate very directly,

sometimes word for word. Because the translation is to serve
as a key to the original, I have often translated literally where
a looser rendition might be more readable. The only major
liberty taken has been in combining many of Wittenwiler's dis-
jointed clauses into compound sentences by adding the con-
junctions implied but not expressed in the text and by changing
demonstrative into relative pronouns. Also, I have omitted
some of the meaningless rime-fillers when their presence would
over-load the English translation.

Sometimes a free translation must be made for better com-
prehension; for example, *hailig öl* (4010) is rendered freely by
"extreme unction" rather than literally by "holy oil;" and the
common German word *Überbein*, when it appears in a nickname
(140), is rendered by "bony bump," since the exact translation
"exostosis" would be impossible in such a context. In two other
verses this word is dropped entirely, since the expressions are
idiomatic and the word merely refers to a lameness (3724) or
to the bruises one will receive (6947). However, in my trans-
lation Wittenwiler's figures of speech are retained, rather than
rendered by their English equivalents, wherever their meaning
is apparent.

In a few cases I have translated one of Wittenwiler's words
with two English ones, because one would not cover all of its
meanings. For example, his word *weisshait* (4466) is rendered
as "prudence" when it appears along with the Christian virtues
of justice, fortitude, and temperance; but it is rendered by
"wisdom" when he says that Solomon preferred it to wealth
(4472).

The manuscript of the *Ring* is written continuously, without
any subdivisions except for its three major parts. However,
for greater convenience in reading it and referring to it, I have
divided it into chapters, to which I have arbitrarily added titles.

No doubt my translation has missed Wittenwiler's meaning
in many spots, but I hope it will at least stimulate interest and
scholarship in this peculiar literary and cultural monument so
that these obscure passages will eventually be illumined. As
Übelgsmack says in the *Ring* (4417), I am doing my best but
am ready to step back if anyone else can do better.

It is both tedious and confusing to read a detailed introduction
to a work before reading the work itself. Therefore, instead
of being preceded by an introduction, this translation is fol-
lowed by an exposition, which is to serve both as an interpreta-

tion of the entire work and as an explanation of various obscure passages. For the latter purpose there is a system of cross-references relating the verses of the poem to the paragraphs of the exposition in which they are explained.

I first became acquainted with the *Ring* in Wiessner's excellent edition, which I have read so many times that I now seem to see the original through his eyes. Also, much of my basic knowledge about the *Ring* came either directly from his scholarly articles, commentary, and personal letters and conversations, or indirectly from literary or scholarly works suggested in them. To him this volume is respectfully dedicated.

THIS BOOK IS CALLED *THE RING*

PREFACE

In praise, service, and honor of the highest Trinity and of Mary, mother and pure maid, and also of all the heavenly host, for the pleasure and joy of the good and for the sorrow and heartfelt pain of the wicked, you shall now hear[33]* a book that is called *The Ring* (It is fitted with a jewel), for it will inform us of the course of the world around us and will well teach us what we should do and leave undone. No finger-ring was ever so good as this, if carefully heeded. In my opinion it should be divided into three separate parts. The first teaches courting, with tilting and jousting, with story-telling and singing, and with other things too. The second can well tell us how a man should conduct himself in soul and body and toward the world. Consider it the best of all. The third part informs you how you can best fare in battles, war time, assaults, fighting, and combat. Thus the fruit of *The Ring* lies in courtliness, manly breeding, virtue, and prowess.[196]   v. 31

Now man has so little constancy that he can not always listen to serious matter without merriment, but rather enjoys great variety. Therefore I have mixed the peasants' shouting with this teaching so that it will convert us all the more easily; yet they are separated with two colors: the red is common to the serious part, the green shows us village life.[150] But listen to me carefully, if you please! In my opinion he is a peasant who lives wrongly and acts foolishly, not he who wisely supports himself with honest work;[177] for, in my eyes, the latter is very blessed,[175] you should believe me. But, in case you see nothing in this that brings either profit or pleasure, then you may accept it as a fictitious tale, said Henry Wittenwiler.[1] Echoing merrily in the heart, the story begins thus: v. 54

---

* Raised numbers refer to the paragraph in the following exposition in which the passage is discussed.

PART ONE – THE COURTSHIP

THE PEASANT TOURNAMENT

In Grausen[45] Valley lay a village named Lappenhausen,[104] charmingly situated and abundantly supplied with wood and water, in which many asstocratic[71] peasants dwelled without sorrow.

Among them was a youth called Bertschi Triefnas, a hero healthy and proud. On holidays[177] he went about as if he had been carved of wood. Be one straight or be one crooked, be one near or be one far, one had to call him "Squire." What more should one tell you? He could conduct himself so well that both old and young women crowded close around him; yet there was one particular one in his heart, and that is the truth.　v. 74

She was called Metzli Rüerenzumph. She was noble, lame, and bent;[73] her teeth and hands were like a coal and her mouth as red as sea sand. Her braid was like a mouse tail; and on her throat hung a goiter that reached down past her belly. Dear companions, hear how her back was hunched: you could have cast a bell on it! Her little feet were so thick and broad that no wind could hurt her by blowing her over, provided she wished to resist it. Her little cheeks were as rosy as ashes and her breasts as small as lard sacks. Her eyes sparkled like the fog, her breath smelled like sulphur, and her garments clung to her as if her soul had fled. She could conduct herself as well as if she were three years old. Do you want another song? She won such praise everywhere that Triefnas never forgot little Metz but became so devoted to her he almost pined away for her.　v. 102

Then began a courting with jousting and tilting. It was on a Sunday [177] that Bertschi was seen coming to the green at Lappenhausen with twelve[76] handsome companions. They rode as undismayed as if they had been drenched with rain. The first was our Triefnas, a hero like a pitcher;[91] his escutcheon was two pitchforks in a dung heap, with which he was very pleased. The second was called Kuontz of the barn, a hero just like wood moss, on whose shield was painted a dead hare in a field of green. The third was called Knotz, well known in all disgraces, who bore two wooden cherry-hooks as his coat-of-arms. They called the fourth one Squire Troll, as courageous as a butter ball, whose emblem was a rake that did not want to be broken. The fifth was Haintzo with the goat, a donkeyman and chivalrous.[71] The pastor had given him his coat-of-arms: three nuts on a grape vine.[86]   v. 131

The sixth one had the name Twerg, a man highborn upon a mountain, whose coat-of-arms was painted with three flies in a glass.[86] The seventh one was called Sir Eisengrein, a real rip-snorter,[38] who wore on his snout[45] nine spoons in one platter. It seems to me the eighth was called Count Burkhart with the bony bump; he had his escutcheon made with two warmly roasted turnips. I'll christen the ninth for you: he was called Pentza Trinkavil, and what he bore on his shield was oxen hitched to a plow. The tenth lived not without harm: he was called Jäckel Grabinsgaden and, because of his ancient lineage, he bore four cow's milk cheeses on a dryer. Be certain of the eleventh's name: he was Rüefli Lekdenspiss; he was the village mayor and his arms were eggs. I do not know the last one's name, but he came riding up to the same circle with a fox-tail.[20] I suppose it was the peasants' scourge, Sir Neidhart, a clever knight who hated all villagers.   v. 160

Their crest[201] was the best of all: a calf in a stork's nest.[86] They bore it jointly in honor of Damsel Metz. Their helmets were woven like baskets[41a] so that no one would smother in them; and beneath them you could see hanging their shields, which were winnowing baskets. Their clothing was of home-spun, well padded with hay and straw; and, if they wished to bind their legs, they used tree bark for that purpose. They sat in knightly fashion on rich pack saddles, on asses and field horses.[101] It would have grieved a Jew,[146] for you could see them cover their horses with blankets and sacks. Their spears were oven rakes. They swept hither and thither frightfully with their piper Gunterfai, who blew his bagpipe[205] in two. v. 182

They shouted with one accord, "Hear, you lords both rich and poor! If anyone desires to joust today and break shield and spear in honor of womankind, he should come against us." But there was no one on the field who dared withstand the heroes; so Triefnas, who never forgot himself,[61] said to his companions,

"And even if it costs my life, there must be courting today with jousting and tourneys! If no one dares withstand us, let's ride against each other."

They were all pleased with his words and called out to

Gunterfai, "Pipe up, dear minstrel! We will pay you well." Gunterfai sounded his bagpipe so that it was heard every-where. v. 204

They tied on their helmets, which were woven with young withes; then they couched their spears and rode against each other. They rode so hard that no one could stay on until help came to him, except for Sir Neidhart, the jolly fellow, who could never be thrown by villagers with crooks. Behold! One could see eleven heroes struggling there on the ground and in the brook, which was to their great discomfort. Triefnas, the very confident man, came to again and saw he had fallen in the grass for Metzi's sake. He was immensely ashamed of that and said, "This year is too long for me! And even if only this had happened to me, you would see me greatly grieved." Then his father's servant came and helped him up; for that was his duty.[168] v. 228

Meanwhile Sir Troll began to wake and shout, "Alack, alas! How hard I've been sleeping!" He began aching in his side, so they had to carry him home. Count Burkhart too was none too lazy as he lay on his back: he asked the lords of the council to help him out of the muck. Knotz had been measured such a blow in his belly that his dinner gushed right out of his mouth; and he could neither sing nor talk nor even bewail his pain. However, help would have been given him but that the others were in peril of their lives, since water was pouring down their throats in the bottom of the brook. They were picked up like friends; for why should they be swelled any more? Yet Twerg had drunk till his eyes sank: they had to cure him of that; so they lifted him up by his feet and let the water run from him until he came to. v. 256

Then Pentza Trinkavil said, "I'll tell you truly, this is the only time I was ever really cured of thirst."

Grabinsgaden was washed without lye and ashes. He said, "I've profited: formerly I was burning, formerly I was stink-ing; in addition my lice are drowned." For that he praised God most diligently. Then said Haintzo with the goat, "Your gain is a straw compared to mine, I'm glad to say. Before I came to the brook, I was a wild heathen, and I was of the order of heretics too! Only now have I become a Christian." v. 274

Behold! That made Kuontz angry. He said, "I think we've lost more than we've won, for we've run into the brook like mice. If you say your lice have drowned, that's a lie; for I've often pulled my pants off and washed them in the brook, but I've never seen a louse drown. And you, Haintzo with the goat, I don't know what you've gained. If you've become a Christian thus, it is a shameful farce; for, according to what wise priests say, no one can baptize himself in a brook in any sort of way. There must be a distinction between you and the baptizer. Also, the baptizer must speak certain words that you can find in holy scripture: yet all that is nothing if the baptizer doesn't have the desire to baptize you when he does so. You've been faint-hearted in serving God, and that's why you've shed little of your blood in His love. Nor do you burn with ardor in your spirit, I tell you. You're still a Jew,[146] believe me!" v. 306

Eisengrein could not refrain from a speech, which you should hear: "Behold! By God's plunder! Isn't it a wonder that Kuontz has become such a good jurist at home on his dung heap? If you'll shut up a minute, I can tell you something for true, without letter or messenger: You have made yourselves ridiculous!"

His message displeased them all, they struck themselves on their foreheads and began to rue their sport. Wow! How loud they shouted, "Now alack, in nommydommy,[182] amen! Alas that we have come together, alas that we have ever jousted! For that we must bear shame and disgrace."

Lekdenspiss the undismayed heard their lament, which caused him pain. He jumped forth noisily: "Hear, all you lords, some words that I will tell you. We'll still have some good sport if you'll follow my instructions. We'll still retain our honor if we tie ourselves tightly in our saddles when we fight with the stranger." v. 334

All were pleased with the advice except for Kuontz of the barn, who alone said, "I don't want to joust and break lung and liver. The sooner I'd try to tie myself, the sooner I'd pass out with pain."

They did not listen to his words; they got on their horses and tied themselves as best they could with withes. Yet Knotz could not stay with them: his riding was of no account, his arse began to pain him however much his heart was set. Thus no more than eight came with all their din onto the field and against the stranger. They called out loud and shouted hard, "Sir foreign fellow, what do you want? If you wish to joust for wealth and ride for fame, then step right up and wait no more." v. 356

Sir Neidhart was pleased with their words, even though he did not show it. He answered courteously and said, "I would like to have my comfort and would like to look for peace, if only you would deign to grant it. Even though it is only in sport, it still wouldn't be right for me to ride against such gentlemen, who are always too noble and strong for me. Even if there were only one of you, I wouldn't dare withstand him; so you ought to let me off."

When they heard his words, their fear was destroyed. They won brave hearts and said, "Listen to the nun, how she speaks and what she says, as scared as a frozen rabbit."

Count Burkhart stepped in front of the others and said privately to Sir Neidhart, "I don't know how you do it, but I well see that you stay in your saddle when we fall. This disgraces us all and pains us in our bellies,[61] and therefore you must joust some more."   v. 384

"In truth," said the stranger most courteously, "may God in Heaven know that I've resolved to do what I have to do."

Thereupon one piped as before. "Helmets on, hey!" how loudly they cried. They waited no longer: swiftly they rode together so violently and hard that Count Burkhart fell right back on his horse's arse. Listen to what else I tell you! One could see his buddy[84] bounce out of his breeches; and now a real misery, fear, and pain arose! The ladies were laughing themselves to death.

Count Burkhart got back into his saddle. "So help me, you bitches," said the man, "you came for adventure, and you've seen adventure!" With that he got up and went away.   v. 405

Then Lekdenspiss stepped up with his sharp countenance and said, "Sir Stranger, you're a rascal, it seems to me in my heart, and therefore you must suffer pain."

The stranger answered him, "Young my lord, what have I done that I should suffer pain? I beg you by God's grace to let me go my way for the sake of worthy womankind." He could have done without his sweet words; for now Lekdenspiss really began rebuking him. He couched a long spear and ran forward just like a plow. He struck the stranger so hard that the calf fell at least halfway out of the nest.[39]

They all enjoyed that and shouted noisily, "Go home, Üeli with the Nose, and help your wife feed the cow."[84]   v. 426

Lekspiss called out of his mouth, "I wouldn't take a hundred pounds for that, but I've got to hit him again. He can't escape me." He took his spear in hand and ran forward against the stranger and struck him by his saddle bow so hard and violently that the straps left him. Because he could not use them any more, the worthy fellow fell three spans deep in the earth. Behold! Then arose plaints of misery such as you have never heard in all your days! How quickly their former laughing was turned into weeping!

The mayor's mouth and nose were bleeding, yet the hero called out freely, "Hear me, all my lords, you shouldn't lament my fall! He didn't hit me, I knocked myself off." He was carried away at once.   v. 449

Eisengrein, a bold warrior, came running up very quickly and said, "May the Devil take him if I don't measure him a blow that'll bowl him over backwards!" He raised a loud shout, "So help me you vagrant rogue![118] If you keep that up any more it'll make me mad and provoke me greatly."

Thereupon Sir Neidhart answered him, "So, my dear sir, so? I'll gladly let the matter drop, if you don't push it any further. I told you before, please note, that I'd do what I had to do."

"Not so," said Sir Eisengrein. "There must be some more fighting. I've got to hit you on your bucket[41a] again, and then may the hangman take you away." Hereupon they tied on their helmets and Eisengrein grabbed his spear.   v. 471

"Up and at him! Up and at him!" the others all shouted loudly, so hot were they against the stranger.

When they wished to come together, the ass under Eisengrein began to cry and flee hither and thither so aimlessly that he could little joust or avenge his injury. His spear fell on the ground and the worthy hero called, "Help me, Lord, and help me quick, or I'll perish on the beast!"

Then a miller came running up after him: "Sir, do you wish to sell the beast? I'll give you ten shillings on the pound right now."[120]

The handsome man answered him, "Just make the ass stand still, and take the saddle along with him. Take him, dear miller, take him!"   v. 493

Hagen was caught with the miller's staff;[207] the others were all running after them, in such a hurry were they to reach the ass. They shouted loudly, "There's nothing to it! Blindfold the ass's eyes and then he'll run straight ahead." Behold! This was done immediately! Hagen was bandaged as if the wolves had flayed him, and thus he sped swiftly against Sir Neidhart's spear. They fought there in knightly fashion, shields and spears were broken without number. v. 506

The stranger could wait no longer: he struck the ass in its side so hard that it at once stretched out all fours, and Eisengrein lay under it. Behold! A new lamentation arose for the noble gentleman who could defend himself so well! Eisengrein was undaunted: he said, "Your lamentation grieves me. See here, in the name of a mare's fart! If my horse has fallen, why should I be blamed? Who can hold on to the sky? I've injured my right hand, and that hurts me more than the shame." With that his speech was over, and Eisengrein left there as fast as he could. v. 525

Triefnas began to stir himself. He started curling his lip, fire gleamed from his eyes, and foam burst from his mouth.[43] My, how he shook with anger! He had completely lost his color, and his sharp tongue began to stammer. No matter what one said or sang, he would not tolerate the stranger, he only wanted to see him dead. And so he began to stutter, "So, you, you, you whore's son, so? Ha-, ha-, have you dared do this? You ma-, ma-, may live no longer!"

Sir Neidhart was a Christian man, and therefore he called to Bertschi, "My lor-, lor-, lord, for God's sake let me, me, me repent be-, be-, before I die." v. 544

Unfortunately that did not help him. His ridicule hurt Bertschi, who said, "Don't pr-, pr-, prate any more." How quickly he tied on his helmet and took his spear in his hand! He wanted to rush against the man and settle accounts with him; but somehow his horse stumbled on a pea so that its knees sank to the ground as if it had not drunk. Triefnas fell over and over so hard on his head that he moaned and also groaned. He cursed all women pure: "You wenches, sluts, and wicked bitches, may evil Death lay you low because of the agony I suffer just for your favor. To what have you now brought me?" v. 564

But then he thought again of his worthy Lady Metz and hushed, for he was sorry. Thereupon he began another song, "I'm a disreputable man if I don't win the ladies' favor, even if I should die four times for it." He began looking up and shouting, "I've not received my due. Help me into my saddle again; and then, if I don't strike him down, say I'm an ass." Thereupon at least three of them came up and helped the brave man get back on the mare.[101] If he had formerly been tied tight, they now tied him three times tighter. They ordered the piper to play again.

"Let go! Let go!" they cried defiantly. They couched their spears and crouched their backs defensively behind their shields and ran so admirably that two oven-rakes fell in pieces. The baker had to pay for that; so he began cursing and scolding about his two oven-rakes. 　　　　　　　　　　　　　v. 592

Bertschi promised, "Don't worry, I'll give you hay and straw; bring me two more oven-rakes," and that was quickly done. Triefnas said, "Now you'll see whether I can serve the ladies!" and he ran against the stranger again. That provoked Sir Neidhart, who gave the lover such a blow they would never have found him, except that he was so strongly tied that he could in no way get down from the horse. All that brought him disgrace. His bonds made him hang in the mare's hooves; and, if I tell it rightly, his hair and beard were combed too hard. Moreover, if they had not come to his help, the dragging would have taken his life. Even so, he was about to faint with pain; and now at last he realized what Kuontz had told him when he last took leave of him.[39] 　　　　　　　　　　　v. 617

The ladies shouted till it rang. "Helmets off, helmets off," was their song. The piping completely subsided. And what were the others supposed to be doing? That you may actually know: they were almost shitting with the fear they had; and they wanted to quit their sport.

Nevertheless Lekspiss said, "We are still sure of our lives, and we could win fame if we killed the stranger. There are still four of us left; if we couldn't defeat one man then it would be wrong for us to eat or dwell in Lappenhausen. Therefore, without waiting, we should ride together against the rogue with bare swords and tear him limb from limb."

Then said Jäckel Grabinsgaden, "Your advice was seldom without evil consequences, and therefore I won't follow you." Pentza Trinkavil was pleased with that.

"Well," said Haintzo with the goat, "he doesn't care a shit about us. I think he's a wild fox, since he has one's tail on his shield."

So much discussion had taken place that Sir Neidhart began to notice they did not dare joust any more. He wanted to end their fear and give them courage too, so he began to run away. Behold! There arose such a chasing that no one could ever tell you all about it and such a shouting at the stranger that one

could hear it for more than three leagues. They were so anxious
to hurry that two of them fell down dead. v. 657

THE MOCK CONFESSION

When the others saw that, they stopped their hurrying and
began repenting their sins. They called after him with great
sincerity, "Dear lord from foreign lands, guard us from evil
disgrace. Forgive us our wickedness. We rue it much and feel
remorse, for we well perceive that you are full of the Holy
Ghost."[57]

The stranger was heartily pleased at that; he turned toward
them and said with a soft heart, "May God free you of all your
pain and also forgive you your sins. Yet I declare it the truth
according to holy scripture: I can't forgive sins without re-
pentence, confession, and penance, which the sinner must do
completely and without falsity. Take my word for that!" v. 679

Then a real repentence began: they started beating their
hearts so hard that blood spurted from their mouths and noses.
Their weeping was great, and Haintzo gave himself such a blow
that he sank to the ground and became sick with righteous de-
votion. Lekspiss, who was no longer joking, looked up to God
and called out loud with all his might, "Lord God, give me mind
and strength to free myself of sin and not to journey from this
earth so shamefully as Pentz and Jäckel have departed from
this heath." Next he went to the knight and knelt down so
sincerely on the field that he might have broken his legs. He
cried out, "Dear my lord, hear my sin for Mary's sake and give
me enough penance too. I have sinned immensely." v. 703

Neidhart sat down in the green grass to hear the peasants'
confessions. He made a sign of the cross over them and said,
"May God free you from care!" Then he turned toward Leks-
piss and said, "For the sake of God, who hath created hay and
straw, and of the Holy Ghost, tell me everything you know."

My Lekspiss began thus and said, "I'm a guilty man and have
sinned here without measure against you. I still remember,"
he said, "a sin that occurred yesterday. Unfortunately it is so
great that I trip with my tongue and don't know whether I
should tell it: yet I trust so well that you won't tell it any further
that my devotion compels me to tell it to you in the place of
God." How earnestly he asked it of him! v. 725

Sir Neidhart said very intimately, "You should believe me

that I would be heartily sad to lose my priesthood thus with your confession. I'd rather choose death. Tell me your sins freely if you wish to be God's friend."

Lekspiss began his confession; yet he trembled with shame at his sin and said, "Then I'll tell you and not despair in it. Sir, my wife—now woe, now woe—I don't dare tell you any more. It's such a great sin I don't like to tell you about it."

The confessor said to him again, "May God take all your discomfort, dear son, and don't be afraid. I'll be a rogue today if I ever tell anyone your thoughts (while I'm all alone)." v. 747

Lekspiss did not hear that right, and that is why he began again thus, "Sir, my wife is not very tall, and therefore she took a bench and climbed on it with her legs and cut a slice off the bacon. When I noticed that, I came creeping up and pulled the chair away so quickly she fell right on her back. I lifted up her dress and kissed her three times on her belly." v. 759

Sir Neidhart began to smirk and said, "So help me. Fie upon you, wicked man! Why, madman, have you thus accused yourself and so damned both your soul and body? Your sin is so great I cannot free you nor can I tell you anything better than that you must hurry to the bishop." He told him that not without reason; for Sir Neidhart, the mock-priest, thought to himself, "Evil sport never turned out well; so one shouldn't toy with his soul. In my heart I well know that, according to wise teachings, I can neither absolve nor bind as a priest. Also, one cannot safely tell his sins to a layman if he can get a priest."[5a] v. 779

Lekspiss went away; and then Haintzo, the very penitent man, came walking up. He began his confession and said, "My lord, help me out of my plight. I have sinned mortally, and I've lost God's grace[161] too. Woe to me that I was ever born here on this earth!"

Then worthy Neidhart said, "So help me, son, you shouldn't despair so. I'll tell you for a fact that God's mercy is so plenteous and copious that no sin was ever so great but that it was at once forgiven, if the person would regret it deeply and sincerely." v. 797

Thereupon my Haintzo began and told what he had done. He said, "My lord, it's a shame. Yesterday I was travelling across country until I came to a brook. Then sorrow and discomfort arose; for I didn't want to strip and wade through naked, nor did I want to turn back and thus spend my money

in vain. Behold, I found a cow there. I led her by the ears
and climbed on her[97] and rode until I got across the water." v. 811

"You craven heretic!" said the knight. "May evil bitter
Death take you, you wicked man! You couldn't have done
worse. I'm not dreaming when I tell you you must betake your-
self to Rome with hands and feet, if you wish to atone your sin."
Thus Haintzo made his way to Rome, and that was to his loss.
Lekspiss went to the bishop, and that hurt him in his purse.
Neidhart gave them his blessing: "May the Devil keep you!
God give you both pain!" said he in his heart. And with that
he got up from the confession like an unordained brother.[57]

v. 829

THE TOURNAMENT RESUMED

Meanwhile Triefnas came riding up on a sledge. He begged
the stranger persistently and said, "My dear Squire, if I have
done anything to you, you should forgive it for the sake of our
very wealthy[161] God and advise me earnestly whether I should
court any further with jousting, talking, singing, and with other
things too."

To that Neidhart said, "It seems to me that you are a hero of
good birth and physically courageous. If you wish to take a
wife in marriage, you may serve her without sin.[189] And I will
help you in that as best I can, believe me. And also I'll forgive
everything you've ever done to me in all your life. Therefore
tell me, you free hero, what do you in your heart think best done
for fame and wealth?" v. 855

Bertschi thanked him for that at once. "It's well that I have
known you," he said to Neidhart and swore to him by his salva-
tion that he would take Metz in marriage even if he lost his
pants.[61]

Thereupon they started scurrying back to Lappenhausen just
like a lead bird[70] and came to his companions, six of whom were
still left. Bertschi said, "I'll be fugged! There must be more
courting and knightly jousting in honor of my dear Metz!"

No one wanted to be the coward; so they all said, "Well then,
so let it be." Thereupon a shouting arose, "We must try a
tourney, even if we should all be crushed to death. If only we
knew how to arrange it!" v. 876

"I'll teach you myself," said Sir Neidhart sincerely, "I'm
not new at the game."

They were all satisfied with that and shouted noisily, "God

has sent us His angel, a man from foreign lands, so that we might be saved!"

Very quickly they were divided into two exactly even parties, according to Neidhart's instructions. In the first party were he and Bertschi Triefnas, Burkhart with the bony bump, and raging Eisengrein. In the other were Twerg, the worthy fellow Kuontz from the barn, and the gentlemen Knotz and Troll. In truth I would gladly swear that no tourney was ever so evenly divided as these four and four.   v. 897

Sir Neidhart began to speak, "Tourneys and jousting were not thought up only for courting the ladies pure; surely they were also made so you could demonstrate and also learn horsemanship. That's why you should gladly practice in such things so you will succeed all the more often in earnest and in battles. Jousting teaches us to ride effectively with a spear: in addition the tourney helps us wield our sword in knightly manner and strike flesh and bone and iron."   v. 913

They all said, "Praised be Christ and all that's in Heaven! May we do what we should and fulfil your commands earnestly!"

Then Sir Neidhart spoke again, "I rejoice in your honor. Therefore we should at once choose two among us fellows from either side as 'bridlers', who have nothing else to do but look back and forth in the tourney and see whether they can find anyone who should be soundly beaten. They should lead the same by their bridles so they can't flee before the other members of their team come up and fight around him[42] and strike him—but not hard—or pull him from his horse. And then, if they throw him, he should pay four pennies (and no bad ones) if he wants to redeem his ass."   v. 939

His words pleased them well: yet they called, "How should we beat or strike the bridled fellows?"

Neidhart answered them thus, "With cudgels woven out of straw."

"How good, how good!" they loudly called. "This straw won't do us any harm." Thereupon Knotz and Burkhart were selected and elected as their impartial bridlers. Both teams went to their corners at once and began deciding against whom the tourney was to go.

Thereupon Sir Burkhart began and said, "No one is worth beating but that whore's son Twerg, who wipes his arse with his shirt. That should grieve us all."   v. 959

That did not seem very good to Bertschi, who said, "It seems to me that we should beat Kuontz's soft hide because he stank in church in spite of all of us."

Eisengrein said in reply, "I'd be sorry for Kuontz. Isn't it better for us to beat Troll on his clod-like head, because he cheats lands and people and pisses in his bed?"

They were all pleased with his advice and said, "So let it be!"

In the other corner Kuontz was saying, "Do you want to hear what happened? It's just as I'll tell you. One Sunday Eisengrein removed the manure from his stable so that it stank all through the street. Therefore we should grab him by his hair and by his beard so he'll pay too dearly for his stable cleaning." v. 983

That did not please Twerg. "I'll tell you something else I've just thought of: the stranger has brought us to this pass, we should pay the stranger back with beating and rebuking."

When Troll heard that, he interrupted the speech and said, "Sir Twerg, you are not worthy of having honor in hill and dale. Don't you know what troubles we have suffered from the stranger entirely through our fault? Now we've been reconciled. Should we foul that up now? Before that, I'd rather pull your hair out!"

Twerg was provoked by his words and said, "You can go to hell! This disgrace must be avenged, or may I be stabbed today!" With that they grabbed for their knives, which had recently been sharpened. v. 1005

Kuontz cried, "Fight! Murder! Fight!" and gave them each a blow and separated them. He said, "I don't like this. If you carry on like this, you'll cause us all trouble. We must stick together if we want to win glory." Thereupon peace was made. Kuontz continued speaking, "It seems to me the tournament came because of love: we should pay back the lover—that's Triefnas. Moreover, I've found out that Bertschi skinned a cat with his left hand; that's a disgrace and a shame." v. 1023

They were all pleased with his advice and shouted, "So let it be!" They advanced from their corners and sent a youth from each side to ring the bells that would announce the tourney. Behold, that was quickly done! Wow! What joy you would have seen among the village maids with their singing and chatting! It was also proper to make a fence all around the field; and, to be sure, that was quickly done. On it a grandstand was to be built for the lovely ladies who were to watch the tourney, and that was quickly done. Meanwhile the heroes bound them-

selves; they ate half a cow and sat on their donkeys with their
cudgels of straw.   But Sir Neidhart's was not that way, as I
shall prove to you.   His club was of iron well covered with
straw, for it could jokingly cause all the fellows in the game a
lot of suffering.   v. 1053

Then they rode into the field according to their old custom
with Gunterfai the piper, whose belly was seldom empty of
turnips[106] and barley.[107]   Bertschi rode around the ring first.
"Hey, hye, hay!!" was his jubilant shout, "How well and young
I am in my heart!"   How knightly he could ride with spurs[112]
on either side!   He swung the cudgel around his head (He's a
fool who believes that).   After that the merry man took his
place among his companions.

The other team endeavored to take position at the other end,
whereupon the stranger gave his orders to the rustic umpires,
who were padded with hay and straw, "Listen you lordly war-
riors, you should close the gates and carry off all who are
thrown; that is meet and right for you."   v. 1079

The tourney was begun and the barriers closed: they ran
against each other just like the sows of Flanders.   Of racket
there was enough and much in the group until Sir Burkhart
found Troll and bridled him with his hand.   He said, "You must
go along with me and be beaten from the arse up."

At the same time one saw Knotz run against Triefnas and
say, "Now give yourself captive.   It's all up with you!   You
have tried to escape, and for that reason you've got to suffer
pain."   v. 1095

They were led away individually from the tourney, one of
them hither and the other thither.   They both grabbed their
saddle bows (otherwise they would have been pulled off) and
held on so tight they lost their breath.   They locked their legs
together underneath so that no one could take their horses.
However, they were beaten with the straw until the ladies cried
out passionately and all too noisily, "Save Bertschi and Troll
too!"

Sir Troll heard that and it went to his heart.   He began
farting at the knight and said, "Let that be a present for the
stranger."   But he was promptly thanked for that: Sir Neid-
hart untied his hood and scratched him until the blood spurted
from his eyes, and he measured him such a blow that he fell
beneath his ass.   With that he ran away and his Hagen was
captured.   v. 1117

Sir Burkhart said, "Now we should save Bertschi. Follow me!"

"That's right," they said; and all three rushed to Bertschi.

Now when Bertschi saw that his comrades had come, he gained strong courage and began teasing. He said, "I'm sitting so softly and so well that no one should save me. Bring me cheese and bread too, I'm almost dead of hunger." They quickly gave him some bread; Triefnas bit a piece off and thrust it whole into his gullet. How loudly he called, "How good! How healthy!"

Neidhart began to laugh; he ran against Knotz from the rear and lifted him from his horse and threw him on the earth. The umpires took him away, and he had to let his mare go. When Eisengrein[38] saw that, it grieved him and discomforted him. He would gladly have avenged it at once; but he had to refrain for fear.   v. 1143

Twerg had resolved to win glory. He said, "May the Devil take him. It's nothing to fight with Bertschi: he has eaten and we haven't."

With that the tourney was over and they ordered the piper to trill up. Then Geri with the jug called out, "Now alas, if it is all over!"

The parson answered her, "So help me, you whore! So help me! So? Do you realize those were groin blows? May the evil Devil take you!"   v. 1155

THE AFTER-TOURNEY

Geri hushed, yet the stranger said, "Now we should exert ourselves and ride against each other with striking on either side. That is called the 'after-tourney'." Behold, they then began aimlessly dashing and thrashing through one another like the wild swine of Flanders! The thing lasted so long that a fog and mist arose from the movement of people and horses until suddenly no one could recognize the other. Now at last we can detect whether Neidhart could strike and overthrow the fellows! It happened that you could have found five[37] handsome jousters stretched out on the field and also so pummeled and beaten that they could have been carried away in baskets. That was caused by Neidhart's little cudgel, which should have been of straw. He was able to conceal this fact; for he laid himself down softly beside his companions and cried, "Alas for my lung, which has been crushed! Because of it I must lie in the manure!"   v. 1187

When the old folks saw that, they agreed unanimously that in all their days they had never seen such violent fighting as had occurred there, even if it was to be considered real fighting. On the other hand they said that, if the unhorsing was to be considered a sport, they had never seen a sport with such disorder. The fellows were carried away.

Another tourney was beginning between the asses and the steeds; and they began jumping and kicking so hard that no one dared approach them to catch the asses and mares.[101] Then Troll's Hagen kicked Bertschi's nag in the stomach so that she promptly stretched out all fours. v. 1207

Neidhart's horse reared up and kicked that donkey's teeth and tongue out so that he fell down dead. That harmed no one so much as the miller from the meadow, who had lent Hagen, and Kuontz's wife Jütz, who, from laughing and coughing, had fallen down from the grandstand and on her head so hard that her soul didn't want to remain but went whither it was to go.

Then a shout arose, "Listen, girls and boys, everyone should go home. The tournament is all over." With that the fence was torn down more quickly than it had been built, and the barriers were knocked down and carried off both hither and thither. v. 1227

As soon as this had been done, everyone went away. One party went with the dead woman who had lost her life there; they began burying her at once, and that was of no harm to the parson.[66] The second party had to haul away the ass that had been unable to escape, and to commend him to the ravens. That did the wolves no harm. The last party, I must admit, went over to see the heroes who had been so severely beaten, without any harm to the surgeon.[122] But the latter could not profit from Neidhart or from the swift warrior Bertschi, who recovered as quickly as if they had never been hurt. That was because Sir Neidhart had been able to spare himself, and because the lover had high spirits, which were good for his wounds. He would have sprung and danced and sung and pranced; but no one could carry the baton[13] for him because the stranger had trotted away. v. 1253

How could they end Troll's pain? He had been beaten so hard he could neither see, nor hear, nor lament his pain. Kuontz had been measured such a blow he had forgotten how to dance. Besides that, his wife was dead, and that brought him pain and sorrow. If Twerg had been more successful, how gladly he would have danced with Bertschi! But his feet could not carry him, so hard had he been beaten. Then Squire Eisengrein and his other friends said, "We've been hit so hard we can't get any pleasure from dancing. And even if that weren't the case, it would be hard for us to wake up tomorrow when we should plow, thresh, cut, mow, and carry. May he drown in the muck who brought us to this pass!" Nevertheless, Burkhart would have sung pure song with a sweet tongue, but he could not feel it in his heart, so hard had he been beaten. Therefore Bertschi had to remain alone, and that's that.   v. 1281

THE SERENADE

However, he would not desist, but served Dame Metzi day and night; for he could not stray from her in his mind or thoughts. At night he would always go out and slink to her father's house; he would tear the clay from the wall, and it was not sour. He swept back and forth, his mind was focused on the little door. Time and tide were too long for him; how often he began and sang, "I'll pine away for you, for you I will die." With that he would waddle up to her windowsill in hopes of getting a glimpse of her; but he did not find her. That made him angry, and thus his song was lost. He did that oft and many times, but unfortunately it did not help him a bit.   v. 1301

Therefore he crept to the piper's house and said, "My dear fellow, get up and help me tonight with your art; for I travail in the fire of love." Gunterfai was snoring loudly, he was dreaming he was fishing in the sea.[92] What should the hero say? His throat was parched. My Triefnas was impatient; he began calling the minstrel louder and beating on the door with two large stones. He knocked with a stick and said, "Get up, worthy fellow!"

Meanwhile the minstrel was beginning to wake, and he started up like a wild hare. "What is this, and what is that?" he began calling all at once. He threw his wife out of bed; for he thought she had done it all. "You deceiver," the man said, "why are you disturbing me all this long night?"   v. 1324

Bertschi would have laughed out loud, but love's fire was martyring him so severely his nose bled. When it stopped, he knocked again and went up and called the man, "Get up for rich[161] God's sake and go with me. I need you."

Gunterfai was very angry, and besides that he had drunk a

lot. He shouted, "Go away, you son-of-a-mare, and don't knock any more. That'll be best for you!"

Bertschi was offended by the scolding, but even more by the familiar form of address.[119] He thought, "I'll be a rascal! If I didn't need you so much, I'd beat up your calf and cow and your back too. Now I've got to sing as you wish; but the day will come that I'll pay you back." He began sweet words, "Don't be angry, dear minstrel. I am Triefnas, go with me and I'll give you seven hellers."[60]   v. 1347

When Gunterfai heard this, he began a different cry, "Yes, my dear sir. Is that you? I didn't recognize you, forgive me." Then he got up and wiped his eyes with straw. He looked for his pants, but they were lost. However, he could well have done without them if his purse had not been tied to them at the time; but he could not be without it because he wanted to put his money in it. His search lasted so long that Bertschi jumped up three times with the righteous indignation that seized him.

"Aren't you coming?" he called to the man.

"Yes," said the latter, "just as soon as I find my pants."

Therefore Triefnas said quickly, "Come, leave your pants there. I'll give you pennies and a purse, I'll give you beer along with the bottle!"   v. 1369

Who was happier then than Gunterfai? He didn't care an egg about the pants but came hurrying and scurrying out in a cloud of dust with his bagpipe, which was new.[39] Bertschi said, "Now play and play, and let us serenade tonight. I'll pay you for it fourfold."

The bagpipe resounded everywhere till it echoed in hill and dale. They came to Metzi's house. She stuck her arse out of the window and Bertschi promptly said, "Well for me that I have known your beautiful face! Hold it out, Metzi, hold it out!"[58]

The din began to disturb the others, who would rather have slept. They said to Gunterfai, "Why are you disturbing us tonight with your piping? Do you want us to whip your hide?"   v. 1391

Schollentrit answered them, "Dear gentlemen, I think he has played to announce the bath. We should hurry over there." They believed Schollentrit; and they were so happy they at once jumped out of their beds, for they had never been able to have a hot bath in all their days. They ran after Gunterfai; but, like a hero, he had fled so fast with Bertschi that he could not be

found. Therefore they had to do without it. If baths had been
rare for them, they were now even rarer. Therefore they re-
turned home again.   v. 1409

THE TRYST IN THE BARN

Triefnas was full of joy; he thought he had done well. How
often my little fool would say, "So help me! So help me, I've
seen her!" His farm work was all over, his thoughts were all
on Metzi. The next night he went out and toddled over to her
father's house. He went into the cow stall so softly it made no
noise. He hid himself behind the door until Metzli began milk-
ing. He came forth and said, "Now hush, dear love! Don't be
grieved. I am Bertschi. Be of good cheer; I'll make you full
of joy."   v. 1425

Metzli was so frightened that she did not hear Bertschi but
began to scream and kept on screaming. "No, no, Metzli, no,
no, no!" said Bertschi. He was not lazy: he put his hand over
her mouth. She started thrashing about and kicking till the
milk was turned over. That went to the cow's heart: she
started thrusting with her horns, lowing, and also rushing right
through the heap of them. She scratched, he scuffled, and the
cow butted: no one has ever seen such a wonder. In that same
struggle the cow measured Bertschi, against his will, two stabs
with one thrust. He would hardly have survived them if it
had not been for his thick jacket. Thus Triefnas was driven
away and Metzli's mouth freed.

Therefore she called out and also shouted, "Here thief, here
thief! Hey, hey, hey, hey!"   v. 1449

When Lady Metzi's cry was heard, all mercy was at an end.
If anyone had weapons, he armed himself until midnight.[69]
Only then did they come flying up with their swords drawn and
shout, "What is this? Tell us, Fritzo, for God's sake!"

Fritzo said, "A thief has been all around in that barn. If you
will agree to it, we should look for him under the earth and on
the earth, to see whether we can catch the whore's son." v. 1463

"That's our duty," they said. Fritz and three of his sons
risked entering first; all the others followed them into the barn
and everywhere. Their shouting resounded very loudly, and
they beat dreadfully against the wall. "Wow! May the Devil
ruin you! If you were ever an honest guy, come forth, and
make it fast!" The pounding annoyed the cow, and she gave

Fritz such a blow that he remained in his house when the others
fled.   v. 1477

THE VIGIL ON THE ROOF

They could not find the thief until the third night. Then
love brought him to the point of thinking to himself, "You must
go out again and climb on my[42] sweetheart's house; then, through
the roof, you'll see what she's doing." How quickly he carried
out everything he had thought of! Triefnas was on the roof,
and Fritz was sitting by the fire with his children eating tur-
nips.[106] Bertschi wanted to take a look and stuck his head
through a hole; but he was heavier than a log and therefore he
had to fall in the fire in front of all the children and their father
like a monstrous devil. Hook and kettle fell down along with
Bertschi, to his disadvantage.   v. 1499

Who could wait any longer? Whoever had nothing to ride
fled with hands and feet, and no one could stop him. Metzi
was so lame[39] she hardly reached the staircase. See, she
stumbled out just like a mill-wheel! The others all fell after
her, in such a hurry they were to flee. Fritz had to remain be-
hind: he could not budge because of the injury the cow had
given him in the barn.   v. 1513

As soon as this had occurred, Fritz began to understand the
situation and thought in his heart: "Flame has fallen in the
flame, fire has come to fire; that is caused by love and romance."
Bertschi was about to burn up both outside and in; but Fritzo
dragged him through the ashes, warmly washed with turnip
water, and farted three times in his face, and thus the lover was
cured. Yet it was a miracle that he survived, since he had
fallen so hard. As a fee he gave the doctor a blow that knocked
him on his back. He trundled out of the back door and left his
host in the house.   v. 1531

Fritzo got raging mad. How loud he cried, "Where shield,
where spear?" He would have begun fighting then, but his
enemy had escaped. He took his revenge on Metzi: he caught
her by her braids and hurled her on the ground three times.
He said, "It's all your fault. I've been hit and beaten in my
mouth and in my belly, and my roof has been broken. See!
I have all that from you." He also gave her a kick and locked
her in a loft. He said to her, "Sit there and shit. Your arse
is too thick and fat," and thus Metzi was imprisoned. v. 1548

METZI'S IMPRISONMENT

"May a fart take him!" said Bertschi as soon as he heard the report. "I'm getting fonder and fonder of her," he said again, "and that's that. I have sworn I must have her, even if she were buried in the earth." This caused him anger and discomfort. How often he looked over at the loft and thought to himself, "Holy Christ! Hidden bread, how sweet you are!" Triefnas loved Metzi so much he thought the heart in his body would burst for the woman.   v. 1563

Metzi was sitting alone and looking at her white legs. When she saw her very brown pussy,[84] such a pulling, plucking, and beating began on the hairy spot, and such a tearing, pounding, pinching, cursing, threatening, and scolding that no one has ever heard such misery. Metzi said to her pussy, "God give you pain and discomfort and also all the agony I suffer so bitterly in my heart just through your fault." Then she beat there again until her mouth was sore. She said, "See there! I'm giving you what people have given me because of you. And may he die who is languishing for you!"   v. 1583

But Metzi had long hair and a short temper, and that's the truth! How quickly the tables turned! Metzi reversed herself. If she had formerly scolded, she now began caressing her pussy all over with stroking and salving. Again she said to her patch, "May God repay you for all your suffering and heal all your pain, I beg Him from my heart. In addition I want to ask you to forgive me if you have suffered anything from me. Upon my oath, I rue and regret it." The patch would have answered; but its teeth were knocked out, its mouth was swollen, and it had lost its wool.   v. 1603

However, a truce was made and she laughed and said, "May he be blessed who is languishing for you." That was directed at Bertschi, who brought joy and delight to her heart so quickly that she completely forgot all her pain. If she had formerly borne him hate, that was all reversed now: the fire of love so increased that she became fonder of her lover than of bright gold.   v. 1617

Now a real courting, a clinging, clanging, and a din began on both sides. Love began riding them so hard that they forgot what they were drinking or eating. This life was much too sour for them. It was natural for them to be that way: the less one lets love go to love, the more one heart yearns for the other. They ate less and less and soon reached such a state that they could not move their arses, and therefore they had to lie down on their benches. Their minds and thoughts had almost foundered.   v. 1634

THE ART OF LOVE

However, Bertschi had drunk sweet mead and beer and wine so that he retained his strength; and he thought in his heart, "Now if she is so well guarded that I don't dare speak to her, at least I'll send her a little letter." Then he made up his mind and quickly sent for the village scribe, who was called Henry Nabelreiber. My village scribe at once came running to Bertschi's house. Triefnas was lying on the bench, his song was "Alack and alas!" When Nabelreiber saw this, it grieved and discomforted him; for Bertschi was his kinsman.   v. 1652

"Has someone done something to you?" he said to the poor man. "He'll have to pay me for it!"

"No," said Berchthold, "I'm so fond of Metzi that I'll pine away and die for her. If you want to save me from this, you must write a letter secretly to my lady, or else I must suffer pain."   v. 1663

Then the scribe answered him and said, "The situation isn't as you think, my dear fellow. If anyone wishes to court correctly, he should be a young lad, fresh and physically healthy, and should choose for himself from all women a single one that pleases him best of all, and he should have nothing to do with any others. She should be his equal in age and family too; for whoever wishes to climb too high will eventually fly into the ditch. Also, she should be alone in all your thoughts, for true love has its strength between two people and wants no more. So much I can tell you: if you wish to win your sweetheart as your wife properly, then find one who is new in love if you don't wish to regret it; for widows and old women are excluded from true love, since they think of their first husbands and thus hurt the feelings of the other fellows.   v. 1691

"Well now, if you have chosen a love who was born for your happiness, then show yourself lively, merry and attentive everywhere. Wherever she sits or stands, you should already be there and stretch out your net: that is, in my opinion, you should often smile at her with playful eyes so that the good one will be aware of what you are thinking; for the first sight is the beginning of the story. You should dance a lot and play on the lute and also sing and spring and tell stories and other things. Yet let that occur with moderation both in the house and on the street with dissembling secretly so that it won't become too public; for ladies' favor is won only by the man who can make love clandestinely.[136]   v. 1715

"Therefore quietly seek out a go-between whom you can well trust, and give her something as one should so she will go to the pure maid and tell her precisely these words: 'God greet thee, tender blooming rose! For a long time no damsel has been as fortunate as you are, for the loveliest youth in this world has now chosen you as his love. He is so courtly and wise that no mother has ever borne his equal. To tell the truth, no woman can ever be worthy of him. With great humility he offers you his service and begs you from the bottom of his heart that you answer him by me whether it can ever be that he will win your favor and also that you grant him to reveal all his thoughts to you with his own mouth at some sweet hour. He will always be indebted to you for it, believe me.'   v. 1743

"But, if the pure one first says, 'Your words don't please me. Drop the matter at once! May the evil spirit take him! Do you think I'm a courtesan? You are one yourself in your heart. Go away and don't come back, or else I'll cause you woe!' Or, if the good one says something else through modesty or for the sake of her good name, you should not despair because of it but go up and down the street singing for your sweetheart's pleasure especially the court song:

> To serve her I have sworn indeed,
> Although today she says me nay.
> Because tomorrow I'll succeed,
> My heart looks forward to that day;
> And in my hope I still persist.
> To serve her I have sworn indeed,
> Although today she says me nay;
> And therefore I will not desist.   v. 1765

"On the other hand send her many messages; then, if you have already implored her greatly, beg her even three times as much until she honors your request; for no heart was ever so hard that you couldn't soften it with constant pleading, as a child knows. Well now, if she grants you the favor of coming to her, then don't tarry but go there unbeknownst to the envious crowd and bow before her.   v. 1778

"Greet her thus: 'May God make you happy in spirit and give you much luck and happiness. I will ask for nothing else.' Right after that you can say, 'Supreme treasure, gem of May, my

beloved full of grace, virtuously deign to listen to me.' Then
ask her to take a seat and sit down next to her (that's the idea!)
and begin your message with propriety (that's the custom).
Speak gently and softly, 'Oh, cherished love, my paradise, re-
ward me today for having borne you secret and sincere love for
so many a day with joyful sorrow, and kindly promise me your
entire and constant love straightway. For me, dear lady, that
is the highest gift, the greatest bliss, the greatest favor; for
nothing was ever so good as two hearts bound in steadfast
harmony and entirely ready for true devotion.'   v. 1803

"Perhaps she'll say, 'God knows, if someone truly loves me, I
cannot bear him hate.' For that you should at once thank her
and say, 'How good, how good, how happy God was in His heart
when he created mankind, and especially you, my tender one,
with such correct measure and pattern, neither too short nor too
tall! A ruby sparkles from your mouth. Happy would he be to
whom you would grant a kiss! That's why I would think I had
won a thousand marks and even more if I could ever have that
luck.'   v. 1819

"Perhaps she is full of cunning and can refuse you this; and
for the sake of her good name she won't admit that she too
wishes it would happen. My friend, don't feel hurt about that,
but grasp her softly by her garment and say with sighs, 'Alack,
my treasure, if you kill me, it is murder; for you well know that
I must languish and also die.' Then don't talk too much but
begin your love-play with sweet works (the time has come),
with kisses, mark you, and other tactics, until the pure one has
become warmed up! Then you can propose marriage without
worry if your heart desires her, for you will surely be granted
it. After that, do like other people; I'll not explain any more of
it to you now."   v. 1839

Bertschi answered, "Oh cousin mine, may you be very happy!
Don't you know that Metzi is so locked up now that no one can
come to her to tell her my heart's desire? You, my friend, must
realize that yourself and go to the loft with the little letter and
throw it to her through the window. Thus she will find some-
thing that will make the tidings known to her."

Nabelreiber began speaking, "May it come about as you
wish!" Then he took out his pen and said, "Tell me, my good
man, how you want the letter."   v. 1856

The lovesick swain started speaking as best he understood.
He began and spoke thus, "God greet you, lindenblossom. Be-

loved, I'm devoted to you. You are my morning star; I'd gladly sleep with you. Because you were locked up all day in the loft, I was so distressed I could not sleep. Also, I have resolved never to eat or drink again until your red mouth comforts me. Therefore accept me or reject me. May God keep your dear soul."

Truly Henritze was clever. "So help me," he said to the poet. "Better stop now, for that's enough of that." He wrote a different letter as follows: v. 1877

"May my tender one be granted as much luck, happiness, and health as she wishes. I have been bereft of all that, I have been plagued by sorrow which I have suffered so painfully for nothing else but your favor. Therefore, my lady, oh bloom of May, sweet virtue, tender goodness, oh my heart's paradise, I beg you assiduously, in the name of ladies' virtue, man's honor, and love's fulfillment, to favor me with three kinds of gifts: v. 1891

"The first is that you have ready for me in your heart a good will with constancy, for which I shall ever be grateful. The second is, that you will soon find a way for hearts, mouths, and eyes to come together privately. And thirdly I will implore you to promise me that no one will share you with me, for I am entirely yours. And, should it turn out that I should never win this favor, then know that I must languish and die!

with that {
May Jesus bless you everywhere[182]
With all His love so kind!
May Venus keep you in her care
With all her heart and mind!
} and not otherwise"
                                                              v. 1912

When the letter had been closed, the scribe at once set out on his way and went to the loft where Metzi was locked up. He tied the letter to a stone and threw it in through the window. He said, "Now go in without feet, for sweet arms will embrace you. Go, letter, whither I send you; white hands will receive you." My letter started flying through the window with a trail of dust behind it until it came to the place where it found Metzi. It missed both hands and also her dear arms so that it could not warm itself there; and therefore her head received it so well that it spurted blood. The letter was not to blame for that: that was done by its friend beside him, to whom it was tied and who hurt people, instead of greeting them, whenever he was sent to them.
                                                              v. 1936

THE SEDUCTION

Metzi had fallen so hard with arse and everything from the bench where she had been sitting that she lost consciousness.

As soon as she came to, she began to perk up her ears and think, "What's happened to me?" Then she looked around and saw the letter tied to the stone that had made the wound in her head. That amazed her in her goiter;[61] yet she said to herself, "This didn't happen without cause." Thereupon she untied the letter and threw the stone against the wall.   v. 1952

Wow! How gladly she would have read it if she had had the skill! She almost fretted to death that she had forgotten how to write in her childhood. She began to lament that ruefully and said, "Woe unto me the day! Because I have learned so little reading and writing, I now feel sorrow and suffer shame, insult, and injury. How shall I reveal my secret to a strange man whom I can't really trust? The world is full of evil cunning. Alas, you skill, you worthy prize, you supreme hoard, you noble heart, certain treasure, flourishing fruit, salvation of the soul, discipline of the body! Had I sown your seeds with care and toil, then I could now reap with pure joy. Had I set out your roots, which seemed so bitter to me, I would now be gathering sweet and aromatic apples into my sack. See, I did none of that; and that's why I must bear this sorrow!"   v. 1982

As soon as her speech was finished, she thought to herself how she would arrange to get to a man who would safely tell her what was written in the letter. Thus it came to her mind: "For this purpose it would be good to shout and call through the lattice to my furious old father and show him the bloody wound and how I swooned with pain. Then he will perhaps take me out and lead me right to the doctor's house so that he can bandage me."

How quickly it came about just as she had planned! The doctor was a wise man and therefore began to ask, "How were you, girl, so beaten? With what, and when? You should tell me that." He did all that in order to find out all the better how she might be helped.   v. 2007

It was hard for Metzi to tell him the truth so openly before the people; so she answered, "In truth, I don't know. The people standing around me are making me so hot I'm afraid my soul will leave me."

Krippenkra caught on to what the maid was up to and snarled at the people, "So help me! What does this mean? Do you want to smother us and stink and stench us out and also learn my art? That makes me mad, and I don't like it! I can't heal her unless you lock her up alone in this room. Medical science says

so, and it's the truth too. Then we can give her spices if we
want to keep her alive."   v. 2028

Then they all shouted, "Get out, get out! We should step
outside."

My door was locked. The doctor was undaunted and asked
her a second time, "Speak up, dear lass, and tell me your
thoughts freely, if you want God to save your life!"

Metzli began and said, "Well for me that I have seen you!
You are such an honest man that I have no fear you'll tell my
sorrowful plaint to anyone else."

The doctor replied, "You shouldn't worry, because whatever
you say will remain secret." The doctor was sure he would
conceal whatever *he* did.   v. 2046

The maid began her confession, "Sir, this happened with a
stone that was thrown to the place I was sitting. I found it tied
to this letter. I'm showing it to you as in a real confession as if
you were ordained as a priest; and I beg you for the sake of our
rich God to tell me seriously what is written in it. For that, may
you be freed from harm." The doctor took the letter in his hand
and told her what he found in it; she thanked him for it and was
happy about it. Then she said to the doctor, "Dear Sir, then
please write back for me what I want to say. I'll repay you for
it, honestly I will."   v. 2066

The doctor said, "So let it be! But first I'll see about your
head, and afterwards about your heart's desire." Then he began
washing her with vinegar and ashes, with onion and sea salt;
that seemed sweeter to her than lard, for she was seized by love
that makes honey out of gall but later turns the honey into gall
that is too bitter.   v. 2078

Meanwhile Metzi was bandaged; so she began and said to
him, "Sir, listen to my thought. Write and let the pen fly. My
little letter should stand thus: 'God greet you, love of lineage
high! I was never dearer to any sweetheart than to you, my
comfort; I tell you that sincerely, believe me! I have read your
letter, for which I must ever be happy. Come to me tonight in
the doctor's house and give me strength; and I'll do whatever
you wish, I don't care a hen about the others. With that, may
our Lord keep you, be you near or far.' "   v. 2096

When Krippenkra saw this, he said to himself, "In truth, you
must be a little whore, unless my senses deceive me." And he
thought of the scripture that speaks thus of women, "A woman's
arse is too broad, her heart too small." As I shall expound it to

you, that means nothing less than that there is not much fidelity among women; woman's inchastity is a pawn that no rook can overcome. What am I telling you? It is nothing new, how small women's fidelity is[189] and how short their constancy, and how great and widespread their sins are. We could pursue the matter for ever; but it is better that we leave the matter and return to the doctor.   v. 2115

He began laughing so hard he farted and said, "Metzli Rüerenzumph, your name well suits my stump;[84] and my stump well suits your mood. Our affair can turn out well; if you will do my will, I'll reconcile you with your father, with your rough father Fritz, who so often makes you sweat. But if you don't do it, I'll cause you a scandal." He took the letters in his hand, "See, I shall show them to Fritz if you don't give yourself to me!"   v. 2128

Metzli did not know what he was saying, and therefore his words troubled her and she said, "I am in your hand. If you want to disgrace me thus, it's truly most unbecoming of you, provided you are supposed to be a decent person. I don't know what you want, and I don't know a shit about the stump." That was spoken most courteously.

The doctor straightened it all out by softly singing, "There, there, little nut,[84] there Metzli! Stand, stand, pricky, stand! The stump is spices,[73] a long one with two short ones.[86] What I want you to do is to hold still and not worry; you must take the spices if you don't want to waste away and die in your sins."   v. 2148

"Well then, my dear Sir, so let it be!" said the maiden free of care. Thereupon she began taking the spices with so little restraint that she soon forgot whether she was standing or sitting. The doctor wanted to pull away, but the damsel said, "You shouldn't run away. Doctor me up a little more, I can stand it better than ever!" Thereupon she grabbed him by his stake[84] and held him by both his sacks. She said, "You mustn't take them from me, I want to have the spices again." Therefore he gave her the spices again on the bench and in the straw; and as soon as she tasted the spices she at once fainted, for such pepper was new to her. The doctor had to pay for that, since unfortunately he could not satisfy her with his stump. He wanted to break away from her; but Metzli said, "Medicate me now for a third time, as is right. Unfortunately I'm still not cured." v. 2175

"What the Devil! Can this be?," said the doctor then. "May

the Devil make you well! If that doesn't satisfy you, go jump in the lake; I can't thrash around[84] for ever!" Thereupon he got up and left like a buck whose horns have recently fallen off. For him the game was over.   v. 2184

Nevertheless Dame Metzli got her share, however lusty she had been beforehand. She began feeling pain in her sides,[87] her belly, and her stomach. Water rose to her mouth, her limbs became so weak that she could scarcely move, and she had to be helped while walking. Time and tide became too long for her. Bitter vinegar was her drink, sorrel and not almond rice, sour apples were her food. She had lost her right color, her nipples were swollen and blackened all around. Things got so bad that the doctor decided Metzi was carrying a child. He began worrying a great deal about this and kept her until the third morning. He said to her, "What do you think good? Do you have Bertschi in your heart, and do you want to take him in marriage?" v. 2207

She kept silent; he asked again, and she said, "Now I'm not a maid. If he knew that, he'd hurt me."

To that Krippenkra answered her, "If he'll take you, just say 'Yes.' Afterwards do just as I instruct you if you wish to keep your good name. Go to Straub, your cousin, and ask him to give you lilly leaves, sloe, and gall,[144] all boiled warmly together, and put it in often (you know where, Metzi, by your leg) and say, 'May fortune ordain!' and your puss will grow narrow. And understand me well, if you please! As he well knows, the apothecary should give you gall from a tree and not from a goat! And have all three of them weighed out for you equally.   v. 2228

"Then get a fish bladder and fill it with a pidgeon's blood, for that will help you on the evening they bed you with him.[42] Metzi, do what I say. On that occasion you shouldn't delay in putting the little bladder where your maidenhead should be. Then, when he comes into his seigneurial land, the little bladder will burst at once and the blood will flow out; and thus you will not lose your wealth and good name. See if I can't teach you! If you want to be even more sure, struggle steadfastly and groan; for then he will really think you are a maid. Do you hear what I've told you?"

"Yes indeed," she answered him. She was pleased with his advice and said, "I'd gladly do all that if he would marry me."
                                              v. 2252

METZI'S LOVE-LETTER

The doctor said, "Let me bring it about. I can write a letter with such good and sweet words that he'll at once take you with both hands and feet as soon as he receives the message." Then he took his pen and began his letter thus: "God, superior and supreme, Father, Son, and Holy Ghost, who with His power hath created Heaven and earth, water, air and also fire, birds and fish with their yield, cattle and also leaves and grass for no other reason than that man might spend his life here on earth with propriety and honor, may He favor you, dear love, with His blessed seven gifts, with the seven sacraments! And may my service also be at your disposal.   v. 2274

"I have received a little letter; I thought it came from Heaven, so delightfully it came flying hither in a rainbow. It was wrapped in a cloud, in which songs of joy resounded, with words on its countenance as if an angel had composed them. Its sweetness so overcame me that I at once lost the bright light of day. A sleep seized my eyes, my senses were gripped by a dream in which supreme Venus, a queen of all women, appeared to me in person.   v. 2290

"Naked she was and also nude, the equal of a woman of twenty years. On her head she wore a crown of glass, on which was beautifully written, 'I am the delightful crown of Dame Venus, the goddess of love.' Under it lay her loose hair, plaited like a chain. She was blind in her eyes and much too swift in her gestures. She carried a bow in her hand with a glowing arrow. She was sitting in a chariot beautifully embossed with gold and silver, behind which a stream of red blood flowed in a yearning flood. She at once called me by name (I wondered how she knew me) and also nodded to me and greeted me nicely, for which I thanked her.   v. 2310

"Then she said, 'Do you know why I have come to you? Confess!'

'No indeed,' I said. Therefore she began and spoke thus:

'I command you by the ban to grant your man Bertschi everything he wants, be it much or little, and to live joyfully with him. That will all be to your advantage; for, as you will surely discover, you will be plagued when old age begins to ride you.'

"A black spirit at her left side said, 'Always obey her.' v. 2324

"With that the apparition disappeared so swiftly before my eyes that I would have swooned if I hadn't found another lady fair and pure, who also appeared to me in my dream and came before my face so brightly I thought it was the glow of the sun. On her head she wore a wreath beautifully made with three crowns one above the other and covered with a fine star that shone like a carbuncle. The first crown was of iron; and around it was written, 'I am a crown of steadfastness, I am grieved if anyone does wrong.' The second crown was of silver; written in it one could read, 'I am a crown of chastity, which is so pure and fair.' The third crown was of nothing less than gold and inscribed thus: 'I am a crown of heavenly bliss, I was ever ready to grant mercy.' v. 2350

"Under her wreath her hair was wound and neatly bound. She had four eyes,[31] so beautiful and magnificent that I felt I was looking in a mirror. She had a cloak that was broad and had many colors set in it. She stretched it out with one hand, and it seemed to me longer than a land. In the other she carried a child that was so delightful and wise that I forgot all discomfort as soon as I saw it. It seemed to me she was sitting on the altar in a church which was painted all over with innumerable tender pictures. That same church also had a sea of honey and milk around it, which was vast and great and flowed around it with a blissful motion. v. 2372

"The fair one looked at me with one eye and blessed me. I nodded to her courteously and wanted to run away; but she called to me and said, 'Stay with me and don't run like that. Do as I tell you if you want to have happiness, and don't follow the command of false love since that goes against God, unless your dear man wishes to propose marriage to you. That you can well grant him, to be sure, with bliss and honor; for God with His counsel hath created holy matrimony.'

"After that the child said, 'Follow my dear mother, if you wish to keep body and soul and never be separated from us.'

"A white spirit at its right side said, 'Serve them at all times.' With that the child blessed me with the sign of the cross, which made me glad. v. 2396

"I awoke with joy and got up quickly and went to my confessor. I told him this whole story and begged him for the sake of wealthy God and all His commandments to expound it to me and also to give me his advice. He was greatly amazed; but, to make the story short, he said, 'We can see in the case of the first woman, it seems to me, that she is false, deceitful love, Dame Venus with her wicked counsel, who has damned many a soul.

'She was about twenty years old? She is older than the world; yet she appears to be youthful, for love wants no age. Naked she was, you say? That cannot be by chance; for love wants body to fit to body nude like that. The glass crown she wears and the writing on it can signify for us nothing more than worldly pleasure and fleeting fame. Her hair, so softly brushed and plaited like a chain, is nothing other than a noose that snares our body and soul. If she is blind in her eyes, that means that often a beautiful well-born maid loves a graybeard. v. 2432

'She is hasty in her gestures? That means that lovers have wild dispositions, they think good whatever they do. She carries a bow and arrow in her hand wherever she goes? With them she shoots young hearts at first sight. The arrow is sharp and much too hot, for it will pierce and burn. If she is sitting in a chariot all embossed with rich metal work, I understand thereby that a lover accomplishes nothing without money. The bleeding brook runs out of the wounds that occur whenever a lover is stabbed or struck for some injury. Now I'll explain to you the black spirit on the left hand: it is surely a wicked angel, most dangerous to your soul.   v. 2454

'Therefore, dear daughter, in order to attain salvation, do not follow that wicked counsel. If you want to avoid wrong-doing, disregard the commands of False Love, I advise you sincerely.'

"When I heard the priest's words, I was frightened and didn't know what I should say. However, I began to speak, as God wished, and said, 'God repay you for your instruction! I will do all you want. Tell me, Sir, what does the other lady in this vision signify?'   v. 2468

"He answered me this courteously, 'It seems to me it was the blessed Mother of God and pure maid, Mary, hope of Christendom. The wreath with the three crowns, it seems to me, is nothing other than is written there with holy hand in profound wisdom. Yet I should not neglect the star, by which one should understand her goodness shining brightly into both Heaven and earth. She had bound up her hair? That means she was always full of pure chastity and has mortified all carnal desire.

'She has four eyes? I'll explain them to you at once: they are the four good counsels that she gives to a good person. They are: if anyone strikes you on one cheek, offer him the other at once. Take a wife in marriage if you can't do without a woman.[189] Sell all your property and give it to the poor. Forgive them who hate you, and beg God to convert them.   v. 2496

'She sees the world in four parts and pours out her virtue

with salvation. In her broad cloak worked with so many colors, note her manifold and widespread mercy. Also know that the child is our creator Jesus Christ, our Redeemer and our Savior, our Lord and our Ruler. Let me tell you that the church is Holy Christendom, the painting suits nothing else but a good mind that pleases God. I believe that the altar where the Maid was sitting was the faith that she has never forgotten and which she has ever strengthened more and more.   v. 2514

'And what does the sea signify? The blood in the New Testament that has run, along with the water, from living wells: tears and blood that have been shed with good intent and are now turned into sweetness, as its milk and honey show us. Let the white spirit on the right hand be straightway named for you thus: it is a good and tender angel that guards you all the time. Through this, maiden full of bliss, you can note especially well what you should do and leave undone, if you wish to keep God's favor.'   v. 2530

"Thus it was explained to me to my heart's satisfaction. Now think, my dearest treasure, of the words of the supreme Master, which He spoke to all of us with His holy teachings and scripture: 'What would it help, if you had won all the world with all its wealth and yet your soul had suffered?' You should keep that in your heart and restrain yourself from writing, from serenading, and from carrying on, unless it is an honorable request you wish me to grant you. With this I shall end my letter. May God turn all sorrow from you and heal all your pain. May the highest Queen protect you if you love me truly, I ask her that from my heart. This letter is written, as I say, in a blessed hour on a joyful day, with a dear hand in good circumstances,[210] and fastened on the wheel of fortune."[31]   v. 2554

THE GO-BETWEEN

Now, as soon as this had taken place, he read the letter aloud to her. She thanked him for it from her heart and said, "How should I regret the disgrace you have caused me? You are such a wise doctor." Then she said, "Who will carry it?"

"Let me tend to that," said the man. Then he quickly found an old woman whom he knew. She could wash and massage[121] too and do business with sluts[200] and also help young maids from their honor; and, if one could not fare any better, she would fall in the grass herself.[96] He offered the woman the letter and instructed her as follows: "Depart secretly and go over to Bertschi's house. Give him the letter into his hand and say, 'Metz has sent this to you.' And greet him a thousand times from her, and tell him nothing else with your mouth." v. 2578

Wow! How much that was to her taste! She raised as much dust as a bag of chaff until she reached Bertschi. She said, "God greet you, young man. May you ever be blessed! Metzli has sent you this letter with many lovely greetings to you from your head to your foot."

Who was happier then than the lad? He said, "Now I'm doing all right! Here are two shillings, drink them for my sake and go to our scribe Henritze Nabelreiber and tell him to come to me, for I can't get on without him." v. 2594

The slut ran off like any other courtesan and told the scribe how things stood. The message pleased him too; so he gave the go-between a penny to her profit and hurried over to where he found Bertschi on a bench by the wall. He shouted, "Up, you happy man! The Emperor is not our equal!"

Triefnas would gladly have got up for shame; but he had become so weak that he fell off the bench, for love had brought him to such straits that he was nearly dead of hunger. But now he was so helped by his joy, as well as by a half a cow that he ate right then, that he really got well again and forgot all his pain. When the letter was read to him, he little knew what it said until Nabelreiber showed him. The latter said, "It can mean nothing else but this: she says she will do your will and even more if you will take her in marriage." v. 2622

PART TWO – THE WEDDING

THE MARRIAGE DEBATE

Bertschi was filled with joy; it all pleased him well and he said, "I will and must have her, even if it killed all my kinsmen. If possible, she must be mine, even if a whole land should perish!"

Therefore he gathered his kinsman, Engelmar Farindkuo, and his cousin, Gumpost, and also Herman Rüerenmost, Nickel Fesafögellin, Jänsel Snellagödellin, Hafenschleken, Nagenfleken, Schlinddenspek, Ofensteken, old Colman (I should have named him before), Nabelreiber with the stylus, and many other honorable[123] people. He called his kinswomen, Jützin Scheissindpluomen, Elsbeth Föllipruoch, Engeldrauden Erenfluoch, Snatereina, Töreleina, Damsel Feina with hers,[206] and old Laichdenman with the bare dogtooth, who thought herself so clever.   v. 2649

They all came into his house and began standing around him and asking what he wanted to do and saying he should admit it to them freely. Bertschi said, "So let it be!" He began his discussion thus, "Listen, ladies and men. Dear friends, hear me well and deign to give me counsel. I can't remain any longer without a wife, even if it should cost my life. I have chosen me one who was born for my happiness. I must have her, it's most urgent. Otherwise I would lie down and die. That's something I ask of you, and I trust you will stand by me with advice and assistance too."

Then Farindkuo, who was his nearest kinsman, answered him, "I can't give any better advice than this, 'Do a thing that must be, and don't care a hen's foot about what people sing or say.' I'll help you in this as best I can. However, I'm really surprised you want our advice about something which, as you say, cannot be otherwise."   v. 2678

Triefnas said in reply, "What the Devil!? What's that? Who can please everyone both in earnest and in play? Nothing was ever so bad but that good advice served it well. Therefore, my clever Gumpost, advise me how I should fare."

Gumpost began and said, "I find that in Christendom there are three things good in themselves which it is never good to recommend because of the great curses people give the recommender. They are: to become a monk,[187] to journey far in this world, and to enter holy matrimony."   v. 2695

"Wow! What a wonder! How can you ever go wrong if you wisely recommend good things? Well then, my dear Rüerenmost, give me warmth in this frost and make me cool in this heat with your astute counsel."

Rüerenmost then said, "Your situation is of such nature that you will surely regret whichever course you choose. If you take a wife, it's inevitable that you'll never stop worrying and you'll never be free from care. Note very carefully what I say! If you don't have a wife, there will never be any happiness in your life; then your own blood will die out and a stranger will inherit your substance."   v. 2716

When Bertschi learned that, he nearly swooned with chagrin. He said, "Alas, woe worth the day! There is fear and sorrow all around! Tell me, Fesafögelli, what should a Christian man do?"

The good man began and replied to that, "We hear that in this stream every ford is bad to ride. Therefore, let's leave the side that's called the worse and turn to the better side. That is, you should remain as you are and pass your time without a wife."

Scheissindpluomen heard this. How quickly she began her prating, which was not to be silenced. She said, "Sir Nickel, know this: a wise man can test all things and choose from them what is supposed to be the best; and in that one can detect his wisdom. You have selected the worst, and thereby you have made a fool of yourself. Isn't it better for a man to have a fair wife who will care for him diligently day and night as best she can than to remain thus poor and miserable without a wife? What troubles will one have who can support himself by working and remain healthy, provided he uses good judgement?" v. 2750

Snellagödellin quickly said, "This matter wants counsel and needs a lot more thought; it's no child's play. Know that it's better to die than to win an evil wife who will plague you the whole year through with scolding and cursing and reproaching and questioning, both privately and publicly. No one can survive her. If you've been out of the house, then she'll snarl in her anger, 'You've been unfaithful to me, and you'll pay for it! You've been going with other women.' But, if you stay in the house, then she'll say, 'The nun never goes out. I think he's a parlor knight. He stinks so sour and farts so bitterly in the ashes by the fire that all my pleasure is gone.'

"If you entrust her with the house and everything in it, then she will dominate in her office; but, if you wish to keep a part

for yourself, she'll say, 'May the Devil take him! If he doesn't
dare trust me, I'll give him poison, the dirty rascal!' Then if
she sets horns on you, you must hide your shame and suffer like
a captured wolf." v. 2782

To that Dame Föllipruoch said, "It seems to me that you're
the curse of women. Don't you know you can find both good and
bad in all things? Therefore a wise man says, 'Seek your wife
not far away; but, if you wish a liege-lord, find one far off from
whom you can easily break if he doesn't treat you as he should.'
By this you should note how a man fares with a skillful and well-
born wife, than which there is nothing better. If you remain
in the house, she is your comforter and waits on you; if you go
out, her blessing goes with you. If you come in, she comes
toward you with her affectionate greeting, which will heal all
your worries. Also, she has sincerely guarded your house and
honor and other wealth." v. 2804

Hafenschleken could not stand this. He said, "Why should
I keep quiet any longer? It's truly amazing what she prates!
She wants to teach us the art of purchase in taking a wife, in
which every man is cheated, no matter how much he knows.
People test everything before they complete the purchase, ex-
cept for the cowardly women who never let themselves be really
seen before marriage. That brings sorrow to many a man who
learns all too late the faults his wife has." v. 2818

Erenfluoch was in such a hurry to answer that she almost
pissed. She shouted out of her throat, "Sir Hafenschlek, you
are a rascal who wants to desecrate holy matrimony against
right and against God; that grieves and injures me greatly.
Tell me, where have you read that every woman must be evil?
Haven't you yet read that you should think well of everyone as
long as he has not been proved a treacherous person?" v. 2832

Nagenflek heard this and shouted, "So help me, for a plum's
sake! In her opinion she's learned fourteen of the seven arts;
yet she still doesn't know that scripture says truly of all women,
'By nature every woman is very unclean in her body.' "[189]

Snatereina refuted this. She said, "And if the matter isn't
settled yet, then listen to something else I'm going to tell you!
If anyone wishes to live according to his own heart's desires,
he's not doing right, be he knight or squire. That's why God
has given us reason, by which we live communally and not like
dogs, to whom honor is unknown." v. 2850

Schlinddenspek stepped forward and said, "High ho! How

much bother and expense I still detect in marriage, enough and
much and even more! At once you must have money and ex-
pensive bed clothes, women's jewelry, household utensils, clothes
enough for four people, wine and bread and flesh and fish and
other things that belong to the table; house and yard and ser-
vants and cattle, fields and meadows. Bertschi, see, note, and
hear what woe[208] you'll get, as plagues us poor people."

Töreleina spoke, "So help me, so? I think you're made of
straw, and that's why fool's speech is coming from your mouth
right now. You say, 'If he wants to have a wife then he must
have money in his purse, and also clothes and other things?'
Hear something else that I sing! Tell me, what did Adam do,
who never had a penny yet lived nine hundred years and more
with honor in the Old Testament? What's the bed good for?
Don't you see how a Hungarian does who has never seen a
feather bed and yet finds himself good comfort? If you want
other clothing, then look at the woman of Spain who has no
other clothes! Her garment is a linen sheet hanging down
from her shoulders; with it she guards the cow and goes on foot,
even while she spins and carries a cradle with a child.   v. 2888

"Woman's jewelry? What is that? That's her virtue, which
should embellish every woman better than a pearl-crowned body.
Household utensils may be all right; therefore do as a mer-
cenary often does who finds his troops kitchenware for a shill-
ing. If he can't get wine, then he should refresh himself with
water like a man from Prussia to whom grapes are unknown!
And who has need of meat? A preacher has rosy cheeks and
also a fat face but doesn't eat any beef.[185] You talk about fish?
You're not wise, for that is a food for lords.[106] Whoever has no
wine and pepper should do without fish. House and yard are an
honor, but hear this! How does a Lombard do who lives in
another's inn yet always gets on three times as well with his
money as he who built the house?   v. 2914

"Then you say, 'Where is man and maid servant?' It seems
to me you're crazy in the head. Whoever can't have a servant
should serve himself; that is right. How often one must wait
on another and yawn in his throat.[132] You say that cattle are
useful. Surely, if they ate neither night nor day and didn't suffer
harm from any spell-caster[147] or from wolves upon the heath.
Fields and meadows would be good if God protected them from
hail and from strangers' sickles, from mice and from swarms of
birds. Bread is necessary for us all, so praised be He who gave

it to us! Yet you don't need much of it if you wish to live moderately. According to the teaching of the sages, no man suffers want if he'll content himself as long as he lives with what his nature requires."   v. 2936

Ofenstek countered that, "Women still cause much sorrow, pain, and discomfort, as I'll explain to you. If she is beautiful and young, you'll get no good from her. You are scorned, and she can do nothing. Then, in my opinion, it is hard to keep for yourself something that others are always chasing after. If she is old and misshapen, then she can do nothing but prate; you are neglected and she brings you no joy. Then, as they say, it is also hard to keep something forever that no one else wants to have.   v. 2952

"If she has many relatives, you'll always be worried that one of them may cause a scandal and cause you to be run out of the country along with him. The poor ones will gnaw you to the bone, the rich ones will pay no attention to you. If you want to remain unbeaten, then you must accept her as your boss. If she is poor and without relatives, then you have never fared worse! How often people will throw it in your face, 'You have degraded and lowered yourself, you have become a beggar and degenerated with wife and children!' "   v. 2966

Damsel Fina said at once, "Everyone is expressing his opinion; so I'll begin mine too as best I can. Ofenstek, you're still a boor. What does the doctor of nature say? Doesn't he say that a sound body holds a sane mind? Therefore no wise man should consider a beautiful woman evil. If she's young and can't do much, then I'll tell you she can learn what a housewife should know. She'll be docile and pliant like a baby in the cradle. But, if you have to have an old one, you still needn't complain; for she'll be your nurse and take care of you, and she'll do everything for you she should. If she can't bear children, then you should have her for a mother.   v. 2988

"If she is not pretty, so let it be; for she'll appear all the prettier because of that! How well I can prove that through clever logic! The uglier a woman is, the more she beautifies herself with painting and fixing up, with clothes and other things. Then, the more she is adorned, the more beautiful she will appear at the time."

"Wait, just wait, for shit's sake! How much sophistry she knows!" said Ofenstek then quickly. "The Devil has taught you that. Well then, that may be all right in the daytime, but tell

what he'll do at night when she's lying by him so naked and ugly
as a log."   v. 3006

She answered him at once, "Let him have no light by the bed.
Also, he might well refrain from lying when people should be
sleeping. Now, if he sees little, her ugliness won't do any harm;
for to the touch all women are of the same leather, no matter
what one does. It's just the way it is with chickens, which bear
so many kinds of feathers in their skin: when they are served
to people at the table, roasted warm, they all show the same
flesh. It seems to me you say it's never good to seek too high or
low for a wife. To that I will answer you: if anyone wants to
find happiness, let him keep to his own kind."   v. 3026

As soon as the speech was ended, old Dame Bertha Laich-
denman called out loudly, "Oh, young children, you're setting the
cart before the oxen. Don't you know that old people have wise
advice for other people? Therefore we should have begun with
our gossip Colman, and not rushed into the council unasked,
one ahead of the other."

To that Engelmar said, "Your words are true in themselves,
but you are speaking them deceitfully; for you are the oldest of
all." The council would have ended in an uproar, if it had not
been brought to order with staves and rakes.   v. 3043

Bertschi began speaking, "My lords, when one should make
crooked straight, it isn't right to make it all the more crooked."
And with that he said to Colman, "You well know that the first
and the last are always supposed to be the best in both council
and combat. Therefore tell us, my good man, what would be
the best thing to do."

Colman said wisely, "I have come here to listen and not to
chatter; for God has deigned to give me two ears and one mouth.
That should teach you that one should talk little and hear much;
thus he will do well."   v. 3062

In reply Triefnas said, "I like wise words from a good tongue
more than silence from a mute. Moderation is good in all things.
Better than that I can't tell you."

The grayhaired man began his speech very courteously as
follows, "I've often heard the proverb 'An old beard has wis-
dom.' In addition I've observed that young brains are clever.
It seems to me, as is well known, that women are not without
astuteness. I have seen this especially in this council, I must
admit. So many points have been touched on and expounded so
very cleverly here that I can tell you nothing but childish words,
which I'll now begin.   v. 3082

"Well now, let's assume that every woman is basically decent and respectable (which, as I have read, can unfortunately never be); even then one would not be good for you. Listen to what truth tells us: no one can serve two masters properly and fittingly night and day. Therefore you cannot serve your wife with activity and your God with contemplation. I tell you that in earnest, however well a psalter may harmonize with a lute. I have also read that, if a man wishes to be saved, he has no need of a wife; and that's true in my opinion.   v. 3100

"Also, if your wife lies down on the bench or feather-bed, you must consider her sick[86] and never leave her, especially when she gets pregnant. Now, when she has borne the child, one says that she has recovered. But listen to what I understand by that! She has recovered[71] like one who has lost a boil and caught an ague. I swear that to you by St. Gall![4] Don't you see that then you'll really have baby screaming, bed-wetting, diaperwashing, and baby bathing? Also, you must have nurses; and wet-nurses drink more than one finds water in the sea, and they eat a lot and claim the baby has done it all.   v. 3120

"Yet all that is almost nothing, until your child grows up. Then you really have to suffer in trying to provide it respectably with food and clothing, with shoes and other expenditures. You must guard your boy, both evening and morning, from stealing and robbing both openly and secretly, from striking and stabbing, from beating and also breaking. You must guard your daughter from vice and dissipation, from scholars and priests[185] in houses and in streets.   v. 3136

"Well now, let's assume that all that has been suffered. Then, when the father has risked body and soul for wealth and position for his child's joy and profit, it usually says to him in its mind, 'Gentle father, if only you were buried so I might get my inheritance!' You'll never be without misery, no matter how well the child is formed. But, if it is lost or born lame or blind or as a fool or mute, then all our joy and happiness are really gone. You can take my word for that! I would have still more to tell you, except that my cough is plaguing me so much I can't finish what I have in mind."   v. 3156

When his speech ended, no one knew how to contradict him (their throats were parched and they all wanted to agree with him) except for old Dame Laichdenman, who now stepped forward. How loudly she spoke, what noise she made! "And if my teeth didn't ache, I would have answered you sooner. Dear children, with your permission I will say that calves grow into strong oxen with which one cultivates and plows as soon as their horns harden. By this you should note: when I was a child, I understood as a child, I spoke as a child, and I acted as a child; but now I have become grown up and put away childish things. Therefore I don't want to follow the advice of any man if I can have something better.   v. 3180

"Sir Colman, you shouldn't hold against me what I am going to tell you. When you were supposed to start advising like a wise man, the earth began to move and rise up. I feared a dragon was going to come. I looked—it was a mole . . . blind, stupid, and ugly. That I will overcome quickly, beginning with the last, which I can do best of all. You say you would have told us more, but that you couldn't because of your painful cough. Well now, your cough is over. Tell me, what did you have in mind?"   v. 3196

Sir Colman answered her thus, "A long speech is unbecoming; and therefore I'll say nothing but a few words. The truest proverb is this: 'A single father can lead seven children through a lattice[45] better than seven children can lead one father.' And now, clever lady, for Christ's sweet sake please show us your wisdom. I was ever ready to learn."   v. 3208

Then Laichdenman said quickly, "Sir Colman, it's a shame for a graybeard of seventy-seven to study; yet it's worse if a man can not or will not learn in his old age, for he will win much disapproval and blame. And therefore mark my words if you want to be better taught. When God created the first man in true love and forbade him to eat the apple, the creature forgot his faith and broke the Creator's commandment. Therefore don't be vexed if your children don't thank you as you have expected; for thus you have rewarded your parents with oat-straw. And yet I must admit to you that a man is much quicker to avenge his father than his child, if both of them have been scorned.   v. 3232

"And you say there has been enough discussion and that much talking suits fools. All that would be true if you understood the words to be vain, annoying, harmful, and useless. But, if the tongue is good and useful, they will do no harm; and thus they cannot be too long. Please keep that in mind. Have you never heard that large cattle need much grass? A while ago you told us of the very great pain and misery we would forever bear if the child doesn't have all its limbs. To that I'll answer you at once: it's nobler for a child to be in Hell[188] than not to exist."[148]   v. 3252

"Hold on," said Colman then, "it seems to me that he who can do the most lies and fails most before God and His spirit. Don't you know that the truth says of the false rascal Judas that he would have been better off if he had remained unborn?"

Well, that made Dame Bertha so angry she almost lost her mind. She said, "Listen here, Sir Colman! It seems to me you are contradicting yourself. You say learning pleases you, yet you want to correct me all the time. That's not becoming, for neither a pupil nor a servant has that right. If you wish to learn, keep quiet and listen with complete humility wherever you are." v. 3270

Colman answered courteously, "Mercy, gracious lady. If I have asserted anything against you, it has occurred for no other reason than that I wished to learn the truth through statement and rebuttal. I am despairing in this obscure wisdom. Help me, lady, for your good name."

"Very well then," said Laichdenman, "but you are just trying to get the best of me. If you would talk that way, we still might reach an agreement. Believe me, I'm not against it. I see that what God does and what He says conforms to the truth, if only one can understand it. Therefore, whenever a text confuses us, a gloss is very good for showing us its right meaning in wise words. v. 3290

"Now my text says, 'The worst thing is never to exist.' But yours says it would have been better for God's betrayer if he had never been born, since his soul is entirely lost. In this your cleverness thinks there is a contradiction. I will reconcile that for you; for it is the truth, believe me! It would have been better for him if he had been cut right out of his mother than that he was born and the mother did not die; for afterwards he often slept with her, and he cut off his father's head.[148] Another gloss speaks thus, 'It would have been better for him if he had not been born in Christ's time; for that caused him this anger.' v. 3310

"Yet this must have an end (everything cannot be told), and we should return to the matter which your stupidity previously mentioned about the children that are born dead and are entirely lost. Here the father loses just like a man who is given a tree that bears empty nuts. Then you have needlessly said that the child desires its father's death. How does that hurt me? As one says, 'Thoughts and wishes never hurt me.' You say one always suffers from the misdeeds of grown children? Instruction is good against this, as well as the punishments one deals

young children both night and day while one can still mold
them.   v. 3330

"And what do you say about expenses, about food and cloth-
ing? Don't you know that a person should be reared on this
earth in sack-cloth and with simple food, if one wishes to make
him worthy and wise, growing old in silk and dying rich and
happy? Therefore no money is good for the young man if the
expenditure will do him harm. If you can't keep other women
as wet-nurses, then commit your child to its mother so she will
suckle it, guard it, and care for it. That is given her by nature.
Why do you prate about diapers and washing, so long as water,
ashes, wood, and old linen are so cheap in the land?   v. 3350

"Along with that you want to scare us with baby-crying and
bed-wetting, with sickness and hardship. Take my word for
this! One's own house and own child make great effort into
nought and a little joy into paradise. I'll prove these words to
you thus. If the smith is in his own house, then he gets up of
his own accord and hammers merrily all day long so he will have
the earnings in his pocket. If he is in another person's smithy,
he thinks he has suffered a year when he has worked one day.
How little he can get up out of bed early in the morning, since
the money doesn't go to him.   v. 3369

"If my child cries, I think it's singing, so well its voice pleases
me. It's just too bad for the neighbor who can't sleep through
it. If I have eggs in the house, I'll make them into big chickens
that will seem fatter to me than the miller's fattening hogs.[120]
Nuts and bread on my table taste better than all the fish[106] the
Margrave of Ferrara[6] would give me if I were visiting him. But
if you say a man can keep house without a woman, that is not
true in my opinion, since it has no basis. Its foundation is a
worthy wife who maintains the house with her person in all
sorts of ways, with cooking and child rearing. If she becomes
sick and weak, then she will become well again, and that is a
joy.   v. 3390

"You have read in scripture that a man does not need a wife
if he aspires to God's kingdom. But what has our case to do
with gray cloth? It is not written there that a wife will harm
him, is it? Concerning the first point, I heard that no one may
serve two masters. Note that that means two that are opposed
to each other! But your wife is not the Devil; so I will ignore
the scripture and return rather to the word I have found some
place that says that not only maidens possess everlasting bliss.
It can also be that married people are saved, hide and all. How

true that is, and not a dream! St. Eustace,[189] a citizen of Rome, had a wife and children too who were saved along with him, and many other great saints. Now, speak up, if any of you on-lookers wants to!" v. 3414

When her speech had died down, those who had sided with Colman now turned away from him; and thus the discussion went awry. Yet the graybeard stirred himself again and said, "The Devil must have granted it, or God with His blessing, that a woman has now so completely surpassed me in wisdom and scripture. And yet I still can't believe Metzi suits any man whom the world holds in honor, she who is so flat and also limps, and whose breath stinks so. She is so hunchbacked and so short and doesn't care a fart about respectability! How swarthy she is, and ugly! No one dares name her for shame.[83] Then too, she has nothing; and that's the rub. What do we want with this bag that the flies have so beshitted and the dogs have so torn up?" v. 3438

Laichdenman began again, "So help me! How much that dingy tooth can say! I'll tell you to your face, if you don't want to believe the truth then people will believe you are an ass and an ox. What are you telling us with your wisdom? You still hardly know who you are. Even if she is goitered, bent and lame, you should still consider her noble. If her breath stinks to Heaven, no stranger will kiss her. If she is short and very hunchbacked, she will need all the less cloth. Even if she sees little with her eyes, she can still bear children, believe me! Dark women's milk is good, large breasts give enough. Rosy cheeks and ruby mouth are much more harmful than healthy, for they often make young lads old in a few days. Beautiful hair leads women astray, and it harms men in their prayers.[189] It is more useful to spin thread than to brush hair. v. 3464

"She is named Rüerenzumph? That is a shame only for him who wanted to name her that when she was christened. And if she can't conduct herself properly, it happens in good faith. And even if the well-born maid had lost her honor in sweet love, one would earn remission of sin, according to scripture, if he plighted himself to her in matrimony. If she is poor, well, then let that be! She will live in spite of it; and she will sleep all the better and not be afraid of thieves and fire. Her life and goods are safe, and she will gladly accept whatever one does to her. And jealousy too can not harm her. We see that those advantages are had by poverty, about which there would be much to say if this little book wouldn't become too heavy.[81] Hear what the wise man commands. People should choose each other through true love, not for money, and then they will be happy in the world. Well now, she loves Bertschi; so I'll sing him this song:

> 'Bertschi as his wife should take
> little Metz; that's no mistake!' "   v. 3492

Then Triefnas softly sang, "I've never heard better singing."

Yet there was so much discussion back and forth about this point that they began to get dizzy; and everyone shouted, "I'll burn up and drown in all the wit, in all the counsel and all the sweat. We could keep this up for ever; so let's let the matter stand or all listen together to the village scribe alone. He has read a lot of books; therefore, whatever he says, let's let it take place."   v. 3506

Heinritze was then chosen as arbiter so that he might give his verdict. He said, "Now just listen to me! You could easily have found a wiser man; yet it often happens that a little fool can think of something clever that a wise man has missed. I well see why you have failed and decided nothing at all: you have been standing while thinking, whereas one should sit and rest. You have been riming and versifying; but wise matter wants no rime,[81] for who can embellish a dispute with metrical language? Therefore I'll sit down and tell you my opinion in simple prose: v. 3524

"In God's name, amen! Here one can pose the question as to whether a man should take a wife. To that I will answer thus. If a man will and can remain constant, produce children, and support a wife and children with righteous wealth, but does not[197] wish to serve God as chaste as an angel,[189] let him take as his wife a woman who will please him and be fruitful, wise, worthy, and his equal."

Bertschi was pleased with the verdict and said, "My situation is just as you have said, and therefore I wish to have Metzi."

"Then take her," said Farindkuo, "God give you luck and happiness thereto."

Colman said, "Let me tell you. He may have luck and happiness, provided he always pleases her and her kinsmen."

      v. 3534

THE MATCH-MAKING

Thereupon they selected and elected two of the best (they were the clever scribe and Rüerenmost, who was his equal) so that they might go to Fritz and begin to discuss the matter with him indirectly, with roundabout words as if they were acting on their own, and thus bring about the marriage cautiously and without scholar or priest.

Therefore they hurried toward Fritz's house, where they were minded to go. If anyone asked them, "Where are you going then?" they answered, "On an errand." v. 3548

"Let's go," Henritze said, "it's an important matter. It's a matter that's so important that no other matter was ever its equal."

Rüerenmost began to think of something else and said, "It seems to me we are in too big a hurry. If we chase and run after Fritz, how dearly we will have to buy what we want from him! Therefore let me suggest something else. We should go to the tavern, for Fritz likes to drink in the evening, and we can tipple with him. v. 3563

"Then you should begin by saying, 'Truly, Fritz, you're a man to whom I don't begrudge honor and wealth. Your friendship has always pleased me; for you are worthy and respectable. Well now, you have a daughter there who is growing gray in your hands. It's high time she should have borne a child and been respected in the world, for she's grown and worthy of a husband. And therefore I have something in mind which might be very good if I could succeed in bringing it about: namely that Triefnas, that fine young man, would marry Metz. He's young and also rich, serious, and of as good a family as one can find in the village.' v. 3584

"And as soon as you have had your say, I'll add mine and advise him to do it and promise that I'll do whatever I can toward it both night and day, since his kinship pleases me too. In this way we will discover what he wants to do."

Now the scribe began to speak and said, "Well then, let that be done." How quickly they brought about that which Rüerenmost had planned!

Fritzo thanked them for it courteously and said, "May God bless you richly. Your friendship has always pleased me, and I seek it as one should. Yet it seems to me he is too snooty and too high-brow in his thoughts." v. 3602

"Don't worry," they told him. "However great he is, he can be had. You see to the wishes of your relatives; we trust that we can satisfy him."

With that he stood up and drank and said, "I shall always thank you for your words. The matter will be tended to early in the morning, and not too late. May God keep you. Drink St. John's blessing,[129] and let me treat you to the wine."

METZI'S FAMILY COUNCIL

They thanked him cordially and left him. Fritz was pleased with the discussion; he slept until early the next morning and then gathered his kinsmen together. The first was Ochsenkropf, the second was named Lärenkopf, the third was called Lastersak, the fourth was Uotz Übelgsmak, Straub and Härtel Saichinkruog, and a lot of other respectable[123] people. His kinswomen came too: they were Dame Hilda Leugafruo, Schürenprand, Nimindhand, Richteinschand, Siertdasland, and many other worthy women whom I cannot name. Fritz ordered them to sit down and wisely spoke thus: v. 3632

"Dear kinswomen, friends, and relatives! Know that I don't like to risk great matters without your advice; for a wise man has rightly said, 'No one is self-sufficient in his cause.' Someone has spoken to me (from where it is reported I do not know); and therefore I think Triefnas would be pleased with my daughter, if she were given him as a wife. Tell me, what would be well to do?"   v. 3644

Ochsenkropf was a respected man,[123] and he also had intelligence and strength. He said, "We owe it to you to help you as much as you wish and also to advise you in everything. Then understand that your daughter wants a husband who is a Christian, young and fresh and healthy too, strong and sound of body, and not too soft like a woman. The best color of all is white partially mixed with red. Hair and beard should be a little bit curly in appearance, not too black, too red, too hard, but a little bit brown in color. The head should have a high crown, not too large, with a suitable forehead and with soft brown eyebrows. The mouth and nose should be moderate, the neck strong but not too long, and the slope of the shoulders not too effeminate. The chest should be broad, the legs strong, and the waist slender at the middle. Hands and arms should be long and large, and the fingers should be their match. Short finger nails are becoming, and the foot should not be too broad. His gait should be very rapid and even. An average man suits us best. Now if Bertschi is of that type, then I advise that Metz take him."   v. 3676

Lärenkopf was not satisfied with that, "A beautiful house

won't suit us," he said, "if a wicked host is constantly cheating the guests. Now even if Bertschi is sound in body and has good color but does not have virtue too, I consider him worse than a cow. Therefore he must also be a highly respected and just young man, who sleeps little and does not stand around idly or like to go around with evil people, who can speak yet doesn't lie or deceive his friends with cunning, who knows nothing of wine or of dice and who is not a glutton, since gluttony would never leave him, who can subsist on his own and leave other people's cattle alone, whose heart is not too faint nor his head too hasty, who suffers and acts as one should if he likes good breeding and respectability. And, if he has all that, I'm of the opinion it wouldn't hurt Metz if she took Bertschi in marriage." v. 3704

Füllenmagen leaned forward and said, "This matter won't help much. What does it help if one is healthy, respectable, and well behaved, if he is not wise and clever too? For it is the way of the world that asses and fools both pull a cart that's loaded with wine yet must refresh themselves with water."[31] v. 3714

Dame Leugafruo rudely interrupted his speech and said, "Don't forget what you have in mind; but first hear what people say, 'Whoever wishes to fathom all things will ruin himself and accomplish little. No marriage would ever have taken place if one had considered this and that; nobody in the world was ever so pure but that he had some shortcoming. See, I'll tell you frankly, I don't consider Triefnas a louse. Therefore I won't lie or deceive the good girl. He's an upright young man, well behaved and respectable, and unassuming too, except that he seems lazy to me and has too large a mouth. But I will answer that myself. A small mouth is becoming to a woman but not to a man; as I have told you before, a big city needs a wide gate.   v. 3736

"If he is lazy and likes to sleep, he will refrain from all that when the hungry child begins to sing, 'Daddy, give me bread.' And how much wisdom should a young man have who doesn't even know how to read? Therefore my advice is that we send to him and wisely discover his intentions, just as he has done. And if he wants to have our kinswoman, have someone tell him to come at once and then place him against the wall and tell him in order everything he should do and leave undone. And, if he can learn and act according to your words, then we should give her to him."

Everyone was pleased with this advice except for Father

Fritz alone. He said, "You all know what Bertschi has recently done to me and my daughter."

Damsel Hächel Schürenprand refuted this at once and said, "You talk like someone who is asleep. If Bertschi has brought you disgrace because he can woo so well, we should give her to him all the sooner; and thus she will keep her good name all the better. Don't you know they say that a mouse in the sack and a louse on the neck, a wench[72] in the house and a fire in the barrel, they all repay their host with evil? I know it well in my own case. When I got boy-crazy, I would have taken four of them myself, if help hadn't come to me in time. As they say, an old maid is poison in any house."   v. 3777

They all said, "You are quite right; we should send for the lad and do as Leugafruo has just advised us." So Fritz and Härtel got up and walked to the house of the scribe, whom they fortunately found there. He greeted them nicely, and they thanked him.

Thereupon Fritz began and said, "Concerning the discussion that occurred last night, we have agreed in this: we want to know what he thinks about it. And, if he will follow your advice, then come back home to your house with him, my friend. Here we will explain to him what he should do and leave undone."   v. 3794

Henritze said, "So be it, so be it!" How quickly this took place! One could scarcely have looked around. When Bertschi came, they greeted him nicely and he thanked them even better.

They said, "What do you have in mind?"

He answered, "It would seem good to me if you gave me Metzi in marriage, I'd treat her well and do even more."

Lastersak began to proclaim, "All that could take place if you would strive for honor and also follow our instructions."

Bertschi said, "I'm well pleased, I'll do all one should."   v. 3809

BERTSCHI'S CATECHISM

"Then sit down," said Fritz, "and show us a bit of your knowledge. Do you know the Pater Noster?"

"Yes indeed," Bertschi answered.

"The Ave Maria and the Creed too? Then recite them and don't delay." Triefnas began and said: v. 3817

"Pater Noster. Lord God our Father, Who art in Heaven, hallowed be Thy name. Thy kingdom come to us. Thy will be done here on earth as in Heaven. Give us our daily bread and forgive us our debts as we should do to our debtors, and lead us not into evil temptation, but deliver us from all evil! Amen.[188]   (line 9)

"Ave Maria. Hail to thee, pure maid Mary, full of all grace. God is with thee. Thou art blessed above all women, blessed is the fruit of thy womb, our lord Jesus Christ. Amen. (line 14)

"Credo in Deum. I believe in one God, Father almighty, who is Creator of Heaven and earth, and I believe in His only-begotten Son, our lord Jesus Christ. I believe that that same Son of God was conceived of the Holy Ghost and also born of the pure Virgin Mary, and I believe that He was martyred under the judge Pilate and died on the holy cross and was also buried. I believe that His holy soul went to limbo and took out from there all those who had done His will,[188] and that on the third day He arose from death, true God and true man, and I believe that He ascended to Heaven and sitteth there on the right hand of Almighty God, His Father. I believe that He is to return afterwards to judge over the dead and the living, every man according to his works. I also believe in the Holy Ghost, in the Holy Church of Christendom, and in the communion of saints; and I believe I will win remission for all my sins if I regret them with all my heart. I believe in the resurrection of the dead, and I believe that after this life I shall possess eternal life if I have merited it.[188] Amen, amen, amen, amen." (line 45)

"Better hold up, that's enough of that." Fritz then said. "You are so wise that I think you must have studied many years in foreign lands."   v. 3821

Bertschi supposed that things were settled and asked that Metz be given him right away. That would have been done at once if Lastersak had allowed it; but he did not like the hurry and said, "A great matter needs caution, and especially marriage. Tell me, fellow, can you do anything else?"

Bertschi quickly answered, "I can do as much as four others: plow, thresh, sow, hoe, reap, and mow; and, whatever pertains to bread, that I can do and do gladly."

Lastersak began again and said, "Man can not live in both body and soul by bread alone, but with God's word, the salvation of the body and the treasure of the soul, which emanates from His mouth and announces all bliss to us. And therefore you must learn better."

"I'll gladly do that," said Triefnas.   "First of all I would like
to hear how a youth should learn."   v. 3847

A CODE FOR SCHOLARS

"That was very wisely spoken," said Lastersak, "and there-
fore learn what I know about it.   Ten things are suitable for
a scholar who wants to become a master and win great profit
and fame.   The first is that he should especially well serve our
Lord, who Himself once said to us with His holy mouth, 'But
rather seek ye the kingdom of God; and ye will be given all
things ye should have in order to live.'   And Solomon says
concerning that, 'Wisdom does not come into an evil soul.   The
beginning of wisdom is the fear of the Lord with the knowledge
of the Holy.'[218]   v. 3865

"The second thing he should have is foreign land, that suits
him well.   According to very true teaching, no one can be a
prophet in his own country, since he is too well known.   Friends,
companions, and women impede him spiritually and physically,
in wealth, profit, and fame, in knowledge, training, and learn-
ing.   Yet if he would refrain from them and avoid evil com-
panionship, he could learn without limit, for knowledge is avail-
able everywhere.

"The third thing is that he have a sound head that's able to
learn; and, if he wants to get ahead, he should study what
pleases him best.   v. 3883

"The fourth thing is, as I have read, that he should be very
humble; for, if he has arrogance in his heart, he will be unwilling
to learn and will think himself the equal of his teacher.   There-
fore he will never become rich in skill or knowledge, since no one
can be big who has not once been small.   Keep that fact in mind,
and know that man is born as artless as a blank parchment.

"The fifth thing, which will help him greatly, is perseverance
in his study.   Diligent study is good, and unsteady studying hurts
everyone.

"The sixth thing that should be included here is that he must
read his lesson over often and understand it well, if he wishes to
gain knowledge.   v. 3903

"The seventh, as the teacher says, is questioning the scripture,
provided he doesn't let himself tire of research and asking.

"The eighth of which I will tell you is good food, but not too
much of it, warm clothes, wine in moderation; that will make
him courtly and clever too.

"The ninth, which suits him well, is to be neither too poor nor too rich. Great poverty will hurt him much, but wealth will impede him even more.

"The last is, hear me well, that he should relax occasionally, but not too much, with singing, lute-playing, or with other things that might give him pleasure, yet with propriety as is fitting. In this way he will acquire knowledge and yet not perish in body, if he wishes to devote himself to knowledge."   v. 3925

Then said Triefnas very readily, "See, I have all that in me, and a good will too. Therefore I ask you, virtuous Sir, to tell me all the knowledge there is everywhere."

Then Lastersak began laughing and said, "That would be a long undertaking. No man was ever so wise that he could excel in all the arts and sciences, except our Lord God, Jesus Christ, from Whom nothing is hidden. Art is long, and life is short; so merely learn what a layman should not do without. I'll gladly tell you that, and I will begin thus with the best:

A DOCTRINE FOR CHRISTIANS

"Every Christian man should be ready to believe, above everything you know or imagine, that the true Trinity actually has three persons in one essence. According to correct report, the first is the Father, omnipotent above all things. The second, which I shall name for you, is the Son, full of knowledge. The third (keep this in mind) is the Holy Ghost with its goodness. The Father has come from no one and never can; the Son flows constantly from the Father and ever rejoins Him in love; likewise the Holy Ghost procedes from them both without ever leaving them. I'll give you an illustration of this that will make this dogma understandable. Coal and heat and light can be in one ember. The heat comes from the coal, the light proceeds from them both. And even if one may recognize or name them individually or attribute power primarily to the Father or wisdom to the Son or goodness to the Holy Ghost, you should still know that they are equal on earth and in Heaven in power and wisdom, in goodness and everlastingness.   v. 3977

"You should also know that no one comes before God's eyes without faith, even if he has performed many good works on many occasions. Likewise, your faith avails nought without good works, as one says.

"Therefore keep the holy Ten Commandments seriously. That is, keep God in your mind, and do not swear by Him vainly. Keep holy what one should keep holy, and honor your father and mother. You should kill no one nor occupy yourself with inchastity. Keep yourself from stealing and from bearing false witness. Don't covet another man's wife nor a stranger's goods, as truth says.   v. 3995

"Also be ready to do the six works of mercy. Feed the hungry and give drink to the thirsty; you should clothe the naked and shelter the stranger, and you should visit the sick and comfort the prisoner.

"And also, for your salvation, you should have a part of the seven sacraments. They are baptism at the beginning and confirmation if you live that long. If you have sinned, penitence is good, God's body and His blood and also extreme unction. However blessed the priestly order[187] may be and however good holy matrimony, one can still avoid them without harm to the soul. If baptism, confirmation, and holy orders have been given to you once, they should not be given to you again. The others one can give now as before.   v. 4017

"But all this is as nothing if you won't also guard yourself from the seven sins, which are deadly and void of salvation. That is: from wicked pride, greed (the way of misers), hate, anger, inchastity, gluttony, and sloth.   v. 4025

"And after this, and last of all, learn that which will profit you the best: always love God above all else (thus you will never fail) and also your fellow Christians with complete love; and also do what the Church commands. That is, as I shall expound, fast earnestly for all of the holy twelve apostles. Yet St. James, St. Philip, and St. John the Evangelist bring us no woe of fasting; and St. Bartholomew does the same wherever people are not wont to keep his fast. Also keep all four of the Lord's fasts, the long fast until Easter, Whitsuntide Eve, the death of our dear Lady in August, and the pure worthy birth of God. One should hear mass daily with pure prayer, for that profits you. If anyone can't accomplish that, let him fulfill it on holy days.   v. 4051

"In addition you and everyone who is a Christian are bound to confess privately to your own priest once every year[186] and to receive God's body at the same time, if you possibly can. If anyone didn't do this and died thus, he should be buried in the field like a straw, provided he is over fourteen years old and has sense and reason. See, that is the Church's custom."

To that Triefnas said quickly, "Woe to me that I was ever

born! I don't know how one should confess, and therefore I suffer grievous pain." v. 4067

Lastersak understood a lot about that. "Listen to what I am going to tell you," he said to Triefnas. "I'll tell you this. You should cheer up and not despair so foolishly; what you can't do, you should learn. Now we will gladly teach you. Listen, I am still unordained, yet I have learned the general confession. Through it one learns how one should confess privately. Just repeat it as I say it to you, and remember it until your last day. v. 4081

"I, sinful man, I confess my debts to our Lord God, to my Lady St. Mary, and to all of God's saints and also to you, priest, in God's stead, that I have sinned greatly with words and with deeds, with thoughts and also with neglect of the ten commandments of our Creator, that I have not kept them, the six works of mercy, that I have not performed them, the seven sacraments, that I have not honored them, with the seven deadly sins, and with the seven gifts of the Holy Ghost, that is fear of God, goodness, skill, strength against sin, counsel, sense, and wisdom. I also recognize that I have sinned with my five senses: that is, with sight, with hearing, with smell, with taste, and with touch too, and also with other things: that is, with lack of virtue, with ridicule, with backbiting, with hate, with lying, with deceit, and also with ephemeral joys, with vainglory, with doubts about the Christian religion, with impatience, with ungraciousness, with disobedience toward my superiors, with inconstancy in good resolution, with trespassing against the holy commandments of the Church. However I have sinned, be it knowingly or unknowingly, I am sorry and regret it with all my heart; and I ask my Lady, St. Mary, and all God's saints and you, priest, to obtain mercy for me and remission of my sins from God, and, after this life, eternal bliss. Amen." (line 37)

Now as soon as this had been spoken, Lastersak said, "Triefnas, that's the general confession. And if you wish to confess all your sins to your priest privately, then do as I have shown you and tell him all your misdeeds one by one with complete contrition; and resolve with true sincerity to do penance willingly and to try to sin no more. If you don't do all that, then your confession is of no avail: you will incur God's wrath and be lost like a Jew's soul.[146] v. 4097

"Therefore, my dear young man, in order to attain bliss, contemplate how the world is like a tent, which is moved every day and can never remain whole and safe. It is undeniably an exile; therefore you should leave it and aspire to paradise, and thus you will be righteous and wise too. Remember also how worldly glory rages like the wild sea, up and down and back and forth, and takes its end like and abscess. Where is wise Sir Solomon, Absolon with his beauty, Samson with his great strength, the power of great Alexander, Aristotle with his wisdom? They have vanished like a dungheap, and nothing of theirs has remained on earth but their names, which are still spoken. That helps them little in their souls, if they are not free from sin. Therefore have no regard for praise, which will do little toward your salvation.   v. 4123

"Remember that God has made you as a man, not as an ape, as a Christian, not as a heathen, as a sane and rational man. You should thank Him for that diligently as long as you live on earth and guard yourself from wrong-doing. And especially flee unjust wealth, for no penance will do you less good than giving it back on your judgement day.   v. 4135

"Remember also how our lord, Jesus Christ, came in such a strict order. He became a man and suffered thirst and hunger, cold in winter, heat in summer. He preached and taught and spent His time here with travail. He sweated bloody sweat, for He knew of His martyrdom in advance. He was beaten and imprisoned, nailed and hanged as a thief; He perished and died miserably. See, He endured all that just for our salvation; for with such pain He wished to redeem sinners from death. Therefore ask Him especially to protect you and help you so this won't be lost on you.   v. 4157

"Last of all, remember that you are no more than a putrid dungheap. You can see this easily in your body, for you are full of stench and putrifaction. Therefore you should not vainly corrupt your beautiful soul in eternity through sinful pleasure and disinherit it from its Creator's kingdom. Know that you are of dust and will soon return to dust. Therefore, in your health, take heed that you are ready to die; for nothing is more certain than Death, and nothing less certain than his hour. He sneaks up most surely and likes the poor man as well as the rich.[173] He shows pity on no one and takes[209] the rich man the same as the poor man. Who then can save himself from him? He takes the young along with the old; he likes the crooked as well as the straight, everything pleases him the same. Do not entrust your soul to one who loves you for your beauty or wealth, but let him guard your soul who loves his own. Yet the best advice is to do good all your life if you wish to be a child of God."   v. 4187

Now when his speech had ended, Dame Leugafruo stepped forward and said, "I have often heard that, if one destroys his body with fasting, his soul won't stay with him. Therefore do as they say, and take good care of your body if you wish to keep your soul, especially when you are minded to marry. Therefore, Sir Straub (you are a man who knows so much about medicine), tell the young man everything that will help him in life so that he can remain hale and hearty and strong and active for a long time."   v. 4203

Straub answered like a real rascal. "No one likes to talk himself into Hell," he said. "Know that I am a man who can support himself only with sick people, with the beaten and wounded.[122] Therefore I won't inform you how you should remain healthy; for my skill would become nothing and my apothecary shop nought."

Bertschi said, "You are a rascal whom the penny well suits.[122] See, here are three old hellers.[60] Tell me fully how things stand."   v. 4217

THE HYGIENE LECTURE

Thereupon the doctor thought for a minute and began his discussion thus: "No medicine was ever so good as guarding yourself from too much and too little; for health demands moderation. You should take especial care to seek good air, which is clear and neither too hot nor too cold. And if the wind is too sharp, you need many kinds of thick well-made clothes of silk, linen, and cotton. Air is also good for sleepers; therefore a person does wrong if he sleeps where no air can come. But if you live near ground that's damp, remedy that in wintertime with clear bright fire that gives heat. In the summer open the door so the dampness will go outside and the air enter in. Also, the chamber should be especially well strewn with herbs that are not too mossy and full of water.   v. 4245

"The second thing that's good for health is the exercise one takes. In this regard, know that one who works little should have little food. On the other hand, one who exercises much is advised to have much food. Also know that before eating it is better to walk than to stand, but not to the point of exhaustion. That will rid you of your excessive humors. After eating you may stand or walk a little; for that is always good until the food has settled.   v. 4261

"The third thing nature wants is washing and bathing. In this regard you should note that, according to common parlance, there are two kinds of baths: sweat baths and water baths. Have a sweat bath prepared for you if you have superfluity between your flesh and your skin. A water bath with noble herbs, which is lukewarm and not too hot, will make you beautiful and fat too; and it will also keep you warm, if you have pity on your body. At the most you should wash your head once a week, and at least you should wash it every month without question, for that is right. According to my teaching, your feet should often be cleaned with lukewarm water; and all washing should take place while your stomach is empty. Now you have been informed of the third thing.   v. 4287

"Fourthly you should know that food suits you better when you are fighting with hunger than at any other time. Yet don't fill yourself up; leave the food an empty space in your stomach so it can digest all the better. If you don't want to regret your meal, then you should chew it well and thoroughly. Many courses will do you harm and take strength and power; but, if you can't do without them, then take the second course immediately after the first without any interruption. Be moderate in eating. Let the coarsest be first and take the most delicate last, unless it is soft fruit such as cherries, figs, and grapes, which should be served first of all. After the meal let one serve you harder fruits that will dry up the food: they are peaches, pears, and others that do the same.[132] May one serve us cheese after meat and nuts after fish at every table!   v. 4315

"The fifth thing you should have is drink to quench your thirst. I mean the true thirst that comes to healthy people only after eating, not before, from the heat of the stomach. But how should the drink be? Appropriate, not too long, in the summer white and clear or rosy, not heavy. In the winter you can better drink strong red wine; and, if it is pleasant and aromatic, it will well suit your sack. Also believe that a new wine that's clear and fine is better than an old one. If your stomach is cold, then drink a little high wine early in the morning, for that is fitting. But, if you wish to remain healthy, guard yourself from all adulterated wine.   v. 4337

"The sixth is necessary for all of us. It is sleep, for nature commanded us to rest well. Yet if you have eaten your fill, don't follow sleep like a beast, even if it has come over you. You should resist it with pastimes, sitting, walking, or standing until sleep seizes you a second time; then it is healthy to sleep quite restfully until your eye is free of drowsiness. Afterwards try to get up and go to stool. Let the water run from you, cough, clear your throat, and wash quickly, and discard all filth. Comb your hair and scrape your legs, and also clean out your ears. But, if you like to sleep during the day especially in summer, then lie down free from care where it is freshest and also as dark as night, without your shoes but well covered. You should also know that the head should be better covered while asleep than while awake. First of all you should lay yourself on your right side; you are advised never to sleep on your back if your head is hanging back in the straw. You may lie on your belly if your stomach has gotten cold. v. 4373

"The seventh thing that's good for you is a heart full of joy, since health depends largely upon that. Therefore everyone should guard himself from ill humor and anger that will scald his blood. Ill humor dries you up, and anger lashes you and makes flesh and bone too hard; yet a little anger is good if it refreshes your blood. Fire also serves this purpose, for it gives pleasure and promotes life. Yet don't turn toward it, since it's not good for your face. And, if it makes you too warm, it will weaken you physically. v. 4389

"And, lastly, let me tell you this. What one likes in his heart to sing, that is his song; what he gladly drinks, that is his drink; what he willingly eats, that is his food. Therefore the wise man tells us, 'Sensuality and bad habits corrupt wisdom and justice and pervert nature so that the nobleman becomes a peasant; and a peasant becomes a nobleman if he can conduct himself accordingly.'"

Richteinschand noticed that Straub was about to finish; so she said, "I have still heard nothing but what might help a monk. The lad wants to have our kinswoman and to get along in this world; so good conduct and other virtues suit his youth."
v. 4409

A LECTURE ON MORALS

Übelgsmack seconded that and said, "An exceptionally wise man says he knows nothing, and he lets himself be begged and implored for a word or two. I don't care an egg about all of that and will tell you how I perceive the matter; if anyone can do better, let him step up in front of me! Learn and hear what I can sing! Virtue is above all things; no one can be happy without virtue, I maintain. It gives strength to that nobility alone which is ennobled by its virtue.[176] It demands nothing of you but a good will; for, if anyone wishes to act virtuously, he is already virtuous. Yet it is more apparent in the rich man; for a proverb says that, if one's purse is full, people listen to him gladly and believe him well. In addition, take my word for this: if you have virtue in you, even though your purse is empty, it will become full and heavy too.   v. 4435

"In this regard you should know what the supreme virtue is. She is an old mother who grows more beautiful every day. She has four lovely daughters whom I'll name for you at once. The first is called Prudence, the second is called Justice; and Fortitude and Temperance can also be reckoned as two. Well now, just remember how quickly these high virtues are named. Yet that won't do you any good whatever if you don't listen to their commandments and teachings, for what you hear won't profit you and what you read won't be understood. What would it help to find gold if one wouldn't keep it? Therefore, my son, gladly learn what the virtues sing. Hear and note and keep their commandments and their teachings too.   v. 4457

"I'll tell them to you in order, but first of all learn this from me. Prudence, or Wisdom, is an arch-virtue and teaches us to recognize what is bad and good, which no other virtue does. She is the first, it's rightly said, since no one can have virtue without wisdom. I'll also tell you that Prudence also makes man partially like God in Heaven, much more than any other two virtues. In that regard scripture also says that Sir Solomon chose and selected wisdom before rich treasure and long life; and therefore God gave him wealth with wisdom, for that follows a wise disposition. One buys hogs by the pound but men by their wits. Next, you should straightway know that Prudence has four handmaidens: v. 4481

"The first is named Memory. Through her she offers you four commandments that you should keep and never forsake. That is, you should remember the lives of wicked men and how hard they have ended, and guard yourself from wrong-doing. On the other hand, remember the life that has been given to good men and how it has ended with bliss, and apply yourself to good works. Remember what people owe you, remember also what you owe so that you may have yours and also give the other person his.   v. 4497

"The second is called Circumspection. Through her she offers you four commandments which you should learn and also follow. That is, consider who the man is who wants to do business with you so you won't fare like those who buy pitch for amber. Consider a thing that concerns you, how it has been brought about and what can come of it, if you don't want to perish suddenly. Consider the place where you go, lie, sit, or stand; and don't linger long where rascals are in power. Consider in what time you live and also how the weather is so that you can quickly turn your cloak against the wind. v. 4517

"The third handmaiden is called Astuteness. By her you are commanded to learn these four teachings and fulfil them promptly. That is, resemble a man who can deceive you with words, and likewise observe and recognize how one can overcome cunning with cunning. Also deceitfully thank a person who has served you and given you something unwillingly, and thus he'll have what he should have. After this, if you have had to swear to thresh and plow for someone, you should turn your back on him if you wish to live by your wits. Moreover, wise men tell us that where fools are better off you should cunningly make yourself into a fool in all things. v. 4535

"The fourth is Discipline. By her she commands you four things which will help you if you learn them as one should. That is, you should consider yourself as poor in knowledge as an empty sausage skin and show yourself rich in discipline; and then you will act like a wise master. Teach the youth according to his ability with true affection, and he will profit by it. Lift a rafter according to its weight, and sow your seed upon the ground. If you want your pupils' favor, teach the best knowledge in a concise manner; teach it and leave everything else aside. If your teaching is to be agreeable, live accordingly; for we are annoyed by the teaching of anyone who shoots himself with his own tongue. v. 4557

"Justice is a virtue that teaches you that you should never injure anyone in his person, reputation, or wealth, but rather that you should willingly grant everyone that which is his. This virtue is considered the greatest in God of Heaven, the highest Judge, who with His power holds justice above all things. Who would wish to live on earth if there were no justice? Now robbers could not live and spend their time together if they did not mutually maintain the law that exists between them. She has ten handmaidens, whom you will see in sequence, each one separately with her four commandments. They are Severity, Mercy, Truth, Liberality, Peace, Love, Friendship, Obedience, Loyalty, and Innocence. v. 4581

"By Severity you are ordered to dedicate yourself to coercing[198] wicked people with mutilation and killing. Head for head and foot for foot; see, that's a just retribution![180] If anyone has taken a stranger's wealth through violence, let him return it at once with all gain that he has received or might have received. Also, if anyone has hailed another person before the court wrongly, you should charge him for all the costs incurred there. Also, if the man wants to be disobedient, give him the punishment he fears most of all, especially if he has committed it often.

"By Mercy you are ordered that no judgement should please you unless it has pity in it. If the case is really confused, don't follow the wicked Jewish multitude,[146] but turn at last to what is best and most merciful. In this regard you should have pity on widows, paupers, orphans, clergymen,[186] and loyal workers. Moreover, in order to have peace or conciliation, you may show mercy to one even if he is guilty, if he is too powerful.   v. 4616

"By Truth, my friend, you are ordered never to lie for any reason, if you wish to guard yourself from sin. If anyone cannot restrain himself from lying, you should never let him swear; for, if anyone wants to falsify his tongue, he will not respect an oath. Also guard yourself from liars if you wish to keep your wealth and good name, for no flesh was ever so wicked as a lying, dissolute tongue. If you have promised someone something, you should keep your promise unbroken unless he would break his word to you or unless you would sin by keeping it.   v. 4631

"By Liberality she demands that you should know what you give, why, and also to whom, be it to this one or to that one. Give your own and nothing else; for truth says that God wants no sacrifice with harm to another person. And give freely, if you wish to give, and avoid procrastination; for if you give in a trice you give twice. If it remains with you, you are taking it from me. And don't be satisfied with giving gifts in return for gifts. Let no one persuade you with gifts or force.   v. 4647

"By Peace you are ordered to hate no one; for where there is no peace in the house, God has been driven out. And if you wish to keep peace with everyone, do as one did who gave thanks for all good but kept silent whenever one did him harm. If you always want to keep peace with your comrade, entrust him with little of your belongings and don't stay with him under one roof. If you wish to turn war into peace, know that you should always use sweet speech, since that is very suitable for a reconciliation.   v. 4663

"By true Love you are ordered to ridicule no one; otherwise, I swear to you by God, you will become an object of ridicule. If you wish to be loved, then do as scripture tells us and love everyone dearly. Hear what else she orders you. If you want paradise instead of hell on this earth, then try to love your wife as yourself. Try to love other things too if you want them to bring you happiness. For nothing will make you free unless you have dear love in it. v. 4679

"Learn this about Friendship. For your own good you should test your friend for a long time. The wise man says, 'Keep the proved friend and don't let him go, be good to the friendly person so that he will be all the more friendly to you.' You should not do evil to your enemy in hope of friendship and reconciliation. Always help your friend unsolicited if he is in need. If he doesn't need your help, then help him only if he asks you. Do to your friend and to every man that which you desire from them, and refrain from that which annoys them and you do not wish to receive from them. v. 4695

"By Obedience it is prescribed that you should gladly obey your master, whoever he may be, in all good and sinless commands. You should always obey your parents and follow their advice if they truly love you and if the matter is proper. Follow your master more than yourself in your training, in commands, and in other things, if you wish to aspire to public approval. Moreover, if you want to be right, obey the serving girl and listen to the serving man, be obedient to a child in matters that are useful to you. v. 4711

"By Faith one calls to you, 'Be faithful, oh worthy man. Faith is a key to a good name, if anyone loses it he will no longer be worth anything.[161] Dice are nought and have no faith in them; so don't play for keeps with anyone you wish to keep as a true friend. If anyone has revealed and exposed his secrets to you, you should keep them especially secret and preserve them as faithfully as you would your own eyes. Yet you should never trust anyone in an important matter unless you have eaten a measure of salt with him. v. 4727

"By Innocence you are admonished not to harm yourself. Also vex no one else; and that will make you worthy and welcome. And, if you wish to be very innocent, guard yourself from wrong-doers, that is, from servants of causes that might bring harm. Preserve your life and your goods, and take careful heed of your good name. Even though you conquer an enemy, you are still not a wrong-doer. If you are a judge and have authority, hear the other side right away. Judge justly, that's my advice, and then no one will consider you in the wrong.   v. 4743

"Fortitude is understood in two ways. The first makes the body strong; but one should not consider it a virtue, since a rascal often has power. The second fortifies one's heart; it is a gentle and good virtue and shows us how to disregard all wickedness. It is the foremost and best in nobility and constancy; for, if anyone won't practice it, he will not maintain the other virtues. It has five lovely little maids: the first is Security, the second is Magnanimity, the third is Confidence, the fourth is named Constancy, and the fifth is called Patience.   v. 4761

"The first comes to you and says, 'If you are afraid, you should tell me.' If you say, 'Yes, I am worried. I shall be impoverished by tomorrow,' she will kindly answer, 'I wish you had lost the greed that is riding you, then you would always be rich.' If you are afraid of backbiting, she will say, 'Do your best and don't worry. Evil people will tell false tales, and not what we have merited.' But, if you are worried about sickness, she can tell us something else, 'Sickness can't stay with you for ever,' and similar things. 'If you are afraid of death, then you are a child,' she'll quickly tell you. 'It's no disgrace and you have to die; no one can avoid it.'   v. 4782

"The second comes up with a happy mind and says, 'My Lady thinks thus. You should apply yourself to great things; for no eagle catches flies. Strive for the common good rather than fight for yourself alone; for the common good enters in but private interest remains outside. If you have a magnanimous heart, grant people respect and wealth; and, if people don't respect you, kick up your heels and don't worry. If you are a man, you shouldn't flee unless you have to withdraw in such great peril that it would be your death to remain.'   v. 4798

"The third too does not delay long. She approaches you with her song, which says, 'Have hope in your heart, for that is good for your life. Do not despair, hero! That's my advice. How often a man has lost his all in a game and afterwards won twice as much. Have confidence and don't lose it, even if luck never comes to you; for often a Swabian takes his end with good hope, which averts pain. And especially have confidence if the wind overwhelms you with rain; and, if the sunshine comes in the meantime, you can mix your joy with care.'   v. 4814

"The fourth clothes itself for its journey in blue cloth and has a gentle voice. She says, 'In your thoughts guard yourself from vacillation. Be as constant as indigo blue in joy and sorrow; neither go with the first nor lie with the second. Constancy has a duty you should be ready to do; do not remain with evil things, and let no one force you from good ones. Yet it were not unfitting if a man took the better and left the good where he has found it, unless he is obligated to it some other way.' v. 4830

"The fifth won't fail to come to you bringing four sacks with her, which will especially suit everyone who wishes to remain at court. The first sack should hold clothes.[41] You should wear them neatly; for, if you are rich in your clothes, people will hold you in greater respect. The second sack is full of pennies; it will do you particular good, it will bring you friends and companions and no one will dare withstand you. The third sack is audacity. It has been prepared for you so that you may come forth freely, not like a dull hibernating bear. The last sack is patience, which will put an end to all your suffering in waiting, fasting, waking, keeping silent, and other things." v. 4850

Dame Richteinschand said at once, "I notice that you are familiar with the court. Therefore I ask your worship to teach him courtliness as well."

To that Lastersak answered very quickly, "If he wants that, I advise him to go to court himself. There he will learn good breeding in many things. With chickens one learns to cackle, with swine to smack the lips sowishly. Yet people often say, if one wishes to become a courtier, let him keep the peasants in mind; and, whatever they do in their boorish way, let him do exactly the opposite, and thus he will become courtly and elegant.[176] I can tell Bertschi this. If he wishes to conduct himself in a well-bred way, he can learn to at his wedding,[131] if it takes place. v. 4870

"And with this I turn my attention to the last virtue. It is called Temperance or Moderation and is unknown to many hearts; for no one ever practices temperance constantly and without interruption. Therefore, when every custom is corrupted frontwards and backwards with evil practices, know that moderation lies in the middle. Take an example of this right now. Here is the spendthrift, there is the miser; the spendthrift is the kind of a man who can't keep anything for himself, the miser hides it all together and can't let any of it out of his hand. They both have evil ways; so the liberal man wins the prize. He lives temperately both in keeping and in giving; that is, he gives what he should and keeps the rest. Also know that Temperance is such a splendid virtue that no one should neglect it for anything else. She has four gentle handmaidens, whom you should see. They are Humility (the raiment of God), Shame, Propriety, and Chastity. In them you will now see not less than sixteen points.   v. 4902

"What the first wishes to say, dear friend, note carefully. She says, 'If you wish to win the prize and be considered wiser than other people, then I will inform you of one thing: you must show yourself humble. If you wish to come into power, conduct yourself humbly; for whoever shall exalt himself shall be abased, whoever humbles himself shall be exalted. If you don't want to be ridiculed, listen to the second two commandments. You should never praise or censure yourself; and don't be too humble lest a fool get the better of you.'   v. 4918

"And what will Shame command you? She says, as I understand it, 'Be ashamed of all misdeeds, if you don't wish disgrace. Be ashamed of behavior that is not of respectable nature; for in my opinion anyone who cannot control himself is a fool. Also teach your children shame so they won't live like cattle, for one often blames the father for his child's disgrace. Yet know that a wise man who is old and powerful should not be too shame-faced lest he appear too childish.'   v. 4934

"What can the third show you? Let me tell you that too. You should be moderate in your house and your clothes. Be moderate with food and also with wine, both old and new; for excess does harm to your soul and body and substance. If you are inclined toward honor, then be content with a small profit. Small profit is pleasing to God, great profit is sought by usurers. Yet you may very well have great wealth, if it all comes from just earnings and helps the poor too.   v. 4950

"And what does Chastity sing to us? Nothing else but that a maid be chaste with her eyes if she wishes to abandon evil thoughts. And she should be chaste in her thoughts if she does not wish to debase herself with deeds. She should not choose amorous ways if she does not wish to lose her wreath. And yet a woman is still chaste if she carries on only in marriage.[189] And with that I'll tell you no more."   v. 4962

Siertdasland was quick. "It seems to me," she said, "that that must be the end of the speech. But there is still one thing left that shouldn't be passed over hereafter and which one must be able to do if we are to grant him our kinswoman! That is, hear me one and all, to keep house wisely. What does it help a woman if her husband can do a lot outside yet is a fool in the house? Therefore tell him frankly what will be useful to him in his life if we give him Metzi."

That was directed at Saichinkruog, for the others said, "No one can do this so well as Härtel, who has done so much housekeeping. He has kept house fully sixty years or more as a married man." v. 4892

Saichinkruog then answered them very courteously and spoke thus, "You know, as I know, 'As many heads, as many minds.' Therefore every house has its own customs and regime. Thus you can learn through experience how you should maintain your house. Man's heart is so blind that, even if he knows something is true, it will still limp after him on crutches. Therefore I need not teach him." v. 4994

In reply Dame Siertdasland said, "Your mouth is too lame. Don't you see that all activity needs knowledge and wisdom? Often one person can jump, dance, and court better than eight others. Likewise one must learn to chop wood, which is easier than keeping house. Why are you drivelling about crutches? Don't you know that it is generally said, 'Help yourself, and God will help you'? I think you are speaking in jest. If one wouldn't learn to look ahead, it would happen to him as it once did to the fly before the ant's door: it had to fast with hunger while the ant had its chests full. Therefore tell the good fellow how he should arrange his house. That suits him right and is his due." v. 5015

HINTS ON HOUSEKEEPING

Then Härtel Saichinkruog said, "Well then, let it be. I'll teach you what seems best to me, if you wish to keep house respectably. First of all you should do this. Try to carry in your pockets a second house made of silver so that you can buy hay and fodder and also straw, wine and grain, and also wood, millet and greens, beans, peas, barley, lard, lintels, meat for drying, salt, household utensils, and bedclothes, cheese and fruits and many things, each in its own season. That will be useful to you on all sides. Sincerely try to buy the best, if you don't want to regret it. v. 5034

"Parties and daily invitations bring one honor and two losses. If you wish to keep your wealth and good name, don't consume your substance with guests and on pipers and treasures. As it is truly written, military expenditures are very honorable. Have especial pity on your poor friends. Don't build houses for death[46] unless you are compelled by dire necessity; for a constructed house, a written book, a laid woman, a cut cloth, and old jugs and junk are so cheap that it's a miracle. You can repair a leaking roof; and a small damage is better than a great one. Respectable clothing but not too rich is praiseworthy, if it is clean, not spotted, well sewed and not torn, and suitable for the season. New fashions ride fools.   v. 5058

"Gladly listen to poultry crying and geese singing, and you will be rewarded. Let your dog be a good hound that will guard your belongings. It is good to spend for your children's instruction; also consume your substance in providing them with portions. Share your goods with the poor, and that will follow you to the grave. Yet see that your earnings each day are greater than your expenditures; for an occasion may come that will take with one fell swoop your earnings from a long period.   v. 5072

"Now I'll tell you quite directly how you should earn and protect yourself from loss. Be the master in your house. If your wife wears the pants, she'll be your scourge and your curse against God and His commandments, and you'll become the people's laughing stock. Therefore sit on her neck and keep her like a fox in a net. See to it that she takes good care of what you put in her hand. Also see to it that she always keeps kitchen, board, and bed ready and clean, if she wants to grow old with you. Order her to scour, sew, spin, milk, and suckle, if you wish to profit; and never let her be idle. You should also demand this of your daughters; and, if they don't know how, then see that they learn day and night as well as four others, for what your wife should be able to do for you will suit another man as well.   v. 5098

"As dear St. Bernard[29] says, don't recommend a staff to your son, but soon teach him to the best of your ability a handicraft or merchandizing and, above all, writing, if you wish to make him happy. If he can't amount to anything with you, then send him out; and let that be his portion.   v. 5106

"If you have servants under your supervision, don't tolerate any surliness from them; and don't trust a dissembler. A servant should be obedient, loyal, perseverant, chaste, patient, not too rich, sensible, quick, and uncomplaining. Likewise he should have a master who is respectable and who gives enough (but rough food, for that suits him) and who does not hold back any of his servants' pay by force but pays them fully and feeds them well and sees that they have earned it. And, if you want to have sure profit, get up early along with them and see to the cattle yourself, unless you want to prosper in reverse.[208] And don't you know what I know? Your own eyes make the cattle fat. But, if you are lazy in your affairs, your servants will take their ease; and, what is worse, they will soon thrive in evil thoughts.   v. 5130

"When you leave your house, remember what you have to do; and, when you come back to your house, see what's been taken out of it. If your grain has not increased, then know that you have lost the day.

"If your neighbors are good, rejoice in your heart. Serve them to the best of your ability, and your house will long stay powerful.

"If you wish to sell wine and corn, you should reach your customers first and sell lower than other people. Also sell most dearly to your enemies. That's your gain and you are avenged without blood, and that revenge is better than all others.[29]

"If you wish to sell a piece of ground or buy it when it is for sale, then guard yourself from an arbiter[29] who is richer and can do more or does not have a good reputation, if you wish to be free of care. Yet I'll tell you personally, it's better to suffer hunger than to sell your substance; yet it is better to sell a part of your patrimony than to pawn it to a usurer.

"Don't lend unless you see to whom, and borrow from him even less willingly; for, if anyone tries to comfort himself by borrowing, he'll surely go to ruin with great disgrace. By this you should see that one should pay back gladly.   v. 5166

"If you want to use your brain, write your will while you are alive and healthy so that you can pay your debts to your creditors before the priests.[29] Also, remember your servants; for sick people often forget that. Leave your wife what she should have. You should also ask her, in case God calls you, to maintain herself in honor and, if she can do without a man, to remain without a husband for the sake of your children and in order to live better and with devotion. Yet you should not compel her to do that through oaths, money, or other things; since a lawful husband is better for a woman than is a master or a servant. Also help your daughter and small child better and more readily than your healthy and strong sons who can support themselves.

"Last of all, if your sons wish to be merchants, advise them to work separately; thus they will achieve all the greater profit. If they wish to be artisans, then let them follow their own voli-

tion. If they intend to live lives of leisure, then tell them to
keep together undivided. That is good, for every head wants its
hat, and every house wants its fire. And now I won't contribute
anything more."   v. 5200

THE MARRIAGE CEREMONY

As soon as this instruction ended, Fritzo spoke right up,
"Well now, Bertschi, do you hear that? If you wish to do that
and even more, promise us it on your word of honor and I'll give
you my daughter." Triefnas was thinking devotedly of his dear
Metzline's body and acted like Renard Fox courting the fat hen,
and he promised on his oath that he was ready for all things
that an honest and wise young man should rightfully perform
and do.

Thereupon two of the best were sent quickly from the council
into the kitchen for the bride. They hastily came to the place
she was and said, "You should reward us for our message:[126]
you have a husband."   v. 5222

Dame Metzi was overjoyed about that. "Who is he then?"
she asked.

"It's Bertschi Triefnas, who has never forgotten you."

If Metz had been happy before, she could now hardly survive
for joy and fell down in a swoon. The others helped her up
again and made her pretty with salve of capon grease and with
brushing and grooming, as is the custom on such occasions. And
with that they led her forth, but Metzi spoke to them thus, "I
don't know how I should conduct myself."

One of the women said, "I'll teach you. When someone begins
thus, 'Do you wish Bertschi as a husband?' you should at first
begin to defend yourself a little. That'll be good for your repu-
tation."   v. 5242

Now when she came to the others, Ochsenkropf said, "Hear
ye, in God's name! Amen. A marriage is to take place here.
You two should answer me this. Tell me, Bertschi, on your
word (God will that you never regret it!). Do you wish Metz in
marriage?"

Bertschi had had such a pang of joy in his heart when he saw
her coming (besides that, he was not used to such occasions)
that his hair stood on end. He could hardly stand on the ground
and could scarcely say "Yay" correctly, and therefore his answer
was "Gray," but no one noticed that.

Then he[42] turned to Metzi and said, "Now tell me, Metzli, do

you want Bertschi as a husband?" Metzi remembered her in-
struction and began to defend herself; with her feet and elbows
she struck about so genteelly that at least four of the women fell
down.   v. 5268

Then Fritzo said, "Daughter, don't be so embarrassed and
take Bertschi in marriage." She hushed.

He[42] asked again, and then she said, "All right, if it pleases
you."[42] And thus, at the desire of both, the marriage was con-
cluded without scholar or priest.[125] Then Bertschi took out a
ring made thus. It was of lead and plated with tin, with a stone
that was called glass sapphire. Around it was an enamel of resin
as blue as water. In addition it was furnished with two pearls
from fish eyes. He put it on her hand, and suddenly there was
such a disgraceful assault on the groom in order to pull out his
hair and beard that he was at once bald and beardless.[128] Bert-
schi wept, the others sang and crowded out through the door.
They shouted loudly and even more: v. 5295

> "Bert has married Metz today, today, today.
> May luck and fortune come their way!"

GUESTS, GIFTS, AND NUPTIAL MASS

The news came quickly to Glarus, Canton Schwytz, Appenzell,
Lauis Valley, and all over the Marchfeld, to Praettigau, the Albs,
the Scherr, and everywhere.[4] They invited their very sweaty
neighbors from the villages of Nissingen, Seurrenstorff, and
Rützingen. Soon a great crowd of them with their village
wenches arrived there with great shouting. You should judge
them according to the way they are named.[88] Listen, for they
are all known to me: v. 5314

From Nissingen was Galgenswank, an honest fellow in spite
of himself, also Gerwig Schinddennak with his buddy Scheu-
binsak, Dietrich of the lattice and Gugginsnest his gossip, Stor-
chenpain and Arnold, Harnstain and Kriembold, and many
other such young louts who were thought to be squires. There
were also many wenches. The first was called lusty Kützeldarm,
the second Gredul Ungemäss, the third Ändel Pfefferäyss, the
scabby[121] Wasserschepferin, and lovely Lady Gnepferin.

From Seurrenstorff came four of them. They were Palstersak
the magnificent, Teufelsgaden, Schabenloch, and scurfy Gug-
goch. They had two girls, who were Dame Lena Fallinsstro and
Sophia, her companion.   v. 5337

There were not many others, except for one fellow from
Rützingen (he was called Jäckel Reuschindhell) and his brother

Farindwand, with a girl named Hüdel. Otherwise from other lands I can recognize and name none except one who was called Bopphart, a born hero from Appenzell.

They came riding up on asses and sledges, each with his good jerkin,[112] two red hose,[113] and a hat,[113] with their broad swords[103] and with other things too. Some of them came on foot with their wooden staves.[103] The maids were all clothed in well prepared white kirtles (their wreathes shone with flowers), and their shoes were whole, except for their holes.   v. 5358

They drew up as best they could that same Saturday night to the village of Lappenhausen with their din and dither. If anyone did not have the comfort of a house, he took the sky as his roof and the street as his bed. They scurried back and forth all night with their tumult such that, because of them, no one could sleep in the hay or in the straw; and they kept this up until day. They let no one carry a candle; and this was to the detriment of the groom, who skinned his ass instead of his cow and brought the meat to the kitchen. However, he would never have thought about it if, on the next morning, he had found the ass on the spot where, to his great sorrow, he saw the skin lying.   v. 5380

Now when the night ended and the bright day began, Gunterfai sounded his bagpipe all over Lappenhausen. All the men came up in front of young Bertschi's door, and the women and the maids went into Metzi's house. Thereupon the bell sounded for mass.

"So that I won't forget the best," said Bertschi Triefnas then, "I have no pennies (that's that) to offer, as I rightly should."

"We'll take care of that," they said. "Have it charged to your account, if you don't want to suffer disgrace." Thereupon they went to church, as the custom was. The young men went in front and the old ones behind; the young women went in back and the old women in front,[128] much too quickly.   v. 5402

Now as soon as the mass ended, the priest began saying, "Hear ye, women and men! Know that it is the Church's law that one should take a wife publicly (thus he will do well) and not so secretly, without a priest. Also we are authorized to proclaim publicly before the populace in church about the bride and groom in case there is or might be anyone who wants to object. Therefore I command, under pain of excommunication, if there is anyone who can prove that this marriage is not in order, let him say it at once."

Then an old woman crept up with a staff and said, "I see that Bertschi has broken his troth with me through the Devil's advice. Not much more than a year ago he distinctly promised me marriage." v. 5426

They all began laughing and saying to the priest, "Know that marriage was created before monks and priests.[187] Therefore let every fellow take a wife whom he likes most."

Concerning the speech made by the woman who accused him, it was decided in Lappenhausen that, if she wanted Bertschi, she should delouse a pair of breeches. If she could see as well as a wife should see and therefore be able to recognize the lice and burn them yet let the buttons remain, then she should step before them all and prove her accusation.[93] Thereupon the bridegroom pulled off his breeches and said, "Now take a look, you whore, and seek. And if you burn the buttons on my laces, I'll pull out your gray pigtail!" And why should one lengthen the story? She let all the biters survive and groped with her hand; and, wherever she found a lace, it would have lost its life. They all laughed at that with righteous indignation. v. 5454

They ordered the piper to play up and hurried over to Bertschi's house. When they came to the door, they set the bride in front; and the groom sat down beside her as the village custom then was. Then Fritz came and said, "I am happy in your honor. May misfortune avoid this house. I will also give you seven hens and a rooster as a dowry. Think of that! And I'll give you a blanket and a straw sack and a fresh kirtle too. Thus she'll be prepared for board and bed in keeping with our circumstances.[168] If you are the kind of a fellow who likes to have linen sheets, then order her to spin night and day."

Engelmar came up next and gave him a housedog. He said, "May God, and the dog too, protect you from harm."[183] v. 5478

Ochsenkropf came up next with a cat whose name was Fach and said, "Have this for another kind of protection. It's good against mice."

Colman pushed in front of the rest with a small kid and said, "I'll send this to your house. It'll become a goat with horns."

Jäckel's friendship was not lost. He brought a new-born calf and said, "This is suitable too. It can grow into a cow."

A fellow named Öttel Kriech brought a sick duck and shouted, "Look here, young man. I wanted to eat it myself."

Another, who was called Blasindäschen, began reaching into his pocket: "One prefers to receive pennies," he said. "Here's a Berner."[60]   v. 5498

Straub had a lot of bogus drugs and gave the bridegroom satyrion and mossberries and said, "That's imported from overseas and it'll help you in your need.[144] You know, when you do the thing."[84]

Dame Laichdenman was of generous disposition and gave the bride three needles, a spindle-ring, two spindles, a tinderbox, and two spools. She said, "Now you must earn with sewing and spinning."   v. 5510

Then Lady Elsbet Föllipruoch gave the bride a hempen sleeve[144] and said, "That's a welcome gift, since hemp is expensive this year." Snatereina handed her a very rusty buckle, a purse, and two gloves[114] as dingy as her teeth. And there was even more crowding around. One gave a broomstick, the second brought a jug, the third offered a vinegar jar, the fifth[43] a basket, the sixth a sieve, and the seventh gave the lid to a salt-cellar, which was good. The eighth donated a hat which he had worn thirty years; yet he could hardly stop lamenting its loss. They also gave innumerable platters, plates, candlesticks, forks, rakes, and many spoons. And realize that I am trying to make it short for you!   v. 5532

THE BANQUET

Meanwhile they should have danced, but they could not lift their feet for hunger. Therefore four of them, who wanted to serve at the table, got up quickly and said they should have the first soup, according to custom. That was done quickly.

One of them was in such a hurry to eat that he almost scalded himself to death in his gullet. He jumped up and struck the tureen with his fist so that the soup sloshed out on the ground along with the bread. Everyone said, "Before I perish thus of hunger, I would rather pick it up out of the dirt and eat it." And no matter how well it was beshitted, not a bit of it remained. Believe me, that really happened! It was to their taste. v. 5553

Next everyone took a sack and spread it down on the ground. See how lovely their table cloth was! It was washed at least once a year, and that's the truth. Their cups and glasses were pitchers,[133] not at all suitable for lifting. Salt and saltcellars would have been brought if they had thought of them. Knives and sliced bread were omitted.[133] They brought in barley loaves and oaten bread, and rye bread was also served.[108] And thus the table was set. v. 5568

The giving of wedding presents also ended, and men and women betook themselves to the table like sows to the trough. No one washed his hands except Dame Els and Farindkuo, who needed to do so because they had fallen in the filth in their hurry. They needed some water, and it was brought to them. Farindkuo jumped in front of Els (I think he was impatient) and ordered them to give him water at once. The servant poured it very neatly, from high up, onto his sleeve and not into the basin, reaching up with his head and stretching his legs straight out.[133] Their basin was a broad sieve that had been bought for the wedding. v. 5588

Damsel Elsa was provoked and ran up to where they were pouring. Her sleeves got wet, and no one helped her with a towel, which, according to court custom, should have been held up between the basin and the clothes of anyone wishing to wash his hands. Also, the servants' finger nails were as long and pointed as ten-pins; consequently no one dared approach them to hold his thumbs along the edge of the basin to lift it, and so they had to set it down. v. 5062

Farindkuo had no cloth for drying, and therefore as a towel he used his breeches, which were wide open. He ran up boisterously and sat down just any old place. Dame Elsa washed her hands until the second course was served. Wow! How quickly she saw that! It caused her pain and sorrow. She had no breeches, and she did not want to ruin her blouse by wiping on it. She thought it too slow and fruitless to dry her hands on the air, and that is why she came running up still wet. How quickly she sat on her arse! Her feet were not lame; she knocked over jugs and tablecloth. v. 5620

"So, you sow, you! So?" said Sir Ochsenkropf, "I don't like your game, because it harms us in our bellies." And if they had drunk more they would have come to blows. Thus the squabble was settled and the table set again. Els ordered them to bring her the first course, which she wanted to have. Therefore one of the servants, who was called Spiegelmäs, became her personal waiter and brought apples, pears, nuts, and cheese[132] in his bare hands. He set the cheese in front of her whole. She was pleased by that and ate it up along with its rinds; for why should she skin it any more? He bit the nuts with his teeth until

the blood ran down, and he began to cut the apples at the stem
and the pears at the head.[133] Whoever agrees with him is a
peasant. Next he looked into the mug and saw that there was
not enough in it;[209] so he took a heavy serving pitcher and shook
it to see if there was any in it. The cider sloshed; he was
pleased and poured it into the mug and filled it so full, I tell
you, that it overflowed.   v. 5652

Yet that was nothing compared with what I am going to tell
you. She did not want to disgrace the host, so she grabbed the
mug with both hands[133] and stuck her mouth and nose in it, so
good the cider[110] tasted to her. Meanwhile she found something
floating in it, which she pulled out with her bare hand, and
drank steadfastly till she ran out of breath. How quickly she
came to again and began glancing back and forth just like a
wild boar! She let her head back and drank until her eyes grew
dim and her ears hung down from drinking. Yet there was still
more liquid; she went after it and hung her head backwards
along with the mug, and that stood her well. She leaned her
back against a tree and shouted as if from a dream, "Woe to me,
woe! Everything is screwed up. The mug is dry and empty.
Fill it up and bring me the second course as I wish."   v. 5680

Spiegelmäs did not delay long but poured her a full mug of
applejack, as he thought best, and went for the food. He
brought the roast from the ass, and she thought it a noble veni-
son.[107] She pulled a loaf of bread against her breast[133] and
sliced it without more ado, always cutting it right in the middle.
Those were respectable slices! She laid them together in a
proud heap just like a stack of wood. No one wanted to take
the knife from her, they broke the meat in pieces for her. All
of that was her own, she gulped the bread and gnawed the
bones. She gnawed and tore so steadily that one of her teeth
broke in her maw. And what were the dogs to enjoy? Her
gnawing began to grieve them; so one of them took a leap and
pulled the bone out of her mouth. Yet she ate on and on until
she caught up with the others.   v. 5704

They had been having their fun too, until nothing was left
for them. They shouted horribly, "Bring us more! We're
hungrier now than before!" If Dame Elsa had drunk well, none
of them could get full.

Next some kraut, prepared with pork and covered with
greaves, was served along with fish.[106] The waiters were court-
ly: they held the platters against their stomachs and laid their

fingers on them and partly in them, spilled half, and dished out
the rest just as one throws grass into the calf's crib in the stall.
The gentlemen thanked them, so pleased they were with the fat
kraut. Lastersak was very hungry; he gazed at it like a steer
and asked them to give him a spoon. The others said, "Give us
one too." Some got a spoon and some did not; so the latter did
this: they made their hands into ladles and ate as daintily as
their companions. v. 5730

Now such a struggle arose for the kraut and the pot-licker
that you have never seen such racing and chasing in all your
life. In one platter you would have seen more than ten hands
and spoons going into the kraut simultaneously,[132] just like
spears. They were in a hurry for the greaves[107] and reached for
them with their oars. Twerg came up and threw some pork into
his mouth so neatly that his beard was at once covered with
lard. Count Burkhart damaged them all. Having loaded a
hand with kraut he brought it up toward his mouth and in-
voked God to keep the weather favorable until he garnered his
load. How quickly Kuntz got revenge by moving so violently
that the spoon broke. Then he piled into the kraut with both
hands and grabbed up a double handful of the food. "Now
good weather or bad," he said then, "you must come into my
mouth!" v. 5758

Geri picked up the platter and drank a deep draught from it.
She said, "May God let you stink to death! If you've eaten, then
I'll drink," and set it down again so hard that a large part of
the remainder sloshed out. Alas, how she chuckled! Then the
others came and sucked it up (I do not know how) so that the
tablecloth remained dry from their sucking. But whatever else
there was, be it leaves or grass, crumbs, rinds, or bones, they left
it all lying. v. 5774

Some sat politely bent over their platters so that the trip
would be all the shorter, since their burdens were heavy. They
had another reason too. If anything fell from their spoons or
mouths it would fall back into the platters; for their mouths
were wide and always open. Therefore they did this. When-
ever their fingers got wet, they swung their hands rapidly over
the kraut, the rest they wiped off quickly on their boots and
clothes. They had to do that for this reason: they had no
napkins before them. Then they started up again and delayed
no longer. Another thing pleased them too: if a diner dropped
anything on the ground from the table, be it chewed or fresh,

it was to be picked up again and set before them all, unless by
chance it landed on his clothes. In that case he might keep it
without toll, if he liked the shavings.   v. 5804

Thus it went in their carousal and noisy gluttony until
their platters were as empty and clean as washed ones. Yet
their hunger was relieved. If they had formerly had to keep
quiet, now they all began to shout, "I'll ruin your wife and sister-
in-law too, Triefnas, if you don't bring us wine and mead and
beer too! And you'll also lose our friendship." No one else
was to blame but those who were serving and yawning at the
diners from far away or else much too near the gentlemen; for
not one of them wanted to see what the table should have. v. 5822

The bridegroom noticed that and wanted to show his power;
therefore he took one of them by his beard and jerked it till he
screamed. Thereupon the other three came up and grabbed
Bertschi and beat him till he fell. They pulled off his breeches
and poured water into his arse and all over the place. They
took him by his legs and beat his backside against a tree so
hard it resounded, and gave him blows without number. The
others enjoyed the event and considered it the best course. Then
he got up on his feet again and said, "You all know I couldn't
defend myself, since three are always the master of one." Thus
nothing more came of it.   v. 5843

All the cider that was in the house was brought out and
served up quickly; and they drank and swilled it until their
eyes were dripping. In spite of all his comrades, Pentza Trin-
kavil[38] drank the first mug to the third and the third down to the
middle. Then he began panting and wiping his sweat on the
tablecloth. He leaned courteously over the table, supporting
himself with his hands and elbows, and that is how he stood
it. At the same time Damsel Feina was drinking out of a mug
and slurping so properly that she was seized by a cough. The
remainder ran down her busom and she licked after it with her
tongue, in such a hurry she was to get the acid. The others
drank so steadily that often one of their belts broke, but that
did not happen to the wise ones; for they first belted themselves
loosely and then kept right on until their belts fitted them. v. 5870

Next they came to the fish that were on the table. Straub
would have tasted them, but he saw such a racing and chasing
on the platter that he omitted the tasting and grabbed for a
piece. To his good fortune it was the largest. How quickly it
disappeared! Who should now wait for the others to be served?

There was no time, it seems to me. The waiters would have cut the fish in half for them; but they could not wait, since the course was so sweet to them. Reuschindhell made a pass at a head that was slimy and seemed good to him. Then he thought to himself, "If you chew on the head, then you've really missed out; but, if you leave it, you'll have no fun and you'll have come here for nothing." Therefore he pulled it through his mouth three times and set it down before himself quite whole. Next he had better luck: he snatched up a mid-section and swallowed it quickly. v. 5900

Meanwhile swift Farindwand grabbed the head in his hand. He supposed it did not please his brother; so how quickly he gulped it down! However, he could not enjoy it at all; for the spines stuck into his throat. Thereupon Galgenswank said, "Gentle God, be ever thanked!" And thus Farindwand's soul departed for the land of Cocaigne as was its due, and his body was carried to the Necker.[4]

How should that hurt the fellows? It seems to me they just ate all the more; for those who want to eat enough guard themselves from too many companions. But, if anyone wants to fight successfully, let him have a lot of friends! Uotz of the hedge thought of that. He wanted to get rid of one of the diners and said, "Sir Guggoch is a man who can compose songs himself about Dietrich of Bern.[127] It would be much better to listen to him than to sit here and eat dead fish." v. 5926

Therefore Guggoch thought himself pretty good. He began his story and said, "Heroes were sitting in a hall, they were eating wonders everywhere . . ."[73] and so forth to the end. Meanwhile the listeners were active and ate up all the fish before the singer noticed it. Now as soon as the song ended, Guggoch wanted to begin eating as he had intended; so he looked around and found nothing. He lowered his scurfy head[209] and shouted out loud, "I'm a child; and you, Uotz, a real rascal, as one can see by this event." If he had formerly been merry with singing, he was now sad with weeping; but it was fun for all the others.

Triefnas saw all the impropriety in eating and drinking. His head began to sink; the expense grieved him greatly and reminded him of the saying, "A small wedding should he have who wants to guard himself from loss." Therefore his fun was spoiled. v. 5953

He had heard of a remedy for that and went up like a true doctor. "Hear ye, lords both rich and poor," he called out.

"Eating is not healthy for you and drinking hurts you too; so get up and don't eat any more."

Thereupon Sir Knotz blew his big nose through his bare fingers and threw it into the bridegroom's face. "Now lick that, and I'll believe you," he said to Bertschi.

The others enjoyed that and said to the bridegroom, "It seems to us you are talking in a dream. Bring us sausage along with bacon if you want to make us well, or we'll go home and eat as suits us. If you want to starve us here, you don't know what a wretch you are. A true doctor believes this, "On a full belly is a happy head!'"　　　　　　　　　　　v. 5976

Then Arnold said forthwith, "Your words would be good and quite true, if you said them at my table. Give us something on top of the fish."

Bertschi said, "Everything's been fouled up everywhere!" He filled a nut-shell with cider, and that was a respectable slug. "Have Kochunsauber bring us the wine," he said to the servants, "and tell him to roast four eggs. We must put an end to this starvation." See, how quickly that was done!　　　　v. 5989

Meanwhile the gentlemen began shouting, "Bring us some wine. The fish want to swim!" But this did them no good: they were served pear cider and appledrink and even sloeberry water;[109] and someone even brought them a pail of sour milk,[109] which they drank up. Then Rüefli set the pail to his mouth and turned away from them and toward the wall, which stood him in good stead, in his opinion. He drank for such a long time that it became annoying to the bride and she began to reproach him.　　　　　　　　　　　　　　　　v. 6005

She said, "It seems to me you've fallen asleep in the pail or else drowned in the milk." Rüefli began laughing at that. And what did the milk do? It went up to his brain and ran out of his nose and back into the bucket. He offered the others a drink, and the bucket went round and round. Lärenkopf, who did not find enough milk, spoiled things and threw the bucket against the wall.　　　　　　　　　　　　　　　　v. 6018

Thereupon the eggs were prepared and set before the fellows. Now the time had really come for grabbing, and they did not fail to do so. They followed their old family customs and shoved toward the eggs (not unlike wild boars) with hands and feet, and no one could stop them from it. The first was the best, and the worst was the last. Kriembold got an egg and Scheubinsak got two of them, Knotz and Troll caught the fourth, and that is the way they were allotted. Count Burkhart with the bump said, "That game doesn't please us, me and my companions here. The worst dividers are those who let one man get drunk and the other die of thirst." With that he reached right out and grabbed an egg from Scheubinsak so firmly and roughly that the yolk ran through his hands. He stuck his fingers in his mouth and licked them off; for it was healthy for him.   v. 6044

Then Jänsel said, "Give me some too."

"Shut up," said the former, "You're a fool." The long nails on his thumbs helped him empty the egg. Scheubinsak held the second one and quickly split it in half and cut right through the middle of it with a great slice. The result was that the yellow ran down along with the white as a complete loss.

"It's a fugging shame," said the man. "If fortune begrudges anyone good, he'll lose overnight a king's hoard and an emperor's might."

Kriembold was aware of that and grabbed a whole egg and threw it into his mouth and swallowed it with one gulp. He would have died of it at once, but his gullet was so wide that the egg passed whole through his neck and into his stomach. He said, "Well! How good, how good! Now my share is safe from you."   v. 6072

Knotz and Troll were regular guys, and no one dared stand up to them. That gave them great confidence; and, besides that, they were very clever. They both grabbed their egg and opened it very calmly. They ate in most courtly fashion; they stuck their slices of bread into the egg and dunked them a bit and then threw them in their mouths. They did not swallow the slices entirely, they stuck the remainder back into the egg and proceeded as before right to their mouths. They both kept that up until no bread remained on the table, and all the others looked at them like wolves at a cow. There was still a bit of egg; they held it tight, it was not for sale. They wanted two more loaves, but no more were found in the house. What should the poor men have then? In truth, I cannot tell you that. They reproached the host for that; they gave the egg to the servants so they would remember it and bring them something to drink.   v. 6100

The guests could not get anything to drink, and therefore they were served water.[109] At first they passed it around respectably; then their business began increasing because thirst had been afflicting them steadily right up till then. It was served without measure, and it made them full and free from pain. Thus everyone began singing and talking; and, no matter what the master began, be it singing or talking, the servants could disturb it with propriety. No one wanted to listen to the other, everyone wanted to be heard and shouted, "Listen to my story."

The disorder lasted until the last course was served; that was cherries, grapes, figs, plums,[132] and no more. If they had grabbed up the first course daintily, the last one was gulped down much more violently. Yet the bride acted according to her position and did not gulp her food like the men but bit more than seven times from one cherry. That was a praiseworthy thing.   v. 6128

Then Bertschi Triefnas saw that there was no salt before them. He brought them a shirt-tail[115] full and said, "That belongs on the plums."

Meanwhile a flea had jumped between Dame Hüdel's legs and bit her till she groaned. She wanted to buck over and squeeze the flea to death, but her skin was too tight. Something went wrong—she let a fart. She wanted to avoid disgrace and started scratching with her feet so that people would believe her feet had done it; but Heinrich was too clever for her and said, "That won't help the matter. I'll sing you something that was well composed: 'Scratching is not like farting.'"   v. 6148

This ridicule pained Hüdel; and she let another big fart like the last, and then three more, which made four of them. She shouted at the scribe, "Look here, you fugging rascal. Do they sound all right to you?" And thus the scribe was paid back. But Count Burkhart paid for the smell, or perhaps his egg was rotten; for his food rose to his mouth and he had to spew it out on the table through his beard.   v. 6160

Now old Sir Gumpost had drunk water, milk, and cider; and his belly was puffing up, raging, and rumbling like the sea. The fish began swimming and plaguing him so severely that he had to get up from the table. He said, "I'm going to go pee. I'm coming back. Wait here." All the others up and ran after Gumpost, in such a hurry they were to piss. Yet Dame Laichdenman remained; for she had done it in her chemise, which had got wet, since she had left her sponge at home. Therefore she got on her feet and did not want to sit there alone.

Now when the gentlemen came back they would have sat down, but the tablecloth had been removed. They could hardly

stop mourning the fact. Since they had sat down without a
blessing, why should they want to say grace? The servants
washed their[138] hands and thus the meal took its end.   v. 6186

THE DANCE

Behold, now it was time to dance in the meadow, which was
far away. A cry arose, "Gunterfai, accept an egg and pipe a
couple."

The minstrel was full of wine, as he could well notice by
himself. Yet he thought to himself, "Now even if I am quite
drunk, I trust they are not empty either. Therefore it won't
be hard for me to pipe a fools' march,[19] for they won't under-
stand a fug about it." And with that he sounded his bagpipe
so that it really echoed through the mountains.   v. 6200

Ofenstek jumped forth and took Dame Jütz by the hand. He
danced forth, she swept after him; the others up and close
behind. The line grew very long. They all jumped up and
down as in a dream, like apples from a tree. Gunterfai struck
and struck for a long time and very wildly. Ofenstek was too
fat for that. He had pranced until the sweat ran down through
his thick jacket; and the fellow got so tired from that that
he could not stand any longer but had to leave the dance.
He laid himself in the grass and said, "May God give all dis-
comfort to whoever taught you to pipe, such pain I have suf-
fered here."   v. 6220

Schabenloch was carrying the baton.[13] He was clever enough
to drop it and grab the first girl and jump high with her; but
the guy was too thin and his breeches too big. He noticed that
only after they had fallen below his knees in front of them all.
That made him stumble in the grass, Jütz on him as was right,
Kuontz on Jütz, and Els after him, in such a hurry they all were
to fall. At this time it occurred that Elsa broke her mirror.[71]
A piece went into her hand. It hurt her, and she cried out loud,
"Stop, cowardly Gunterfai, for my mirror is in two."

The minstrel stopped, and Gumpost cried, "God give him
pain and woe who is to blame for the mirror." Because of this
everyone understood who had bought the mirror and whom he
revealed with his curse. They laughed it off, for it was not time
for a fight to begin.[59]   v. 6246

Now they left off dancing. The men sat down from exhaustion,
but the ladies stood. That was well, since they are never full

of dancing. They would have sung before the boys, thrown stones, and jumped;[15] but they were not very used to it and therefore soon stopped.

What should one bring them to drink? The mugs were all broken, and therefore the second shout came, "Pipe up, dear Gunterfai."

He answered, "I can't any more. My skull is hurting."

"I'm sorry, but you deserve it," said Bertschi merrily. "Therefore we should sing a number and jump all around." They were pleased with his words; so Bertschi began thus:

v. 6266

> Thaat's all caused by love, you see,
> Thaat's all caused by love, you see,
> That we live so senselessly,
> That we live so senselessly.
>
> That's all caused by wine, you see, etc.
> That we must ever happy be. etc.
>
> That's all caused by gold and pelf, etc.
> That one loves no one but himself. etc.
>
> That's all caused by pledge and pawn, etc.
> That people borrow on and on. etc.
>
> That's all caused by dice, you see, etc.
> That I can't hold back much for me. etc.

Et cetera. That lasted so long that finally everyone was jumping with one foot so that he might rest all the better on the other when he lay down without stepping, as a lazy person likes to do.[202] Such leaping and bouncing, dancing, prancing, and pouncing had begun in the circle that you have never seen its likes in all your days. Eventually the singer ran down and said, "Well, woe worth the day for me! It grieves me in my heels[71] that I don't know any more of the song."   v. 6292

The others had had enough dancing; so they all said, "That suits me fine." They fell down in the grass and rested there, for that suited them better.

Then Galgenswank took an egg and jumped up in front of Gunterfai. He said, "Take this, and play a good one. I don't feel sick." Now as soon as the piper had had his pay, he struck up and it sounded nicely. Galgenswank took Dame Schürenprand by her snow-white hand[79] and sprang up and away with his partner without ever stopping. He swept around and around and around until they had all become dizzy from it. Then the piper was almost strangled by the dust that entered him and hindered the good man so that he had to stop his merriment.

That was to the benefit of the others too, who had become dizzy from the turning and fallen down. That angered the dance-leader,[13] who shouted, "I've lost an egg on the whoring minstrel. May he get a hunched back today, and may God also give him the cramps. Let him have that as my thanks!" v. 6322

If they had formerly lain in the grass, now they really had to sleep. But Uotz snored so loudly and stank so sour in honor of womankind that their drowsiness ended, whereupon the scribe began and said, "Get up! We must dance. I know a courtly song[124] that I'll sing." They were pleased with his words, and he began thus: v. 6332

> "Whom shall I give her to as his life's companion true?"
> "What is that? Tell us, tell us, Sir!"
> "It's Lady Gredel Erenfluoch. Who's best for her?"
> "It's Lady Gredel Erenfluoch. Who's best for her?"
> "No one else but me! My heart's desire is she!"
> "Jäckel Gumpost, you're a guy, so yours she'll be,"
> "Jäckel Gumpost, you're a guy, so yours she'll be,"
> "God bless my lady fair, of her I'll take good care."
> "Whom shall I give her to as his life's companion true?"
> "What is that? Tell us, tell us, Sir!"
> "It's lovely Lady Gnepferin. Who's best for her?"
> "It's lovely Lady Gnepferin. Who's best for her?"
> "No one else but me! My heart's desire is she!"
> "Rüefli Lekspiss, you're a guy; so yours she'll be."
> "God bless my lady fair, of her I'll take good care." v. 6355

Et cetera. So went the song until everyone at the dance had his partner.[14] And with that their pleasure was complete. There in the grass they sang, "Flowers were sprouting through the clover," and "It causes pain to leave one's lover."[218] Then Bertschi Triefnas came up to Gunterfai and said, "Pipe up and take this egg."

Thereupon old Sir Colman and Dame Berchta came up impetuously and said to him, "Here are two, and there are lots more of them. Play us one in the old manner."

Bertschi had a lofty sentiment and said, "Then have three from me, and play me for my pleasure one in the new style. I don't know any of the old ones." v. 6375

The competition was great between the two; but finally it was decided that Colman and Dame Laichdenman should promenade in front, the groom should lead the dance with the bride high up, and Gnepferin and Grabinsgaden[38] should form the tail. Then there really arose a swinging, ox-like shoving, calf-like springing. The minstrel piped so loud there had never been

such lusty rustling and dusty bustling! They romped thither
and stomped hither just like wild boars. Wow! How high
they sprang and swung their arms! The one cried, "Hi yu, hi
yo," the other, "Yo, how goes it so!"   v. 6393

Storchenpain, being very young, undertook such a high jump
he thought he was flying; but he fell down again so fast he sat
on his backside in the grass. The lasses were so lively and
jumped so nimbly that one could often see up to their knees,
but I do not know how. Hilda's neckline was too low; so her
breast jumped out of her busom. Her love of dancing had led
her to it. Little Hüdel got so hot she lifted up her kirtle in
front; so they saw hers[84] and many hearts were made glad.
They all shouted, "She wants a man: she has a mouth with hair
on it!"   v. 6413

Many buttons and laces were broken; and, as I will shorten
it for you, the dance became so close from the jumping and
bumping that the bridegroom did not know where he was or
where to go. He was stuck in the middle just like a sled in the
snow. But why should that bother the lads, who were doing a
little wooing with their hands?[85] Bertschi shouted to the piper,
"Stop, and don't pipe any more."

The minstrel did as he ordered, and with that the dance was
over. They wanted to sit down, but Troll shouted to them,
"While we are still so warm, join the circle and I'll sing some-
thing solo that suits for dancing." They were all pleased with
his words, and thereupon he began thus: v. 6435

> "There ate my father Eberhart,
> And drank my uncle Rimpart,
> There slept my cousin Oll, Sir Oll, Sir Oll, Sir Oll,
> Sir Oll, Sir Oll, Sir Oll, Sir Oll, Sir Oll, Sir Oll.
> There slept Sir Oll, Oll, Oll, Oll.
>
> There sang my son, my Berchtold,
> There sprang my nephew, Hilpold,
> There danced Sir Scholl-lo-lo-lo-loll-lo-lo-
> Lo-lo-lo-loll-lo-lo-lo-lo-lo-lo-lo-loll,
> There pranced Sir Scho-o-o-o-o-oll."

Et cetera. He sang better and better; and, when it reached its
best, the Devil sowed ashes in it. That was caused by trouble-
making Eisengrein, who was about to burn up in his love for
Gredul and wanted to let her know it by scratching in her hand
secretly. That was not right and it was a disgrace, since the
maiden at once began to bleed from the scratching. Therefore
the peasants' sport turned into disorder, according to their
custom.   v. 6457

PART THREE – THE CONFLICT

THE BRAWL

Schinddennak saw this when it happened; he got angry and started curling his lip. He said, "I'm not joking any more, Sir Eisengrein. You ought to know that. It seems to me you have spoiled our fun. What did you have against my niece? Why did you damage and foul up her hand? One should treat guests with honor and not flay them."

"What are you jabbering about?" said Eisengrein. "I'll ruin your mother too, along with your niece, if you don't cut that out. Do you hear that?"

Schinddennak shouted, "Eisengrein, if you ruin my mother, I'll ruin you and all your family."   v. 6474

With that the peasants' quarrel turned into a brawl, and that is a fact, for the one of them fell into the other's hair. The women took flight; but the men showed their training, they all jumped to their friend and pushed and fought their way through the others. Fesafögili in particular fought so hard it was a miracle. He grabbed just a few locks and pulled on them so hard that his hand got full of hair. Dietrich paid him back well for that: he took him by his long beard and pulled him so hard his chin fell on the ground, and he had to die. The longer they kept it up, the better they did it, until there were no more locks on their heads or in their beards and the hair-pulling turned into fisticuffs. They struck around so violently that many a one of them had his nose bleed, and his mouth too, which served him well as blood-letting.   v. 6500

Snellagödel conducted himself thus: he wrapped his thumb around his fist and struck at their ears till it resounded. He pointed his knuckles and thrust up at their noses, against their hearts, and at their goiters. That caused them pain and made Scheubinsak very angry; he wrapped his cape around his fist and stuck it into Snellagödel's big mouth so that he strangled at once. They got tired of using their fists and grabbed for their spears. They began defending themselves with their heavy swords and also with their big staves. In all your life you have never seen such a striking and stabbing as arose among them! The Seurrenstorffers and Rützingers watched from a distance. They were pleased by the others' harm and said to one another,

"The gentlemen have been too strong for us; if they fight, then we'll survive." v. 6525

Meanwhile much fighting took place, and Arnold was thrown into the millstream. The water went into his mouth; yet he splashed and dripped his way out and ran into the house of the miller, who lent him a spear. Now he fought like a hero! He stuck Knotz by his navel and said, "Now see! Lie there and kick!" v. 6535

That displeased Sir Troll, who began fighting so hard he stank. With his halberd he struck Arnold such a gash that his stomach fell in front of his feet. With that Knotz was avenged and the halberd broken too. How quickly Troll found a cloak and wound it thrice around his hand! He pulled out a broad sword and fought like a louse in a scalp. But it was not the time for a sword, since the field was too wide. It was more suitable for spear shafts; and therefore Sir Galgenswank came walking up with a spear and stuck him, despite all he could do, so hard he fell and lay on his arse till his last day, and thus Squire Troll was lost. v. 6556

Then Twerg,[75] a high-born little fellow, came with his cunning. He could not carry a staff; and therefore he had to overcome his enemies with choking, scratching, and wrestling. He attacked Galgenswank. He caught him by his waist and lifted him up and threw him down so hard he never stood up again. He had another trick too. He stepped on the points that Harnstein wore on his shoes[115] and pushed him so violently that he fell in his own tracks. He stepped on his neck and held him thus (I do not know how) until his soul departed. He was not satisfied with that but ran up, that same dwarf, and grabbed Sir Dietrich,[75] the big man, by his legs and swung him around so fast that he stretched out like an ox. Yet the latter protected his neck so that the little fellow could not grab him. v. 6581

Now something else was started. How quickly the juggler jumped on the big man with his bare hands! Wow! How quickly he made him blind in one eye, for he could injure his enemies with jabbing and scratching! He wanted to tear his mouth, but the latter began to bite and held him with his teeth until he could catch him by his belt. Then he hurled the brave Twerg against the ground more than three times and threw him over Bertschi's roof so that they never saw him again. v. 6597

Anger had seized him. He drew his sharpened sword and struck about so that from one stroke a crowd of people fell

before him. No one dared approach him, and they hurried to
run away. When the bridegroom saw this, it pained and dis-
comforted him. He ran to the winding staircase and rang all
the bells for an attack, and that made great noise all through
the community. They jumped up, "Where shield and spear?"
With unwiped arses they rudely came with bows and crossbows,
with bolts and arrows. Great was their haste against the war-
riors from Nissingen, with stabbing, striking, and shooting, with
hurling and thrusting with stones and great staves.   v. 6619

Many pitchforks and rakes were seen broken, and thus the
foreign guests at last realized that departure was too difficult
and too perilous for their lives. They gathered spiritedly with
their backs together and held out their lances. Then someone
(as I remember, he was called Fladenranft) came running up
on an ass and wanted to avenge himself on them by breaking
through their wall. Thereupon one of them attacked the ass
and the other went for the man so that my Fladenranft fell
down (it was not soft), and the ass along with him. Death was
his loss.   v. 6639

When the others saw that, they really began hurrying with
their hurling and shooting. That discouraged the guests so much
that they did not wish to suffer any longer, nor should they
have remained. Therefore they took comfort in hare's defense
and ran away quickly, and that was their glory. Then no fleer
was seen without his pursuer. The others were in such a hurry
to chase that they hurried after them right up to the gate of
Nissingen.   v. 6652

You have surely seen already that every dog on his dungheap
is braver than three others, and the smallest will bite the largest.
That is what those in front did: they turned around to defend
themselves and fought so well and even better than they had be-
fore. Thereby they sounded the alarm with undismayed blows;
for their bell had not yet been cast.[70] Many appeared on the
bridge and gave the lie to the pursuers' might. If the latter had
previously hastened a great deal, they now had to hurry three
times as fast until they crossed the bridge half way back. They
threw it over; then they were free and thereby came home com-
fortably. They grabbed the visiting girls by their hands to at-
tack and dishonor them, and no one could stop them. But all
the maids from Seurrenstorff and Rützingen had been led away,
and that was to their honor and advantage.   v. 6679

THE NISSINGERS' WAR COUNCIL

On the other hand the Nissingers raged madly and ran riot. Soon the burgomaster shouted, "Up, you gentlemen, to the council! We should know how things stand and what is to be done." Therefore twelve aldermen (the very best born) came walking to the council, barefoot both hither and thither. The first was called Strudel, who was their burgomaster. The second was called Packenflaisch, the third, Eckhart Rindtaisch, the fourth was Sneck, the fifth was Zing, the sixth was called Schilawink. Wüetrich and Luodrer, Püetrich and Marner, Eselpagg and Fülizan make six more men.   v. 6699

Their city hall was a barn with straw. They sat in it and spoke thus, "We should send for our lads so that they can tell us just how the thing began, and also how it came out." For this they called to Deupenpain, who was the scribe of the community, and sent him after Kraimbold. The latter came promptly, as he should, and told exactly how the matter stood. Now when Eckhart heard that, and how Arnold had been slain, a great lamentation was begun by the father for his son. You have never heard its likes in all your days!   v. 6715

He said, "Alas, you bitter Death, you gruesome end, you painful sorrow! Why have you taken my dear child away so swiftly? I shall never cease lamenting this sorrow a single day as long as I live." With that he fell down, bereft of consciousness. He was acting like a loyal father who has suddenly lost his own heart's blood that he has reared for so long with great effort. Yet he had much more reason to lament that his son, a man just like a mountain, had been killed by a dwarf,[38] shamefully and without confession, and with damage to his fame and soul.   v. 6733

Sneck too had heard one thing: that his father Harnstein had lost his life. He trembled with righteous indignation. He wanted to avenge it at once; and therefore he began to speak thus, "My lords, I have long known that one should reflect for a long time and perform quickly what he has decided, for anger and haste are always contrary to good counsel. The rule fails, as you well see, when one should avenge an injury with striking, plundering, and burning. You may recognize that in this. If one has injured me and I do not avenge that at once, then other people will come and make peace, and then all is settled. They won't say, 'Stab him back.' Thus my honor will be lost;[170] and my shed blood and pierced flesh will remain wholly unavenged.

Therefore listen. My advice is that, while we still have the time, we summon every man on horse and on foot, under pain of forfeit, and at once make an attack on the people of Lappenhausen in order to strike and burn, to rob and skirmish, with spears, fire, and marksmen. That will be an honorable rustling! And if this is to occur, then do it fast and don't delay." v. 6769

That would have happened that way, but Pütreich thought to himself of his daughter Kützeldarm. He could not help but pity her, and he said, "Sir Sneck, I'd like to do that; but we must refrain for one reason. Don't you know that our daughters are captured? Are you blind? Therefore take my advice and don't hurry to your revenge so quickly. First let us wisely regain our daughters. That is, we should try to give the enemy sweet words and make promises until we have our own. Afterwards, if they touch us at all, then we should beat them one and all and also fall upon them on horse and on foot with shield and spear, with striking, hewing, and thrusting, and thus avenge our old injuries."   v. 6791

Now as soon as he had had his say, Wüetreich looked up toward Heaven. He wished to show that he was concerned with honor and said, "My friend, in my opinion your suggestion is useful, but it is not honorable."

To this all the others said unanimously and noisily, "Whatever does not have the appearance of honor cannot be useful."

With this the council became silent, and the matter rested. Strudel began to ask what would be well to do. They all answered him and said, "Sir, you are the one who is set over us to advise and protect us at all times. Therefore you should start off; and, whatever you wish, let that be done."   v. 6811

Strudel cleared his throat and began to make his speech. He said, "War was created for no other reason than that people might be able to live calmly and in complete peace and without violence. Therefore we can fight with God and with right[169] against anyone who mistreats us in our person or property. Well then, you have already heard (I suffer great sorrow because of it) how the Lappenhausers have murdered our people today, captured and beaten them roughly in their village as scoundrels are wont to do, and have pursued some across the heath. That should rightly grieve us; for, according to wise teaching, it is better to die bravely for honor than to live in disgrace. Now in the Old Testament God ordered his servants Moses and Joshua to fight against false hosts and helped them therein greatly.[177] A nation may also fight whenever it has to defend itself. This authority we have from the Emperor.[102] v. 6840

"But let me tell you one thing. A man's great arrogance often harms him so much that he is defeated even though he is otherwise in the right. Therefore we should begin the matter in a friendly and gentle manner. With complete humility let us hope for a favorable outcome and send our messengers to Lappenhausen to demand that they send us all four of our daughters back again, and also Wasserschepferin, and that they also make good all loss and damage and henceforth molest no one who is from this village, if they wish to be free of war. I advise you that and find it very good."   v. 6860

They were all pleased with that, and therefore two of the best were now selected and elected as an embassy in the matter, they being wise Sir Albrecht Zink and also Squire Schilawink. That did not please Zink, who said, "If anyone wishes to catch hawks and merlins, he shouldn't ask me to be his decoy. By this you should understand that I don't dare go to an uncanny gang that's so criminal and wicked, so wanton and so dissolute. Besides that, they are drunk too. Do you think I am such a fool that I want to carry so serious a message and perish defenselessly?"   v. 6879

But Schilawink was very young. He got up with a jump and said, "Now should I be a coward? Do you want something? Am I needed? I am so comforted in my lady-love that I'll be heartily pleased if I should carry the message all alone." That pleased them well. He had lovely Gnepferin in his mind as a sweetheart, and that was the reason he was so obedient.

Therefore the merry man ran until he came to Lappenhausen, where he found them all still at the dance, jumping high in true merriment. He went to them at their game. "Hear what I want to tell you," said the messenger to the gentlemen. "It seems to me that you are happy in your disgrace that so many good heroes have lost their lives here today; yet you are acting I don't know how."   v. 6903

Behold, they ceased their dancing. No one had heard exactly what the messenger had told them; but now they were immediately ready for it and said, "What does this fool want? Tell us so we'll hear it too."

Undaunted, Schilawink began his message and said, "You are quite right. I am a fool, a child too, and also mad. Consequently I can neither lie nor deceive people like a rogue, for lying requires cunning. Therefore I'll tell how things stand, truly and simply. My lords from Nissingen, the burgomaster and the council, order you through me to give back all four girls, and also Wasserschepferin, immediately and to make good all loss and damage and henceforth to molest no one who is from this village, if you wish to be free from war."   v. 6929

Now when that had been heard, he who could chide best (that was their mayor Rüefli) began and spoke thus, "My friend. I don't know who you are; yet we still wouldn't care a fart about you or about your lords of the council or the peasant-master who has sent you here so foolishly, or about all the Nissingers. Know that he was no friend of yours who would send you here. And if it weren't such a disgrace to violate envoys, you would have to die at once for your act. Take hope from that (but not too much) and return home promptly, or else you will get a thrashing."   v. 6947

Schilawink got so anxious to run that he soiled his breeches. That was the blessing he gave the people on that Sunday. He would have been paid back for all that if he had sprained his legs, which were in such a hurry because the people were running after him so hostilely. Yet he got away from them and back home and told his story to them all.

Thereupon they sent out everywhere, to Uri in Schwytz Valley and to the people of Gaigenhofen, to Gadubri, to Ofen, to Kengelbach and Libingen, to Hofen and Vettingen, to Rützingen and Fützenswille, to Seurrenstorff and Wattwil, and also downstream to the Rhine where their friends should be so that they would come to their aid, for they were minded to fight. The envoys were so quick that their missions were completed by morning, and that is that.   v. 6972

THE BRIDAL NIGHT

Meanwhile in Lappenhausen the wedding had been celebrated by both men and women. They had sprung and drunk and sung and devoured the evening meal. Then too, one should not forget what Bertschi Triefnas did while he was in bed with Metzi that same night. I'll tell you that to the best of my ability. He embraced her with his arms and kissed her on the mouth seven times to his pleasure and pressed her little breasts against his chest. Then he wanted to proceed further, but Metzi was able to block the way and began shouting so loud that one could hear it more than a half a league away. She held her legs together

tightly, which was to the maiden's honor. Therefore the bride-
groom abandoned the struggle and remembered how a man
should win the thing[84] from women with clever speech. v. 6997

Thereupon he began and said, "Well for me that I have seen
the place where mouth has fitted to mouth in a sweet hour. Your
little breasts are pressed against my chest with such great de-
light in true love, and so close too! For that I thank God in
Heaven, who has created this delight with His wisdom so that
mankind should increase. Therefore, my love, be so good as to
remember what God has said, 'A man shall leave his father and
also his mother and cleave to his wife, and the twain shall
become one flesh' (according to the gloss that I know, that
means to bear a child); and deign to grant me that which the
geese do in the brook. Dearest love, that is something for which
I must and will always love you as myself."   v. 7021

Then, sadly weeping, Metzi said to the lad, "Yes, I well
know how the matter stands. You're a fellow with false cun-
ning, like one who wants to catch birds: he pipes sweetly and
all that; and, when they come into his power, he wrings their
necks."

"No, no, Metzi," he said, "I think you are mistaken in this
bed,[61] I tell you. Don't you know that holy matrimony has taken
place between us with our mutual volition and without guile?
And you are lying in your bridal bed. Therefore let's try at
once to consummate the marriage that we have voluntarily con-
tracted." Then he acted like a man and grabbed her strongly.
How quickly he turned up her legs as the scribe had taught him
and put himself right in between them! He was keeping the
custom of his ancestors. Metzi too was none too lazy as she
lay on her back. She writhed and kicked violently and also fol-
lowed the doctor's instruction.[39] Now as soon as that had hap-
pened, everyone knew it; because the bedstead was too weak
and made the best song that anyone could ever sing. v. 7054

By then the bridegroom was about to burn up with great
thirst, so he called out, "Bring water here, bring water here."
Therefore one brought him a soup from Venetia made of
Traganth and Malmsey too. That was the best custom of all.[126]
Then they ate and drank there until they had recovered, where-
upon the guests went outside.   v. 7064

The bride got up at once and locked the door from the inside
and laid herself back in the bed; yet she could pretend to feel
very bad and lament, in her joy, the loss of her flower. There-

fore the groom said, "Don't cry any more. Cheer up, I advise you. Now if you have lost your flower, in return a child will be born. That is a blessed and very good thing. Also resolve to love me and do what I order you, provided it is useful and honorable. See, I will swear to cherish you with true love and never to leave you." She thanked him for his words and promised to do accordingly. Therefore there was no more delay, and he did it to her another time. Now they were tired from it and slept until morning.   v. 7087

Whereas the bride had had only one man, Kützeldarm had four of them. Annie's arse was rubbed raw; for she had more than seven of the fellows. Gnepferin took care of ten, each as he wished. Ungemäss had eight of them; and they filed[84] all the long night. The bath woman[121] was so scabby that she outdid them all.

Now when the day broke, the watchman on the embattlements said,

> "If one on lover's arms doth lie,
> He must get up, for time doth fly!
> The sun her battle of the sky
> Hath won with mighty power.
> The moon doth part, I know not where,
> The stars have all but faded there,
> The night has lost its quiet air.
> I see it at this hour."

Et cetera. He sang it to the end.   v. 7108

Metzi became aware of it and thought to herself, "If I were to awaken him, he'd do it to me a third time before they found us in the bed." That's why she began stirring and searching through the covers until Bertschi had to wake.

Bertschi up and said, "How so?"

"I lost my ring," she answered, "and that made me mad, and I have searched until day; and now the day has caused me to find it." Wow! How quickly it came about the way Metzi had planned! After that all the fellows came with pipers and great noise into the bedroom in order to wish them much luck. v. 7127

"You shouldn't keep it secret. Would she allow it? Did you enjoy the cutting?" they asked Bertschi.

He answered them and spoke thus, "No girl has ever pleased me more. Know that she was a virgin! And therefore I will now give her a pair of shoes as a morning-gift."[126] Then they lifted them out of bed, and the wedding festivities were over; for grave and distressing tidings had come to them that the Nissingers wished to fight with them and that their envoys had

been sent into all countries for help. The young people were
pleased with that; but the old ones were not, for they well knew
what one can get from war.   v. 7148

THE LAPPENHAUSERS' WAR COUNCIL

Therefore they rang the bell of the council; and at least
twenty or more of the lords came up. Some of them have been
named before; the others were Ruoprecht, Gacksimacks, Nie-
mandsknecht, Hilprand, Grämpler, Gnaist, Gumprecht, Helle-
gaist, Künckelstil, Ochsenkäs, Fützenpart, Fleugenschäss, Peter
Stumpf, Riffian, and worthy Sir Pilian, also Lienhart with the
flail, Simon Kegel, Judas Schlegel, and grayhaired Höseller.
By then all of them were present on the threshing floor of a
barn.   v. 7165

Then Mayor Rüefli began and said, "My lords both rich and
poor, you have all seen how the wicked Nissingers with their
cowardly dissolute hearts reproached us yesterday in the grass
for no other reason than that Eisengrein had tickled Gredul's
hand with all his love. Now a dog licks his master in friend-
ship and to show his joy; and therefore they didn't do right
but acted like one who, without right or reason, wishes to create
disorder. They weren't even satisfied with that but sent us a
worthless rogue with a bad message and with threats, just as
mice do to lions.   v. 7184

"In addition they have sent into all lands for aid and advice
and desire to fight with us. What should we wait for then?
You know we should not stand for it or keep silent any longer.
Therefore my advice is that we should be the first to declare
war on them and provide ourselves with good weapons and ride
against the mice and scratch their lice as undaunted as lions.
Take that as my advice."

His words pleased the young people well, for they were in
high spirits because they had been successful on the previous
day and thought that no one could ever hurt them on any oc-
casion. They all said, "So let it be! If anyone knows better, let
him speak up."   v. 7206

At that Riffian, who was one of the old ones, got up and said,
"The situation is not as you seem to imagine, judging by what
you say; for I have often heard that no one can lead a campaign
properly except a prince of high rank or someone with authority
from him. Therefore you cannot fight, as the imperial law
states."

Lienhart at once began speaking, "Tell me one thing that I ask you. What are the princes made of? Where does their sovereignty come from? Aren't they Adam's children as we are?[174] Tell me that." v. 7223

"In truth," said Riffian, "it is quite true that everyone has come from Adam and his wife Eve; yet some individuals were so worthy that they were chosen by the people and elected as lords. Some were good and some were bad; goodness always made its way inside and wickedness begged at the door,[171] just as it happened to Sir Noah's sons. When one of them saw his father drunk, he began to ridicule him and therefore became a bondsman; but those who honored their father then became honorable free men. Therefore we are not equal. One is poor, the other rich, one a peasant, the other noble."[174] v. 7244

Then Lienhart with the flail said, "Well then, that suits all of us well, since we are worthy and full of virtue. Besides, we have a seat superior to all villages, well walled with a pallisade, around which runs a brook full of water. The village has two gates and four blockhouses as its wall, along with a splendid deep ditch, too sour for any enemy. We are so mighty and so rich that no nation was ever our equal. v. 7257

"Therefore I can speak thus, if all my colleagues approve. You, Rüefel Lekdenspiss, be emperor over us all; and you, Walther Fleugenschäss, be king in the Grausen district. Also let Fützenpart be duke on the campaign, and let him have his dukedom in the land of Antertal, to his own personal renown. That will make him famous everywhere. And you, Bertschi Triefnas (I can't advise you any better) be margrave over all the territory of Nienderthaim. Count Burkhart has already been a born Count of Nidrentor; his county is in Hungary, where they make many counts. Let the rest of us be free lords, which no one can deny us! Then, if anyone wants to be a knight, let him come to the combat; for we'll make many of them there. Let our servants be squires." v. 7282

The young men said, "That's right."

Ruoprecht began laughing at that and said, "Well then, even if that were so (but that can never be for a single day, as long as you live), we still shouldn't fight with the Nissingers right now, if we wish to see rightly what combat is and the many kinds of combat and the cause of unjust war."

"Tell us that," said Farindkuo then, "we'll gladly listen to you." v. 7295

Thereupon Ruoprecht said, "Know that combat is a war that consists of striking and piercing, of shooting, crushing, and breaking too. Now there are many kinds of combat. People call some of them spiritual, and some are quite temporal. Spiritual combat has two armies. The first is the Heavenly Host, which defended itself so strongly against Lucifer and all those who followed him that he fell into Hell with all his retinue. It was right that he had to suffer that punishment, for he wished to set himself above God. The second spiritual army consists of the clergy, who in God's stead harmfully excommunicate people day and night and also close the churches to them and deprive them of profit and honor. This combat can be sometimes good and sometimes bad, according to what one does.   v. 7319

"Temporal combat is of two kinds. The first is communal warfare, which is waged against another country if a high-placed prince, or a nation with his authority, fights it. The thing is of such nature that combat can arise rightfully or else just come from violence.   v. 7327

"The second combat is individual and often occurs when a man defends his life. That is granted him by fortune and justice. Individual combat also arises when a man is personally injured by one person but wishes to avenge himself on the community. That can never be just, for only that soul should suffer that has personally sinned. Thirdly, you see it when one fights with another in individual combat. May God give him pain and cramps who first thought of it and made so many men lose their lives without sin![179] Yet, when people fight, the just man more often prevails than the guilty one because he has faith in his just cause; for that gives him courage and strength too.[179] Yet hear another thing, and take note! Other sins often bring it about that he remains in the snare.   v. 7355

"Combat comes from many causes; yet, to make the matter short, the cause of all causes is of five kinds, which should be made known to you at this time. Therefore know that the first is the fact that a wrong is not corrected as it deserves. The second is a full chest that supports the war steadily. The third, hear me well, is that we don't want to give our tithe to the priest;[186] and therefore the mercenary takes it. The fourth is that we don't want to resist the Devil; for whoever fights for his soul pays no heed to the combat of his body. The last reason why we desire the act which creates wars and conflict is that we cannot know soon enough all the damage to our soul and body and goods that we can suffer from the war. I'm also thinking of oversea journeys to colonize distant lands; for, if anyone really knew all the suffering involved, he would drop the whole matter. By this you can note whether it is good for you to fight."   v. 7387

Eisengrein quickly contradicted that and spoke thus, "First Lekspiss told us how we had a right to our cause. Now, if we have a right to it, then we should ever strive to bring it to a successful conclusion. And let no one prevent us from it, for we must win fame! And what harm should those suffer who are so mighty and brave that they don't give a damn for anyone when peril arises?"   v. 7400

The young men thought his words good. Thereupon Sir Pilian began his rebuttal, since he was an old man who knew more about war. He said, "Know that no one should trust himself too much; for no one is so strong or rich that he cannot find his equal. They say, according to military science, that a campaign must have an army of seven thousand one hundred men on foot and seven hundred and nineteen mounted,[139] who should be all together and well and completely armed. There should be a large troop of marksmen who should advance and strike the enemy at a distance. Well now, you don't have all that; and therefore the combat will be of no avail."   v. 7423

Squire Haintz jumped up with anger and said, "So help me! See, for a horn's sake! Does he want to give us figures on how one should live in combat? I have heard of the combat of warriors, of Alexander, of the Trojans with the Greeks, and of the Romans; but I've never heard of any counting. Therefore my advice is that, if one doesn't have ten thousand armed men for his combat, he should come walking up with a log, if he can't do any better, and knock the enemy into the grass. A pepper seed is much faster than a large dung heap."   v. 7441

At this point Dame Laichdenman came to the door and knocked, and was therefore admitted. She entered and spoke thus, "I have always known that no wise man should come to the council on his own if he has not been invited. Now on the other hand I know that, if anyone can advise better than another in a matter that affects him so greatly, he has a right to do so and will be praised for it. Therefore I've come here to tell you my message with many plaints of the great pain I bear in my heart.   v. 7458

"Our mayor is a youth, and the council is of young people.

That can only mean what I have found written, 'Woe to the land that must have a child as its king.' For I wish to swear this to you now: should the fighting proceed, this village can scarcely last a day, I well know. It will be burnt to coals and all its wealth stolen; and, if I dare say it, the child in its mother's womb will be murdered along with the woman, and the men will be slain, or captured and hanged on high. v. 7475

"I have read all that in scripture; and so it must be, for the Nissingers are the children of the planet Mars.[146] You can easily detect that in the fact that their village is full of smiths and that they have many butchers, as that star wishes.[103a] Also, it will be on Tuesday, which is his too,[146] as I tell you. In addition, that star will be in his house (he likes to stand there), which is in Taurus, where he is at least twice as strong as if that weren't the case. v. 7490

"Moreover I'll inform you that we are dedicated especially to the star Venus. You can quickly see that, since this village has only weavers and tailors,[103a] who are reckoned in her number and are supposed to be her children. Also, that star has the disadvantage that it is going backwards and stands in Scorpio. It has an angry countenance, and that will harm you on the occasion. Therefore, my dear children, in order to remain happy restrain yourselves from fighting and wait for a better time if you wish to save your body and soul, children, wives, and wealth and reputations." v. 7509

Now as soon as this speech had taken place, how cruelly Nickel looked at her and said, "Get out, you old whore. May the evil spirit take you with your star-gazing. I'll tell you this. If there were a staircase in the house, you'd have to fall down and out." Laichdenman ran away and left the young men with their own mind.

Colman was a wise fellow, and therefore he spoke weeping hotly, "Well then, my dear young gentlemen, tell what you wish to do."

All the young men answered, "We want to fight for one reason: so that we can give the lie to the old heretics' prating. May the executioner wrack them, if they should frighten us thus." v. 7529

Colman said, "Then be so good as to send for help, as one should do in such great danger. The matter is not far from fatal. It is not for a single strap, the entire hide is at stake. See, that won't harm you, for wisdom speaks thus, 'One can test a friend in time of peril better than any other day.' Also, asking won't hurt us. If someone won't hearken to us, at least he won't hurt us; and, in addition, we'll know even better than before whether he is loyal to us or not so that we can act accordingly later on. v. 7545

"Also, it is the law of warfare[170] to send the enemy a messenger in rose-colored cloth with a sword and gauntlet sprinkled with red blood; for that is a good sign that one wants to fight with them. In addition the fellow declares war against their person and wealth so that they can better watch out for themselves. Do thus if you have a desire for combat." v. 7557

This pleased all the young men, and they shouted out with a great noise, "So help me, it was truly a favor for us that Colman spoke like that." They sent the sexton to the enemy in hopes he would deliver the message and be slain by them, for they bore hate against him.[185]

That was all to his profit when he came to Nissingen and began his speech thus, "My lord, the mayor, and the council of Lappenhausen have just sent me to you to announce their greeting, in accordance with what you have deserved, believe you me! In addition, I declare war, in the name of all my lords, on your persons and property. Take the gauntlet in your hand, and the bloody sword too, to defend yourselves tomorrow morning early. They can be found on the Nissvelt by the linden tree." v. 7584

When the message had been delivered, Strudel was undaunted and said, "You must be a regular guy. Here's an ass. It's yours. I'll give it to you as a messenger's gift[126] from me and my burgesses, for you have made us quite happy with your good tidings. Take back sword and gauntlet, and give them our curse too; for we'll ruin them with our own swords if they come to the place where they have summoned us." The messenger was pleased with this revenge. If formerly he had walked, he now rode back to Lappenhausen and related the answer to them all. v. 7601

THE NISSINGERS' QUEST FOR ALLIES

That made them leap for joy, rage madly, and sing too; and they straightway sent from their general council to the best cities that could be found anywhere. The first was called Rome, situated in Campagna; Venice was the second, and also Bruges in Flanders. Galicia has Compostella, Navarre only Pampilona, in Catalonia Barcelona. The largest in Spain is Seville, and in Provence Marseilles, Palermo on the Island of Sicily, and Naples in the Kingdom of Sicily. Bari lies in Puglie. All these lie right on the sea; Genoa does the same too with a city that is called Savona, and also Ancona in the March. All of them lie on it too. Constantinople is known to the children there in Greece.[5] On the island of Cyprus is Famagost, and Mallorca with its territory has an island for itself too. v. 7630

Now I will turn back to the mainland. In Tuscany are Florence, Perugia, Assisi, Lucca, High Siena, and Pisa. A Lombard can show you Bologna, Verona and Milan, and also Padua and Ferrara, if you do not find the asking too difficult. In Friuli is Udine, which was not to be omitted. Peuschendorff maintains the best highway, without interruption. Bozen lies on the Adige, and Fortress Tyrol too. Lausanne is in Savoy; in France, well built Paris, Toulouse, and Montpellier are three very magnificent cities. v. 7648

Leyden in Brabant, Cologne in the Netherlands, Worms, Speyer, Trier, Mainz, and Aachen all lie near together by the Rhine, as Basel does. Also the good city of Constance lies in the land of Swabia; in addition, concerning Ulm and nearby Augsburg, one should also ask which is the best one there. Zürich lies on the Limmat, Wiener Neustadt in Steiermark, Rastatt and Strassburg in Alsace, and Erfurt in Thuringia. In Franconia one finds Würtzburg and the market of Frankfort. One should find Bamberg there and seek for Münster among the Frisians and for Nuremberg in Swanfelden. v. 7666

Prague lies on Bohemian soil, Brunn in Moravia on the March, in Bavaria strong Regensburg, Salzburg, and very rich Munich; yet Passau is their equal. Vienna has grown up in Austria, and Halberstadt stands in Saxony. Meissen stands alone and has a march of its own. Ofen, Gran, and Pressburg lie on the Hungarian ford. Crakow is in the Polish Empire, and also Breslau[5] its equal. In Carinthia one finds Villach not very far from Friesach. Prussia and other lands too are not so well known to me; and therefore I cannot name their cities. However, so that you will not get discouraged, I will return to the place where I recently left the peasants' envoys. v. 7688

The cities took note of the letters. How quickly they came together to consider to whom they should give their help! And when much discussion had taken place, the Senator of Rome said, "The Lombards are wise enough, and they of France are especially clever, and German men are learned too; and therefore let the honor be given to them. Whatever the Prior of

Florence and the Magistrate of Constance[1] and the Captain of
Paris say, let all that be done."   v. 7702

The Prior said, "That's too much for me; but let it be not
what I wish, but what you wish. And I'll expound a little word
that a wise man spoke, which is, 'It's better to arbitrate between
two of your enemies than between your friends; for, if I lost
one of my friends, that would be too dear, whereas I may gain
one of my enemies as a friend.' That's what I think, and there-
fore I can say here that everyone well knows that both the Nis-
singers and the Lappenhausers are our friends. It seems to
me we should not choose the one party and lose the other, to our
great loss."   v. 7722

The Captain was also asked. He answered at once and said,
"Sir Prior has just answered so wisely that I have nothing better
in mind. Therefore I will second him and corroborate his words
with another speech that says, 'If a man is on slippery ice, he
will be wise to go softly and keep to either side, and thus he will
make his way safely.' Therefore I advise in this matter that
we remain at ease. And we may do that very properly; for we
break neither peace with nor promise to the villagers if we do
not wish to follow them, and we can keep the other party in our
good grace without any wrong.   v. 7742

"Yet I'll add one thing that people often say, 'Cursed be the
skill that makes copper out of silver!' For that reason we should
receive the envoys well and treat them properly as one should do
to strangers, and especially to those who are sent on a mission
to foreign countries. We should also politely decline the Lap-
penhausers' request and tell them that their old friendship is
still so new in our hearts that we would certainly do all that is
fitting, but that the nobility's hearts are so ardent against our
persons and property that we can't fare from our cities at this
time. Therefore we ask them the favor of considering us with-
out blame."   v. 7764

Afterwards they urgently begged the learned Magistrate of
the city of Constance on Lake Constance, if he knew anything
more than the others, that he tell it to them and advise them
better. Therefore the Magistrate began and said, "Those who
have heretofore advised in the matter are so correct in what
they say that I don't think I can improve upon it; yet, as I was
taught by one who was a jurist, I will say that, correctly speak-
ing, help is of two kinds, which are protection and good will.
We are all obligated to help a Christian whenever anybody does
a wrong to his person, honor, or property. Yet let that happen

in such a way that everyone is left unbeaten and unstabbed; for it would be avenged on us if the beaten man were the subject of another. v. 7790

"One finds three kinds of good will. The first is counsel, the second is influence, the third is collaboration. With counsel we should help everyone who requests it, if his cause is worthy of counsel. Then, if he does as he should, we should agree with him and quickly give him our favor and our influence. Also, we can collaborate with someone if he does the right thing at the right time. Yet we are not bound if the assistance demands great effort and expenditure, unless the same man has done a similar thing for us or would gladly do so if we asked it of him. However, we should accept the request if the matter can proceed in such a way that we need give neither our good name nor our life with the help and that no one would thereby free himself from the priesthood[186] and that the assistance would not be too grave for our friends; for we should not displease them, as virtue tells us. v. 7820

"Nevertheless, if both parties are equally valuable as friends, then we should arbitrate between them. Then, if we can't reconcile them, we should go to the weaker and protect him, if he is in the right.[169] See, all that seems meet and right to me. However, if they are equally obstinate in their wills, then we'll let them struggle till they get tired. And what I say about friends you may note vice versa about the enemies, as is the way of this world that sells the soul for money. Therefore it is my advice that we at once send two of us with their embassy, who are to settle their dispute, if they can, with completely fair words. But, if their decision doesn't help, then let's let the chaff-bags get satiated with fighting, if that pleases you." v. 7846

The Doge of Venice said, "Better words have never been spoken," and the Podesta of Padua said, "That's my advice." There were three justices from Prague, and they all said, "So let it be, so let it be!" v. 7852

THE LAPPENHAUSERS' QUEST FOR ALLIES

Therefore their honorable embassy was sent straightway to the council at Lappenhausen. They quickly began their discussion about peace; but they were answered thus, "Tell your people of the cities that we have asked them to help, and not to make peace. Therefore in this matter we swear to all the saints that we won't honor their request." What were the envoys to reply then? They might have known beforehand that a peasant never does what you ask him courteously. His head swells greatly if you dare beg him, and he only does what he has to. Violence is the best cure for him.[175] That became too serious for Höseller, and he thought how it would be better to live on foreign soil than to die there at home; so he removed himself from there secretly, as wise people are still wont to do. v. 7878

The others now sent to the villages in hopes that they would come to help. The first village was Narrenheim, where they had many kinsmen. The second village was called In-der-Krinn. They sent over to the hamlet that is called Rupfengeiler, toward Torenhofen in the valley to their friends everywhere, and to Leusau under the Heuberg,[147] where witches and dwarves dwelled. Near these, heroes and giants too were sitting on the green meadows. They also sent round and round, even into heathen lands. The Jews[146] and Greeks they considered weaklings and nuns, and therefore they did not want any of them. v. 7898

The witches thought themselves quite good. Wow! How quickly they were ready! Each sat on a goat and flew forth so that I do not know what the devil was in them, each in a light shirt on which was their common emblem: Pelsabuk's crooked nose. They rode into Lappenhausen with long swine-bristles and boxes full of salve, which they had to have. That was well known to the dwarves dwelling on the Heuberg,[75] who did not want to be with the witches in any affair because they did not like them much. v. 7915

These began considering the matter, and each jumped on a roebuck with his many-colored cloak. They sprang high all the way to the village green at Nissingen to defy the witches. Their arms were brought after them on high camels; their emblem was a crowned lion with a motto: "No one threaten me!" Before them many wandering minstrels played especially well with pipes and stringed instruments and filled their friends with joy.

Hereupon came the giants (each carried an iron spear) with their banner, which was an angry lion. They trod with seven strides right to the green in the middle of Lappenhausen, to the joy of everyone. v. 7935

The heroes, whom the giants hated, saw that and resolved to journey to Nissingen. That took place as it should have done. Their swords were long and broad, with much steel laid on them. What they bore as an emblem was a beautiful picture of the Virgin.

The heathens well knew how one should avenge himself. When they heard how the Christians' love had been destroyed, they were well pleased and spoke to one another thus, "A man who wishes to avenge himself should overcome enemy with enemy." Therefore a large crowd of them moved up to the Lappenhausers' territory, some on foot and others on horse, with their tridents and their missiles, with a star along with the moon, for they were never without that coat-of-arms.   v. 7958

Now why should the Switzers[102] wait? With their sharpened halberds a great crowd of them came up, only to aid the Nissingers. Some went on foot, the others hung from their saddles. They were frightful and evil too. Their banner had a milk-pail[72] from the village of Uri, that always surpassed the others.

The Narrenheimers went forth too (their minds were set toward Lappenhausen) with their ass ears[19] that made them feel quite noble. As their defense they carried rakes, which struck firmly and hacked hard.

The Torenhofers came up too. They bore a cow's tail and came walking up with thirty-one men, each with his staff with which he gave great bruises. Fifty had come there from Narrenheim alone. A thousand and more heathens had come for the Christians' woe, all armored with leather. Their captain was called Sir Mägeron.[78]   v. 7986

There were seven giants.[77] The first was called Sige, the second they called Ecke, the third was Wecke, the fourth was named Goliath, and the fifth one they addressed as Roland.[76] Reimprecht and handsome Siren were the last two.

The witch-mistress Hächel had brought up eleven hundred cursed damsels. Then the Lappenhausers' army was three hundred and twelve, so erect that I wondered what they had eaten. They were undaunted, each with his lance on horse or on foot, I do not know how, so that all together there were, according to my figures, two thousand five hundred free warriors. The other villagers did not come and said that, in this affair, it was better to watch calmly or sleep against the wall than to take a hand oneself.   v. 8014

However, from In-der-Krinn, the flat country, an old and gray man was sent, for no more of them were to be found there. He wanted to become a knight, so pleased he was with the order. But he was at once rejected. "So help me! What do we want with the shabby dog?" they said. "Go back home. You are repulsive to the young people."

There would have come Sir Gawain, a worthy knight from Montalban, Lancelot, Sir Tristan, Astolff, and other lords together;[76] but they had to save their castles and other properties from the cities. Yet Sir Bückel of Ellerbach,[81] whom one never saw in indolence, would have chosen to fight, except that he was still unborn. v. 8034

Meanwhile the Metzendorfers joined the Nissingers uninvited for their fight. They were seen marching up grimly like magnificent heroes with swords and spears. On his coat-of-arms each bore a groundhog on a stump.[86] They had come because of a matter that had taken place a hundred years earlier. It was an injury and treachery the Lappenhausers had done to their ancestors for no reason, and now at last they wished to avenge it. From the other villages no one came except one man from Libingen, a real huntsman with a horn who had sworn the enemy's death. He wore a rusty breastplate and carried a pitchfork too, with which he gave three wounds with one thrust, whenever he wished to exert himself. v. 8056

As I wish to tell you, there were many Metzendorfers, at least seventy-nine; and that made at least eighty. There were a hundred and twenty Swiss lads, and that made precisely two hundred by a hair. There were only four heroes, whom I shall name for you. They were Dietrich of Bern[75] (believe me), his armorer Hildebrant, Dietleib of Styria, and worthy Wolfdietrich.[78] There were exactly one thousand ninety-eight dwarves. Now watch carefully how many that makes! Of the Nissingers sixty regular spearmen were ordered to ride up to the village green; and for each spear three well prepared horses were counted, just as a lance should have. One would have seen there thirteen hundred and sixty honorable soldiers all together. v. 8081

Innumerable other soldiers came to both parties, hosts of camp followers and light-armed troopers, marksmen, and shield bearers, who also helped fight. The strangers were well received by the ladies and the men, and they were all given drink. What else should they do? The wine rose to their heads; they jumped up brusquely and wanted to strangle the enemy right then like dogs. In truth, that would have been easy; but the old people pulled them from it. All the Nissingers shouted with great noise, "Come here, you lords. Don't be in such a hurry to fight. We should have a discussion and agree as to what we should do jointly." Then they were obedient. v. 8103

STRUDEL'S SPEECH TO HIS TROOPS

Strudel climbed up on a roof and began his speech and said, "Hear, you lords, both rich and poor, great and small and all alike. God, who does all things for our good and benefit, often gives a sinner a pain in his body or mind so that he will be converted all the sooner. Therefore my advice is that all of us Christians should confess our sins completely. I'm not saying that because we should fear the enemy, who are always so dissolute, cowardly, wicked and foolish. I'm saying it only so that we may please God better; for, if He is with us alone, no one will trip us up.   v. 8124

"After that we should all merrily and jovially eat bread and pork and also drink red wine; for that will give us strength and power too. Next, toward evening, we should move out to the field to erect huts and tents. There we should all remain and pass the night very restfully, yet with good vigilance and fire until the lovely bright day. After that let everyone get up and put on his armor and bless himself. Let him suck an egg, or three or four or two, with a glass of good wine; for that will help him in his peril. Then let him proceed to his rightful captain, of which there should be five here.   v. 8145

"Let the first be Laurin, a praiseworthy king ruling over all the mountains. The second is Sir Dietrich of Bern, whom no man ever equalled in prowess and might; and let the giants take note of that! Yet they are all so handsome that everyone of them could be a captain over all the world, as I tell you on my word of honor! The third captain is called the fiercest in Christendom. He is a well-known hero, Sir Packenzan of Switzerland, who has led my lords here from Uri so far away. The fourth captain is the strong man of Metzendorf in the March, who is given to much fighting and defeats them all. Let the man from Libingen be his own master, a free warrior. And I am the head and master of these burgesses—God knows how! I am quite unworthy of it, it seems to me.   v. 8172

"And may my nephew succeed too. He is the best from Nissingen and is called Fülizan. I shan't praise him, since he belongs to me. You may see in his deeds what the man has in his heart. If it suits you, we will select him to be the leader for the sake of our gain and honor and to direct our army with our banner to the place where we shall fight in the morning, for he is full of strategy."

They all said, "That pleases us well. But who, by rights,

should have the privilege of leading the attack? You should tell us." v. 8188

"Truly," answered Strudel, "our order should be thus. Here are Christians, dwarves, and heroes. They should take to the field on horse and on foot in five completely separate companies, just as many as there are captains. Also know, as I'll explain to you, that the enemy's force is divided into witches, giants, and heathens. In addition they have a Christian army of at least six or more companies. Now tell me, for you know it better, whom do you hate most of all? To them you should give battle; for that's fitting and suits you well. I well know that the Switzers, as one of their ancient rights,[168] have always had the privilege of leading the attack whenever they fight with other Christians. I don't know the custom of the dwarves or of the heroes when they fight. They enjoy great respect; may God give them what will suit them well." v. 8212

They were all pleased by his words, and the dwarves answered thus, "No witch and no monster was ever truly our friend."

"Well now, join the battle at whatever time they come," Strudel answered at once.

The heroes' party also began shouting, "We don't like the giants, for they are full of all wickedness."

"Then you should wait for them until they begin to fight," Strudel answered immediately.

The Switzers called from their mouths, "Know that we are Christian people and hunger for the heathens' hides."

"Then take them" Strudel answered. "Yet I'll advise you thus. Let everyone take a scythe[72] and cut off the heretics' legs." v. 8232

The Metzendorfers also spoke up, "Know that we have always hated the Lappenhausers. That's the truth."

Then Strudel said publicly, "They should fall to our lot, we won't sell them at any price. Yet I can say this. If you want to get revenge on them, then attack the Narrenheimers; for a wise man said, 'Destroy the servants, and you destroy the master along with them.'"

The Metzendorfers spoke thus, "You should do just what you hope to get from us. We consider that quite fair."

Strudel had a clever mind. "That would be meet and right," he said, "but there are too many of them. Therefore we will not and should not let you perish thus; for we all know that if any-

one strikes you dead he'll bring us to the same pass." They were
satisfied with that.   v. 8257

Fülizan began stirring and said, "My very dear kinsman, may
you ever be happy! You say I should carry the banner and show
the army the way. Isn't that the duty of a captain to whom the
troops are subject?"

"No," Strudel answered then, "you are standard-bearer and
have nothing else to do but carry the banner forward firmly and
high during the fight, and then you are a man. And see to it
that you don't turn back and that no one forces it down. You'll
be given helpers who'll guard you. The duty of a captain is
something else.   v. 8275

"First of all he should be a man of generous disposition, un-
daunted so that he can encourage the others and urge them
forward as best he can; for whoever is not in good spirits will
give the others no confidence. The second is that he should be
clever and conduct himself like a man who can play chess, at-
tacking while keeping himself from suffering loss. Therefore
let him do this first in peace time and order his troops to prac-
tice horsemanship day and night, with jousting and tilting and
other amusement; for an untrained man can outdo a trained
one as little as a naked man can outdo one who is wearing com-
plete armor.   v. 8298

"Therefore everyone should first of all know especially how
to ride well and neatly. One should always mount and dismount
on the left side, and the stirrup should be of such length that
one can rise in the saddle so that you can put a bullet[5] under
him. One should stretch out his legs yet hold his knees to-
gether and not wear his spurs toward his horse. Let him keep
his reins in control and sit erect with straight posture. Then,
if he wishes to ride with a spear, let him see to it that the stirrup
on the opposite side hangs a half a span in front of the other.
Let him crouch forward a bit so that one can harm him all the
less. First of all he should pace slowly and then quickly, for
that's the smart way. And, if he wants to hit every time, he
shouldn't take too long a run. One should buy weapons in peace
time, if one doesn't want to run naked before the enemy when
the battle has begun.   v. 8326

"Meanwhile the captain should keep watch and not sleep;
and he should not lead his knights and squires too recklessly.
He must look out for his troops' safety and lead them to a place
where they will find oats and straw and wood and water; for that
is necessary so that the horses won't die and the men won't

suffer such want that they lose their strength. The water that they are to drink should have been tested in advance, and all strange food too, if he wishes to avoid poison. He should neither remain in any forest nor pass the night near moss. Also he should have scouts who can tell him daily the intention and strength of the enemy. Behold, that will give him the best power.   v. 8348

"And if there are too many of the enemy, I advise him to sneak up on them secretly if he wishes to win the victory. Or, if that can't be, then let him at least follow my instruction and wait for them in such a place that he have the advantage of terrain. If they are weaker or equal, then a spirited captain can freely let his men run forward and strike and rush wildly into their army. And yet I'll say that if something occurs so that at last one sees nothing but death, then he may flee in his peril. That is the best fight one can find at the time. But if someone is willing to take them captive as one rightly should, without killing them, then I advise them to surrender rather than be sent a hare's tail to their disgrace.   v. 8372

"Especially in order to be spared on this earth, he should set out to battle with his horse troops on the plain and his foot troops on the hills so that he will have the advantage. If the land is mountainous, let him send his marksmen out in front of the others; their shots will do the first damage. In addition he should keep his forces tight together and put those who are weakest into the center. Let no one advance before the others, for that is moderation.   v. 8388

"If the land is all even, you should place behind the marksmen the horsemen, who run their spears through the enemy, and after them those with swords so they can crush their helmets. Let footmen also be on hand so that they can help the riders up again if they fall down out of the saddle. They should stab the enemy's horses and break the necks of their fallen and also struggle, strike, strangle, and cut down the other foot soldiers. And, if the victory has been won, let them take the remainder captive.   v. 8404

"But, if the land is all hilly, then appreciate the high ground as valuable, the marksmen forward, the riders dismounted. Let them tie their horses to the hedge and let them hurl their lances[138] so that the enemy will be aware of them. They should also assault the enemy, and thus they may succeed all the better. And if God grants them luck so that they loot and ransom the enemy,[161] then the captain should share with everyone according to his just earnings. It is also proper for the captain always to look after his troops to see whether he can find any discord among them so that he can reconcile it in hopes of reproving the guilty man. Thus his company will remain free of ill repute, for no war scourges a land as much as one that arises between friends." v. 8426

A CODE OF ETHICS FOR THE SOLDIER

Then the man Packenzan said, "Alas! How little I can judge. I little know what the books sing, say, or establish."

Then Strudel answered that and said, "Don't feel uneasy about that. Hold your court according to custom and pay little heed to books. Act according to your knowledge and conscience, for that is the wisest thing."

The captain from Metzendorf then began another question. "Tell me, what is your advice? If someone has lent me a horse or armor for the battle and I lose it there, must I give him anything back?" v. 8443

"No," said Strudel then calmly, "for he knew in advance that war is full of losses; for four could never win enough in battle for one to ride with God and with right.[169] Such is the profit of war. Therefore the law decrees that he wanted to give it to you and not lend it, unless he has stipulated that he be reimbursed for his losses."

Laurin was lying in ambush and also asked Strudel a question, "Wise master, tell us. How will we treat the captives?" v. 8458

Strudel would have answered, but he wished to honor Laurin and said, "The question is of great importance, and much too difficult for my brain. Therefore I must seek an answer in the books." Then he came back a while later and said, "It's still too much for me; yet, as I see it, I find that one may kill the prisoners if one knows for a fact that their life would do harm or that their word would not be kept, unless the man's life had been assured in open conflict and he is not otherwise a rascal. Such a man should be left unharmed. However, he has lost his wealth unless that too has been promised him. Yet it is the Emperor's right, according to the law of the ancient books, that his prisoners become bondsmen when he himself fights.[168] v. 8482

"You should capture a whore's son however you can and hasten to wring his neck even if you made him a promise, provided he can't be captured without a guarantee. If he says, 'Respect my rights,' he should be answered thus, 'How can you now invoke justice, after you have so often acted against it? Your due is a noose that will choke you by the neck.'[170] Through this you may well know how we should dispose of the Lappenhausers in such peril; for their joy is our death. We should let the strangers go so that we can survive all the better." v. 8500

Sir Dietrich of Bern also wanted to hear how it would be in the case of a prisoner who did not want to keep his parole; and Strudel answered quickly, "That is not the least question. In this case one should consider whether a man has been captured by wicked people for his wealth. If so, he may properly break his parole, however much he has promised, for no one should profit through his evil deeds. This is the custom in open battle: if a man is captured and wishes to beg off and go home to his house and promises to report back at an appointed time, then he should very rightfully keep his word unless he knows that he will die or lose a limb through keeping it. And even if another has vouched for it, it should remain unavenged." v. 8526

After that some old people came from Nissingen and said to Strudel, "We have rights[168] that say that age is never obligated to fight. Therefore we herewith request that you release us from combat service."   v. 8534

Strudel rejected their words. "It's the old ones I need," he said then to the graybeards, "I'd be pleased if there were many of you. I well know that combat strength doesn't depend only upon physical power, courage, horses, and iron. The best part lies in wise men who, with a small tongue, strike through all the enemy. Yet you should observe that in old people, who are much better for it than the young ones. Let the others tell you that a lad of less than sixteen years and anyone who is over sixty should rest in time of war (let no one force him into battle), and also anyone who has five or more legitimate sons living, if one of them died while fighting for the common good, even if he died with honor. Women are also excepted, unless they wish to help with stones. No sick man should fight." v. 8561

"He was an ass who said that," said the others then.

And while they were speaking there, the Lappenhausers were also holding a discussion nearby. Both parties kept that up until early in the morning, as one should. Yet the Lappenhausers remained without confession, for the priest would not hear them, just as he should not have. They said in jest, "Now may the Old God help us!"[132]   v. 8574

THE BATTLE BEGINS

Now when the day was first born, the Libinger sounded his horn, which they regarded as the army trumpet. They were all happy because of the day. Rüefli and Saichinkruog carried the Lappenhausers' banner, on which, I trust, a spool and tailor's shears[103a] were painted, and departed from their tent toward the linden and to the field where they were going to fight. v. 8585

At the same time the mayor spoke to the army, "Well for me that I have seen an army as you are, so beautiful, with complete power, and with such charming youth. Be happy in that, and conduct yourselves today so that we will win fame and wealth, as a free warrior can well do if he sets his mind on fame and wealth and gain. Therefore I command under pain of death (blessed be he who believes me) all knights and squires to present themselves today to fight in knightly fashion, without fleeing. Also, no one should advance before the others without my word. And even if he won a great hoard for our army, that wouldn't help him, for I'd treat him just like a whore's son. Gunterfai, play up! Then both horse and man will be merry."

Everyone, I swear, shouted thus, "Up and at 'em, up and at 'em!"   v. 8610

Triefnas had eaten his steed,[39] and therefore he had to walk his way. Meanwhile Sir Fülizan came with his banner, on which stood a stick on an anvil with a bare skinner's knife.[103a] Strudel was not the weakest, he had given his troops confidence. The mayor moved out to the linden and let himself be found. The enemies were so near that they could see each other. Emperor Lekspiss was a real guy. "If anyone wishes to become a knight," he said to his followers, "let him step up quickly." Therefore Berchthold of the cherry tree, a nobleman and effective warrior, stepped forth as if in a dream. After him Tirawätsch and Kuoni of Stockach came riding up; and Haini of Gretzingen also came at this time. Then the emperor drew out his sword and said, "You are worthy of the honor." He struck them with the side of the sword[129] and began singing this verse, "Here better knight than squire."   v. 8639

The others said, "That's right."

"Yet you should not ride in front of the strangers," said

the man. They would have been given sword and gauntlet, belts, and golden spurs of nobility; but these had all been lost here and there.   v. 8646

THE WITCHES VERSUS THE DWARVES

Then Lekspiss began shouting, "Ladies are very pure and gentle, and therefore we should honor them too. Well then, Dame Hächel, be so good and lead the first attack with your daughters. The time has come. Conduct yourselves as splendid warriors, and do not tire of shooting." Dame Hächel was pleased by the honor. How quickly she advanced! She jumped out before the others high up on a wolf, her daughters all with her (they thirsted for the enemy) and shot bristles from their fingers against the crowd.   v. 8662

Meanwhile Strudel stopped dubbing knights and addressed the master of the dwarves, "How gladly I grant you the honor of striking down that thieving woman and her followers like cattle." Sir Laurin advanced to the center most confidently, and his vassals hastened to follow their king and to throw with their slings into the host of women. The pipers and minstrels were safe and joyfully gathered together in one place. They blew into their instruments and beat on them until the battle took its end.

The banners advanced toward each other; the women flew, the dwarves trailed dust on goats and roebucks. Who should ask for quarter? It was time for cursing and chiding, so equal was the fight. Hächel did that and said, "Hey, Sir Nürggel under the roof, you're a mannikin from the Rhine,[75] and you'll have to suffer pain from me."   v. 8690

Sir Laurin's spirits were quite high. He said, "You whore, you're not worth my prating with you. Defend yourself, or you'll go to Hell." With that he began throwing much, he and all his men. The witches did not tire of shooting, there was so much shooting the day became dark with arrows. The bristles struck many a dwarf so that he fell to earth; for they were pointed and so swift that many a man's eyes were blinded. Many a man lost both his eyes and his life, for they had poisoned all the arrows in front. A message was sent to Laurin so that his left hand swelled. Many and even more witches were thrown down so hard that many of them in their peril were fatally wounded. The battle was grievous for them both.   v. 8717

Moreover, a wild man[14f] on a large stag rode through them
with many a blow from his monstrous club and struck the
women along with the men, many of them mortally. He threw
many of them down his maw. He had two teeth so long and
sharp that he bit many of them to death and wished to kill all
the combatants himself; for he thought in his mind, "The fight-
ing that you are doing among yourselves is my gain."   v. 8731

Both Laurin and Dame Hächel understood the rogue, and
therefore they followed the example of wise people and left off
from their undertaking just to spite the wild man and to harm
him and get revenge. They all hurried toward him with throw-
ing and shooting and never let it get them down; but he was too
quick for them and rode through their two walls with blows and
running, with stabbing and pulling. He struck the monsters
with his iron club such that they fell on the ground by fours.
The stag too caused the enemy much pain with its horns. It
lifted the little dwarves high up from the earth and pierced
them through and stuck into them so that they fell three at a
time.   v. 8754

That was a wild commotion; it was hard on them, and few of
them would have survived if it had not been for a courageous
dwarf. He was so swift and small too that he came between the
stag's legs and grabbed its tail with his hand (he was called
Sir Äschenzelt) and held the stag so strongly that it had to
remain there. Another one pulled out a sword and stuck the
stag in the belly so that it fell on its feet. The wild hero fell
off, and thereupon all the witches came up and tamed him, I do
not know how, so that he sat there like a little lamb and forgot
his life. But this was not without peril. Many fell over him
to death, and many of them were also lost on the dead stag's
horns.   v. 8776

Now when this matter had finished, a new battle started
between the witches and the dwarves, in which even more of
them had to perish. Alas, how much blood was shed then by the
stones and the missiles! And when there were no more arrows
they ran all the more readily against the little men and struck
many down with wolves and goats too, both thin ones and fat
ones. They sprang up to the sky and fell upon the poor weak-
lings so gently and softly—in just the manner of a falcon, which
strikes the birds with its breast and knocks them apart.[148] The
dwarves too made their bucks spring and knocked them down
like sticks. The witches were increasing on the ground, and

their horses flew over to the Heuberg whenever one of them was riderless. v. 8800

When Laurin saw this, how quickly he said to his men, "Dismount and stab the whores' horses to death, and afterwards kill the women if you wish to save your lives." Wow! How quickly they carried out what Laurin had thought up! Yet Dame Hächel's wolf was so charmed that they could not cut it or her in any way; and as a result Laurin really had a hot time of it. She ran against him so violently that he fell down often; but the others helped him up again, or else he would have been entirely lost. The disgrace made the prince angry, and he grabbed the staff of the banner. He thrust it toward Dame Hächel and reached her breast; but that was quite in vain, since no one could fell her. She had done that with her magic! She struck the man's spear aside and stepped down to him; she spit on his cheeks so hard that blisters bigger than a snail's house grew on him. v. 8830

Also, the wolf gave off a vapor from its mouth just like a flame. If it struck anyone near the heart, he swelled up like a jug; and that cost many a one his life. Next a dwarf named Trintsch came up carrying a net in his hand. He approached the woman from behind and threw the net around her and the wolf, whereupon the others came up and strangled both in their blood, as one still does to foxes. Thereupon they started forward again, going back and forth. The witches' banner went down, for one misfortune rides the other.

"Help us now, for it's high time!" the weird women shouted toward the linden tree. "We are lost and expelled, there are few of us left." They fought there until they waded to the ankles in blood. v. 8854

THE GIANTS VERSUS THE DWARVES

Then the emperor shouted in the grass, "Well now, Sir Giants, do you hear that? You are the lovers in the army; go forward in honor of womankind and don't leave any of the dwarves undamaged or untorn. I value one of you well worth a mountain full of dwarves." The praise pleased the giants and they marched forth into the battle against the dwarves. Meanwhile the latter had picked up many rocks and thrown them all against one target, that is, against the giants.

Then raging Reimprecht said, "What the Devil? Who is it that's injuring us from so far away? How much better we'll succeed when we push a bit closer! I must try that. Forward, my lords!" he said, and thus they came very close.   v. 8877

"Sir Chickenshit," said one of them to Sir Laurin, "How do you dare remain or approach me? Don't you know I can lay all your followers dead on the ground with one blow?"

The worthy king then answered him, "I don't well know what you can do, yet I have confidence in my strength. Even though I am a little dwarf, I'll grow to be a mountain in your eyes, believe you me! And I'll also tell you I think you ill-bred; and what you say is a lie, as I'll now prove." He then loaded his sling and struck the giant on the forehead so that the stone went through his head. Goliath fell dead, and naturally that angered his companions.   v. 8898

Meanwhile three of the heroes wanted to join them. "Not so," said Sir Hildebrant, who was their captain's armorer.[78] "Let's remain here a bit until we can better see how a little man can protect himself from a large one and survive. Thus we will also learn against whom we should rather fight. Also know that the giants too will get tired from this exercise, and thus we will advance fresh and strike them down on the field."   v. 8912

Sir Dietrich said, "Sir Armorer mine, what you have ordered, that should be."

Then horny[77] Reimprecht jumped in front of the other giants right through the middle of the dwarves and struck many of them to the earth. Consequently they had to back away from him, since no one dared attack him. However, a letter was sent to him so that the shaft fell from his hand. Then the others ran at the giant's legs so that he fell to his disadvantage. They crowded on his belly and pulled out his dagger, but he was entirely of horn so all their stabbing was wasted. Meanwhile Sir Reimprecht was not idle as he lay on his back; he bit many of them and tore even more; and that was to the woe of many a dwarf.   v. 8936

"At his eyes," they shouted; and he was promptly blinded. Yet he still was not too lazy but yawned widely with his mouth, for he wanted to swallow them. However, one of them came up with his knife and stuck it into his throat; and thus he too found his end. The other giants were swift and ran up with their rumpus just like wolves against geese. They struck with their staves, and it was all over with anyone they might reach.

Who should approach the heroes? Everyone hastened to withdraw—except for Sir Laurin, who was ashamed to flee and

came running against great Sige from the side, so that he too
fell and lay. But he jumped up and saved his life. He said,
"He didn't get me." If he had fought hard before, now he slew
three times as many of them. v. 8961

Sir Trintsch had lost his horse; and therefore the high-born
fellow sat on another dwarf, since his head was too low. He
took his net again and ran upon Weck from the rear and threw
it over him. However, the giant was not lazy, he tore it to
shreds in all directions with his teeth and said, "I'll screw your
mother. Do you think I'm a bird?" v. 8973

His words hurt Master Trintsch, and he ran against Weck
just as before. He grabbed at his eye and jerked it to his dis-
advantage so that it hung down by his nose. Thereupon the
giant grasped his eye and pulled it the whole way out and said,
"I don't care a louse about that. I still see enough." With that
he swung around against the enemy at a venture and struck
Trintsch with his horse so hard neither of them ever wanted
to eat again when one should drink. Thus the dwarves' help
was lost. The little warrior Äschenzelt was angered by that and
ran forward. He came between the giant's legs and tried to
stab him in the belly from underneath with a knife; but the
hero was so well protected by his good iron breeches that no one
could do anything to him. Thereupon he squeezed Äschenzelt to
death between his thighs like a chicken. All the dwarves suf-
fered that and had enough pain and were struck by one mis-
fortune after the other. Sir Roland soon advanced and threw
their banner on the ground. v. 9003

THE HEROES VERSUS THE GIANTS

Sir Hildebrant perceived that, "Well now, you magnificent
heroes, take part in the battle freely. Up and at them, the
time has come!" Sir Dietrich was pleased by his words and ran
forward with his men so that the earth trembled under them.
They pulled the trees from the earth and hurled them against
the worthy giants.

Then Sir Ecke said, "Alack, alas! One should punish chil-
dren with switches," and picked up a big mountain and threw it
against the heroes.

"Look! Isn't that a vulture?" said Sir Dietleib of Styria.
"Do you want to bury us thus? We haven't been slain yet.
Clods of earth and manure are thrown by a woman who is angry.
If you have iron, show it to us!" v. 9024

"Yes indeed," said Ecke and presented his steel staff in such a way that Sir Dietleib became so clearly aware of it on his hard head that he fell down as dead. This sport angered Dietrich, who thought his comrade was lost, and he struck Sir Ecke in two at the middle; for that was Dietrich's habit. His sword had an edge that cut without any pain through flesh and bone and whatever it found.   v. 9036

Sir Ecke said, "It's a shame you've pulled your sword out of its sheath without causing any injury. Fools' daggers and whores' breasts are often seen bared in vain." Dietrich laughed at that to himself and struck out a second time, but he missed Ecke and hit Sir Roland so hard he fell on his arse. Ecke forgot the stroke and wanted to lunge at Dietrich, but he fell down in pieces,[59] so that of those giants four were now lying on that meadow.   v. 9051

There were still at least three of them, and just as many heroes there too. They struck against each other so hard that a blow resounded more than seven miles through hill and dale. A fog arose from the fight a half mile high and wide. Their pounding was so monstrous that wild fire could be seen bursting out through the fog. That came from their swords and also from their breath, which they were breathing so hotly. Here was hard against hardness. At this point Sir Dietleib came to again. He got up and, as I will shorten it for you, he avenged himself so well that evil Death finally seized the giants for himself, and their banner went down with them.   v. 9073

THE HEATHENS AGAINST THE HEROES

Then the emperor without a crown shouted, "Come up and against them, Sir Mägeron, with your retinue (for they are enough) and shove the heroes in a jug." Thereupon all the heathens advanced on horse and on foot and shot at the heroes' army thickly and often with their bows.

Therefore Wolfdietrich would have said, "I think a fly has stung me;" but one of the bolts hit him, and they did not know what he was saying.   v. 9085

Then those on horse came up. They had trained their horses to spring backwards and forwards and up and down so quickly that no one noticed it until he felt the tridents that they skillfully threw with their hands at the people and with which they pulled them back to themselves by their hides. By that they did great damage. However, as I will shorten it for you, Sir

Hildebrant held a shield in front of himself and ran against the heathens' animals so hard that sixty-one of the horses fell from his blows, and their masters along with them. Then the other three slew all the remainder right to the troop of foot soldiers. There were so many of them, I think there must have been two thousand against one. They caused great damage to the strength of the tired heroes, for water will break through stone if it runs over it continuously.   v. 9111

THE SWISS VERSUS THE HEATHENS AND HERETICS

However, the magnificent warriors from Switzerland thronged forward quickly and struck such gaps with their halberds that many heathens fell. Packenzan made such a stroke that twenty-six of them fell down like straw. The heathens' clothing was hard; therefore the leather began thudding so loud from their blows that it could be heard more than ten leagues. With his fork the Libinger stuck all the Russians, heathens, and Turks with one thrust, so that they all stumbled backwards. v. 9127

Then a great throng of heretics gathered at a distance and shot a second time so that many a sharp arrow stuck in the flesh of the Switzers, and that caused them pain and did them harm. Then the latter ran with their scythes against the heathens on the field and began mowing down the heathens' legs like hay and straw. With that it was all over, the others fled from there overseas with their banner. The Switzers are still honored for that.

Now see, it was evening; and also know that everyone on foot was wading in blood up to the knee. When the heroes knew that their side was the better and that their enemies were so beaten, they took their friends' blessing and withdrew from the battlefield, just as Laurin had done.   v. 9151

THE LAPPENHAUSERS VERSUS THE NISSINGERS

The mayor saw that too. It pained and grieved him that the Switzers with their power had driven off the heathens and had held the field. Therefore he said to his men, "Well now, up! For it is time for us to advance to the battle and let none of them live. That will be to their harm and our advantage."   v. 9161

Thereupon he arranged his troop into a wedge and advanced with the marksmen in front and with himself next on an ass with his spear and with all the spearmen after him (they were in a hurry to get at their enemies with shooting and thrusting, with striking and crushing), and with those on foot in the rear. Again the combat gained vigor and became so violent that more than seven hundred lay dead there from the great peril. There were enough Lappenhausers for that, and the Switzers died in great numbers. One heard swords resounding and helmets and chain-mail bursting. The field became wet with blood. If any-one could do better, he did so. The knights showed their might too in their new knighthood, until they all smothered in the heat. That occurred not without cause; for a wise man has often said, "An old beard has wisdom, a new hide has heat."   v. 9189

What should Strudel wait for then? To his troop he spoke thus, "Well now, you merry gentlemen, think of the insults the dissolute Lappenhausers have so often shown us with their evil will. Because of them we should be ready to avenge insult and injury too. Also hear what I am going to say. If you wish to win fame and profit, you should set your mind to fight bravely and strike on both sides and never lose courage as long as there is a breath in you. And surely, if you do that, we'll succeed and survive. Therewith we'll win fame and wealth and horses and cattle so that we and our dear children will be made happy by the battle for a long time in complete peace. And last of all realize that, if we don't do this, the reverse will happen to us."   v. 9215

Then they advanced hostilely and with great noise into the other host with striking, stabbing, and shooting. What was there to discourage the heroes who might so well avenge their insult with their own hand? If the Switzers had actually done harm to the Lappenhausers, then the Nissingers really com-pleted it in their anger. Sir Sneck had not forgotten the death of his dear father,[39] and therefore he caused the Lappenhausers sorrow, fear, and peril thus: he couched his spear and rushed hostilely against their army on a sturdy field mare so that twelve of them staggered backwards from one thrust. Seven remained on the spear, and the same hero lifted them up like chickens on a spit. No one was safe from him, he would have been enough for a giant. Who could escape from him whose heart was so hot to fight and who had the greatest strength? See, he made a lot of trips!   v. 9244

Likewise Eckhart had not forgotten how his dear son had been slain[39] by the enemy's revenge. Therefore he was in a hurry to avenge himself, and especially on the best. He attacked them all, from the first to the last. Thus the first was the king, the second was their duke, the third the count, etc. All of them fell before him then. When he found Emperor Rüefli, he gripped his sword in his hand and gave the captain such a blow that he fell to the earth; but a troop of those on foot came up and set him up again. They stabbed Eckhart's mare so that he had to part from it; but he got up, the well-born fellow. He had lost all his arms; and therefore he lifted up his right foot and kicked the emperor's stallion in its belly so hard it fell on its side and its master fell off.   v. 9269

Eckhart was not too slow, no matter how bad off he was. He pulled out Lekspiss's sword and struck him on his mangy head so hard he was seized by a long sleep that never left him again. One would have helped him up again as before, but he could not sit any more. They would have beaten Eckhart all over the place; but they did not have the fortune that breaks through might and power and wit. After that a large crowd of his combat soldiers[172] came up and helped him from his plight. The enemy also fought desperately, so that, with much pursuit, the mayor's body was carried from there toward the Lappenhausers' tents.   v. 9288

Then real suffering began in the world. Strudel had enough wisdom, luck, and power, as was fitting for him. With two others he advanced into the band of rugged enemies. He pressed toward their banner and grabbed its staff so that it fell to the ground. His arm caught the points of the nails so that he at once began bleeding; but he paid no attention to that because he was happy in his victory. The Lappenhausers fell down just like sheep and rams that have no shepherd or dog when the hungry wolves come into the defenseless flock. They would have given themselves captive, but one would not have let them live and they would have perished anyway.   v. 9310

Thereupon the Narrenheimers came with axes and fell upon the enemy. These had better luck than the others and struck many a man into three. See, now the tables turned! The wheel of fortune turned back again; and, if it had previously helped, it now harmed three times as much. Saichinkruog of Lappenhausen took heart as became him and came to his senses quickly. In his clothing he had a little banner, on which his village's emblem was painted. He stuck it on a spear and held it high aloft, and then a strong force followed the banner and advanced very rapidly to where their enemy's standard was. They pressed forward steadily and struck hard until Fülzan was hacked to pieces along with his flagstaff.   v. 9333

Now it was Sir Strudel's turn; and he spoke thus to Count
Burkhart, "Hey, you guy, you guy, you guy!! Now you can go
to Hell! You have caused so much death that we shouldn't stand
for it any longer."

But the worthy man answered him, "Know that I'm still stir-
ring and still warm in my heart, so how can I go to Hell?" Then
Strudel pulled a knife and stabbed Count Burkhart so that he
fell dead.

"Now go to Hell! That's your house and suits you well!" he
said to the dead man. As a result Strudel would have remained
there with his very wild company; but the Metzendorfers came
up so quickly, I do not know how.   v. 9353

How loud they cried, "Attack their gang! It's not really all
over as you think, you whoring rascals. You've got to leave
your hides here and pay on the battlefield for what your fathers
have done." Then they struck with their spears against the
Lappenhausen warriors, and the Nissingers returned against
the crowd of Narrenheimers so hard that, with their combined
power, they again crippled the enemy's auxiliaries and main
force so much that the Narrenheimer captain and the Lappen-
hausers' banner fell to the ground with one fell swoop. The
flag of Nissingen was raised quickly; and in their struggle the
losers had to call to the Torenhofers, who would have overlooked
them because such great darkness had occurred from the dust on
the field.   v. 9377

Now when the cry for help had been made, the Torenhofers
heard it well and ran forward full of courage, well rested and as
strong and fresh as pigs from the trough, and charged against
the Metzendorfers. They struck many of their men with their
staves so hard they fell down to their disadvantage. For them a
man was like an egg; and they crushed flesh and bone apart.
They advanced with high spirits and with lead balls firmly
fastened to their clothing[138] with iron chains. These they threw
against people's hearts and thereby caused much pain. They
slammed them against people's heads so hard they lost their
senses entirely.   v. 9396

If the previous battle had been lost, a new one was now born
so fierce and monstrous that (to be brief) Strudel's banner got
heavy and went up and down three times. Yet they held their
field and strength and struggled so far into the dark night that
both sides stopped and, as was appropriate, declared a truce
until early the next morning. I heard that one waded there up
to the belt in blood; but how many were slain I dare not report

to you. If anyone had fallen there, he lay; and if anyone could walk, he got up and went back to his tent or laid himself down on the field to sleep like a cow.   v. 9417

THE BETRAYAL

Dame Laichdenman thought to herself of the treatment she had suffered at the Lappenhaus council through Nickel's words. Therefore she wished to cause death and betook herself secretly out of her house and through the village gate and ran over to the enemy's army, who were sleeping soundly from their exhaustion. She waked them up and spoke thus, "I have always rejoiced in your fame and wealth. Therefore try the strategem of riding early tomorrow morning to Lappenhausen; meanwhile I'll set fires at four points in the village and give you one of the gates. I tell you that on my honor." They were all pleased with her words and thanked her most diligently. They also promised her much wealth; for that is the custom. Then she, Dame Laichdenman, proceeded until she came to Lappenhausen and fulfilled what she had promised. How that was brought about, I should not tell anyone; because evil can well instruct itself.   v. 9446

Meanwhile the Nissingers quickly came together to discuss the words that had been spoken. An old man began and said, "This matter requires some thought, for we are lying on the brink of death. Our enemies are much stronger than we, as I wish to tell you. Therefore we should cleverly prolong our dear lives and, to our advantage, divide into two even parts. The first would battle with the enemy and the second ride stealthily to the gate of Lappenhausen and halt a bit in front of it. And then, if we are let in, we should be very thorough with looting and stabbing. Thus we can avenge all our insults and injury. No more can I tell you."   v. 9468

Then old Sir Pütreich said, "Your advice doesn't suit us, and you are contradicting yourself like a fool. You say that there are too many enemy, yet you want us to send out half our force against them all? Alas, how would we come home?   v. 9476

"Instead, I'll suggest something else. We should load our wagons full of plunder and armor and send a company of our troops secretly into the forest. The other party we will soon send with the banner onto the plain where the conflict is to arise; and, when the enemy forces advance toward them, they will try to flee to the forest, the wagons after them. Then the enemy will be in such a hurry to pursue and plunder that they will disperse themselves across the field, one of them here, the other there. The wisest thing is that all our forces together attack their straying troops with shooting, striking, and stabbing, thrusting, crushing, and breaking. And, if we are able to capture them, we should hang the guilty and let none of them survive.   *v.* 9499

"And, if it turns out this way, let us ride with one impulse to the bridge at Lappenhausen; and, even if the murderess would not do as we want (just as no one should trust any murderous person), they would still have to lose courage and quickly surrender when they saw their main force and other troops defeated. And then if they wouldn't do it, we would think no more of them than a chicken and assault their wooden wall with fire. That will be too sour for them!   *v.* 9514

"But, if the woman opens up for us at the right time, then we should all be ready to enter and not to roam in the streets, for people could throw wood and stones down from the houses and kill us all. We should break into the first house and then out of it and into the next one and kill everything that is alive there, excepting only our friends. Afterwards let's take everything we can take and divide it by daylight; and we'll burn to the ground what's of no use to us."

That was all he told them. They were pleased with the advice; and all that Sir Pütreich had planned was soon accomplished. That made them all happy and rich, and they all set out on their way home.   *v.* 9539

THE SIEGE

When they came to the bridge they saw how Triefnas, who had fled from the battle, was sitting on a high haystack. Behold! Then a crowd rushed at the haystack. That did not remain unavenged on the first fellows; for they fell into the ditch that Bertschi had previously made with his strength around the fortress and had covered with grass so that he could harm them all the more. He had piled a lot of sharp thorns on top of each other so that if they came they would find them with their feet. That occurred, and many a bare trooper bumped against them. That caused them pain and made them angry. If they had sworn Bertschi's death, they wanted to complete it now; and they began sending hither and thither for ladders, mantelets, and ballista, and for a battering ram that they were to drive against the wall. In addition they wanted picks to undermine it here and there, and other things that are necessary for an assault.   v. 9568

See, they brought all that up! Then Strudel called to the host, "My lords, take note of what I say. In my day I heard that you defend a house by throwing and you knock it down by shooting. Therefore you should load your crossbows and not tire of shooting, and then he won't be able to stir. We should bring up the battering ram and knock his wall in two."

See, that did not help a bit! The tower was solid inside and not hollow like the others. Therefore he ordered them to bring up the ladders and throw them up and climb up them (and promised with his mouth to give the first man ten pounds) and to keep on shooting. Triefnas noticed that and climbed up out of the straw. He threw something at the first one's belly so that he fell down from the ladder and on his head so hard he remained and spent his last day there. Triefnas had anticipated that in advance and had filled his shirt-tail[115] with stones and also had a shield, which protected him well from the missiles.   v. 9599

Then the speediest of them, a certain man called Spötzinn-kübel, climbed up; but Bertschi threw something on his head so that the ladder fell and broke in pieces along with him. Now when the others saw that, no one dared approach him any further. Therefore they wanted to undermine him with picks and smoke him out of the house as many people are smoked out; but the earth was much too soft and crushed a crowd of people. See, that caused them effort and pain. Therefore they began shooting with their ballista; but the stones stuck in the grass and reinforced the wall all the better. How gladly they would have fired at him with their cannon;[138] but they had no powder,[5] and therefore their assault was of no avail.   v. 9620

Then they began to threaten the man with words; so he cursed them with farts that he aimed at them. They would have liked to get him out of his nest with kind words, but he would not trust them, for a proverb says, "Guard yourself from sweet messages from old enemies and from twice boiled fish." Therefore they agreed that they would take position around the house until hunger should drive him out. For this there were three hosts of them. Each constructed a bastion and camped there in great strength until the fourth night with great consumption and vigilance.

In truth, Bertschi was really hungry! But the hero was besieged; so what should the poor man eat? Behold! He still was not lazy, he shoved some hay into his mouth and bit into it and chewed it well. Strudel in his army saw that and shouted, "Away from here! He's a demon. We can't accomplish anything here; he's eating hay along with the straw." Therefore they all fled from there and hurried across the bridge. v. 9652

THE END

Bertschi took a different way across the heath and came to the place where the battle had begun and ended; and consequently he saw many a great heap of dead men lying there, as if the piles had thrived from the torrents of blood. Then he came to Lappenhausen and saw how all was ruined, house and yard, leaves and grass, man, woman, and children too, honor and wealth, and his dear wife dead. That caused him sorrow, fear, and distress; water rose to his eyes and a severe swoon seized him so that he lay fully half a day like a dead man.

Then he came to his senses and began a mournful cry, "Alas, miserable day, that I have lived to see you! Through you I shall ever suffer pain with lamentation in my heart and shall suffer much bitter sorrow through my own guilt alone, because I was so wisely instructed and inclined myself so little to it. How little I wished to believe it, but now I see it with my own eyes: who lives today will die tomorrow. How quickly a man can lose all he has ever won!"

At the same time he remembered how all things perish if they depend upon our works and how only fear of God and God's eternal love are never lost. Therefore he soon journeyed to the middle of the Black Forest; and there, with complete devotion, the wise man surely earned eternal life after this sorrow. And may we receive the same from Him who provided water out of the rock and also turned it into wine. v. 9699

Amen

EXPOSITION

We know nothing definite about the author of the *Ring* but what he tells us in his preface, namely that he called himself Henry Wittenwiler (*Haynreich wittenweylär*, v. 52). Attempts have been made to associate him with the Lords of Wittenwil, a noble family of Toggenburg in northeastern Switzerland. However, the evidence is not entirely convincing; and, as we shall see, his economic views were those of the middle class. Of the many documented Henry Wittenwilers who could have written the *Ring*, the most likely was an advocate at the episcopal court of Constance, for the legal and theological knowledge indicated in the *Ring* suggests that its author may have held some such position. Perhaps it is more than a coincidence that he praises the magistrate (*amman*, 7700) of Constance in his poem.   #1

It is also possible that Wittenwiler was a scribe. At least he seems to show a predilection for his scribe, who is clearly the cleverest man in the village; and he passionately champions the art of reading and writing (1969-80) and recommends it for young people who want to become merchants (5103). Perhaps it is significant that he has given his scribe the name Henritze, the Latinized form of his own Christian name. Likewise, Deupenpain, the other scribe in the poem, is also an important man in his village (6706).   #2

Most scholars assume that Wittenwiler was an old man at the time of writing the *Ring* because he constantly sides with age against youth. However, it should be remembered that an aged point of view in a literary work need not indicate great age in its author. Many critics first assumed that Thomas Mann's anonymous *Buddenbrooks* was written by a worldly wise and therefore aging author, whereas he was only twenty-four when he wrote it. The youthful works of Hugo von Hofmansthal also suggest a world-weary and therefore elderly author. Such contradictions were even more usual in the Middle Ages, when it was conventional for propounders of wisdom to write as old men; for it was an accepted fact that age has wisdom and youth has ardor, as Wittenwiler tells us in the *Ring* (9188). Also, since the knowledge in the *Ring* came largely from written sources, we need not assume that the author needed a long lifetime to collect it. Whereas it is probable that Wittenwiler was an old man, this need not have been the case.   #3

The setting of the *Ring* is revealed when news of the wedding reaches Glarus, Schwytz, Appenzell, and other regions (5300 ff),

which encircle a spot near Liechtenstaig, the diminutive capital
of Toggenburg. This fact is confirmed when Farindwand's
body is thrown into the Necker (5912), a little stream not far
from that city. Also, Colman swears by St. Gall (3112), the
Irish missionary who converted that part of Switzerland. The
author himself was probably from this region, since he wrote
in the High Alemannic dialect found in that area. The manu-
script shows a few Bavarian peculiarities, for example the
second person plural pronoun is *es* instead of the more usual
ir, and the verbal prefix *er* is written *der*. However, these do
not affect the rimes and appear to have been introduced by the
scribe.   #4

The exact age of the *Ring* cannot be ascertained. However,
the reference to gunpowder in v. 9619, and probably that to a
bullet in v. 8307, show that the work was written sometime
after the middle of the fourteenth century. Most scholars be-
lieve that the reference to Constantinople in v. 7625 proves
that the *Ring* was written before the fall of that city to the
Turks in 1453. However, this argument is dubious. Firstly,
the wording is vague, for the passage can mean either that Con-
stantinople in Greece is known even to children or else that
Constantinople is known even to children in Greece. Moreover,
even after the Turks captured the city, it was still in Greece,
which continued to be a geographic area even after it ceased
being a political entity. Moreover, neither interpretation of
the passage proves that the city had already fallen; because me-
dieval writers often followed their sources slavishly, even when
obviously obsolete. This seems to have been the case when
Wittenwiler placed Breslau in Poland (7680) instead of in Bo-
hemia, to which it had belonged since 1335.   #5

I think that a better *terminus ad quem* is to be found in Wit-
tenwiler's statement that one may not confess to a layman if a
priest is available (778). This naturally implies that one can
confess to a layman if no priest is available, a practice condoned
by the Medieval Church. However, Wittenwiler must have sub-
scribed to this dogma before the year 1418, when Pope Martin
V published his Bull "Inter Cunctas," for this decreed that the
follower of Wyclif and Huss was to answer "whether he be-
lieves that the Christian is bound as a necessary means of salva-
tion to confess to a priest only and not to a layman or to laymen
however good and devout." This implies that an affirmative
answer would be heresy. Surely this Bull would have come to

Wittenwiler's attention at once, especially if he was an advocate in Constance during the Huss trial.   #5a

Attempts have been made to date the *Ring* through supposed allusions to current political events such as the Zürich War; but these are unconvincing. For example, the Appenzell War some years later offers considerably more parallels. The reference to the Margrave of Ferrara in v. 3379 could refer to any of several such rulers known for their splendor. In any case, it is apparent that the *Ring* was written near or not long after the turn of the fifteenth century.   #6

Basing his judgment on the calligraphy of the manuscript, Edmund Wiessner believes it to have been written between 1390 and 1405. That would mean that the poem itself was written sometime before that period. If the *Ring* is actually that old, it should be considered an exceptionally original work in many respects; for it contains much material that appears in later German works but not in earlier ones. Besides that, it should be noted that the earliest extant manuscript of its chief source, "Metzi's Wedding," was written at least a half century after the *terminus ad quem* set by Wiessner. Also, of the many extant drawings depicting scenes similar to those in the *Ring*, nearly all were made at a much later date.   #7

Northeastern Switzerland of Wittenwiler's day offered a splendid cyclorama of the medieval social system in all its variations. Toggenburg, to which he probably belonged, was a feudal state under a petty ruler. A short distance to the northeast lay the domains of the wealthy abbot of St. Gall, who well represented the secular power of the Church. In the rugged hills nearby, the sturdy Appenzell peasants were maintaining their ancient rights and resisting the temporal encroachments of their spiritual leader in St. Gall. To the southwest the Abbot of Einsiedeln had lost his lands to the surly peasants of Schwytz, who, with the help of the other Forest Cantons, had beaten back the armies of the Dukes of Austria for over a century. To the west of Toggenburg stood the proud free-city of Zürich, whose prosperous patricians looked down their aristocratic noses at the crude mountaineers to their south yet did not disdain to join their peasant confederacy. Thus, within a day's march of Liechtenstaig one could see the whole gamut of medieval society: abbot, count, burgher, and peasant—all professing allegiance to an absentee emperor who was powerless to stop their constant squabbling.   #8

The chief source of the *Ring* was a short Swabian poem called

"Metzi's Wedding" (*von Metzen Hochzit*), which tells of the marriage of two young peasants named Metzi and Bärschi. The poem restricts itself to the marriage ceremony, the gift-giving, the banquet, and a dance that ends in a brawl. Out of this brief poem of 672 verses Wittenwiler has built a comic-didactic epic of 9,699 verses. He took over most of his source, some verses even verbatim, and expanded its motifs greatly; but far more important is his addition of many new motifs. Some of these are similar to the source in origin and purpose, but others are of a very different nature, being serious and didactic.　　#9

Whereas some of Wittenwiler's additions concerning the peasants may have been based on personal observation of real life, it appears that more were based on popular traditions, many of which were connected with Shrovetide practices. These Shrovetide or Mardi Gras practices were derived from ancient fertility rites celebrating the return of summer. After enduring the long winter months, the ancient Germanic peoples had welcomed the summer with unrestrained joy, which they expressed in song, dance, and pantomimic rituals.　　#10

This *inductio maii*, or welcoming of the May, was more than a mere frolic; for it served to confer fertility upon man, livestock, and crops. The pantomimes usually represented the struggle of summer against winter and the eventual defeat of the latter. In these rites masked actors performed specified choral dances, including sham-battles representing the victory of summer or May, the two terms being synonymous. The fertility principle was symbolized by fresh foliage; and the dancers crowned themselves with wreathes, danced around a May-tree or May-pole, and touched each other with *Lebensruten*, or leafy branches of birch or linden serving as fertility-producing wands.　　#11

The Christian missionaries combatted these heathen practices with more fervor than success, since popular traditions die hard. Eventually the Church adopted some of them and gave them Christian significance; yet it continued to combat the others for centuries. Gradually these customs lost all pagan significance and lingered merely through force of habit as a form of popular merriment. Even then the Church continued to attack them as wicked because they led people into sin and distracted them from the more important task of saving their souls.　　#12

The Germanic dance was usually a *Reigen* or out-door round-dance in which the dancers formed a circle, often around a May-pole or May-tree such as the linden. Although Wittenwiler fails to mention the linden, we may assume that he meant it to be there, since his source included it and his public would have taken its presence for granted. The circle of dancers could also break into a line of individuals or couples, which was led by a dance-leader or *Vorspringer* (6317) carrying a *Lebensrute*. Many fifteenth-century poems about popular dances, in Great Britain as well as on the Continent, make allusion to these *Lebensruten*; but in all cases the significance has been lost and the object is explained away, often as a rod for breaking up fights when they occur. The *Ring* appears to retain this pagan symbol in the *haber* which no one will carry in v. 1252 and which Schabenloch drops in v. 6221.   #13

One of the functions of these fertility rites was to pair off the young people; and this was often done as a kind of game, which is now called a *Mailehen*. Perhaps the best description of this custom in any European literature is found in the *Ring* in Henritze's song (6333-55), in which he presents the lassies to the lads. Whereas the peasants in Wittenwiler's day seem to have been unaware that their merriment was derived from fertility rites, we may assume that such dances did increase their fertility, especially if we believe what Wittenwiler and other moralists said about their erotic behavior during and after the dances.   #14

Originally all classes of society had taken part in these celebrations. However, after the German nobility began aping the culture of the French nobility in the twelfth century, they began to look down on these rites of spring as boorish, and they preferred to import French songs and dances to their courts in place of the vulgar ones of their own peasantry. The courtly dances were more stately; and for them the verb *treten* (tread) was used, whereas the verb *springen* (jump) was used of the more boisterous peasant dances. Therefore it is significant that Wittenwiler uses *springen* but not *treten* in describing his peasants' dances. Early songs about such dances indicate that people originally sprang high "in honor of the May," but Wittenwiler's peasants seem to do so wholly out of joy or perhaps as a form of sexual selection. Another ancient practice is alluded to in the *Ring*, even if only negatively, when Wittenwiler says the girls would have thrown stones and jumped for the boys (6252), for these female sports were long connected with spring festivities. Perhaps it is significant that Brunhilda could excel in these sports.   #15

As previously mentioned, the German courts of the twelfth

and thirteenth centuries disdained the native songs and dances, or at least the court minstrels did so. Walther von der Vogel-weide, the greatest of Germany's medieval singers, wrote a particularly bitter diatribe against the boorish melodies then being heard at some of the German courts. His attack may have been aimed at Neidhart of Reuental, a competitor of his who was then introducing village dance tunes into courtly circles.   #16

To his tunes Neidhart composed humorous words describing the peasants' dances, and for this purpose he used many popular motifs from the folksongs of the villagers. Like these folksongs, Neidhart's creations were divided into summer songs and winter songs, the former of which clearly show their debt to the ancient fertility rites as well as an influence upon Wittenwiler. Neidhart often appears in the songs himself as an impoverished and no longer young squire who competes with the arrogant and prosperous village dandies for the favor of their village belles. In most cases the dance ends in a brawl when two of the swains fight over one of the girls. In several of these poems the immediate cause of the conflict is an altercation ensuing when one of the men trips a girl and causes her to break the mirror which another man has given her; and this motif explains the situation in the *Ring* when Gumpost damns the person who causes Elsa to break her mirror (6240).   #17

As mentioned, the Church never ceased combatting the spring festivities, be they obvious pagan rites or merely boisterous but worldly merriment. Ridicule is a powerful weapon, and the clerics used it skilfully to discourage such worldly behavior. Anyone participating in such dances and pantomimes was automatically considered a fool; for only a fool would willingly jeopardize his immortal soul for the sake of such ephemeral pleasure. For this reason such practices became symbolic of folly. However, that did not put an end to them. Instead the participants accepted the accusation and donned fools' costumes. During the period of Shrovetide madness, the burghers of the German cities would run riot in such costume, playing pranks, performing pantomimes, acting plays, and indulging in mock-tournaments.   #18

At many points in the *Ring* one feels that Wittenwiler is not thinking of the peasants of the villages, but rather of the make-believe peasants in urban Shrovetide processions. This is indicated at the beginning of the dance scene when the minstrel Gunterfai decides to play a fools' march (6197). Later, in the

battle scene, we learn that the Narrenheimers think themselves
very noble because of their asses' ears (7971) ; and this suggests
that Wittenwiler was visualizing a fools' procession rather than
a real peasant expedition. Likewise, the names Lappenhausen,
Narrenheim, and Torenhofen, all of which mean "Fools' Town,"
suggest that Wittenwiler was thinking of fools' masks rather
than of flesh and blood peasants.   #19

Although Neidhart had usually let himself be bested by the
prosperous and husky village lads, he lingered in popular memory
as the knight who fought against the peasants. Eventually he
developed into a legendary figure known as Neidhart Fuchs
(Fox), who bore a fox-tail as his coat of arms and amused him-
self by playing various pranks on the peasants. It is in this
guise that Wittenwiler presents him in the *Ring* (157), where
he not only trounces the rustics unfairly in the tournament but
also dupes them in the mock-confession.   #20

The inevitable brawl in the summer songs was probably de-
rived, at least in part, from the sham-battles that played such
an important rôle in the spring fertility rites. Perhaps the
peasant participants in these sham-battles appeared to be fight-
ing in earnest. Naturally, under the influence of drunkenness
and sexual competition, such sham-battles probably did often
develop into bloody fracasses; yet their ritualistic origin can
not be completely denied. In like manner it is probable that the
mock-tournament, which was also performed mostly at Shrove-
tide, resulted from sham-battles representing the struggle be-
tween summer and winter. Later they became vehicles of social
satire, and the riders appeared in peasant costume in order to
ridicule the awkwardness and crudity of the lower orders. #21

Even though some of Wittenwiler's additions may have been
based upon personal observation of folk-customs, most were due
to literary sources. Some of these may have been oral, for
example those of the folksongs, the proverbs and proverbial
sayings, the humorous farces about Bertschi's courtship, and
the elements of popular epic parodied in the battle scene. How-
ever, as a true child of his age, he put more faith in the written
word than in personal observation or hearsay.   #22

No doubt some of his written sources were in German, for
example those furnishing the matter for the peasant-tourna-
ment, the mock-confession, the banquet, the dances, and the
brawl. His courtly love-songs were surely taken from, based
on, or influenced by vernacular works; and many passages in
the battle scene are parodies on popular epics which must have

been written in the vernacular, since scholars capable of read-
ing Latin generally scorned this vulgar and worldly type of
literature.   #23

Whereas Wittenwiler used many German sources, he depend-
ed even more upon Latin texts in the serious parts of his poem;
for in his day Latin was considered the only language of truth.
Of ancient writers he seems to have borrowed most heavily from
Theophrastus and Vegetius. The former's *Liber de Nuptiis*, as
quoted by St. Jerome, furnished most of the material for the
marriage debate (2623-3534); and the latter's *de Re Militari*
furnished much of the material for the military discussions in
the last third of the poem. Much of the love-lore in the first
part of the book derived originally from Ovid's *Ars Amatoria*,
possibly via the *Liber de Arte honeste amandi* by Andreas
Capellanus.   #24

The *Ring* also shows the influence of Juvenal, Horace, and
Seneca. However, quotations from these last three authorities
and other classic writers do not necessarily prove that Witten-
wiler read their works, since their maxims were common prop-
erty among medieval scholars and were often used in school
texts. For example, the twelfth-century *Moralium Dogma*,
which was the chief source of Lastersak's moral lecture (4410-
5015), contains quotations from Cicero, Seneca, Sallust, Boe-
thius, Isidor, Gregory, Horace, Terence, Lucanus, Virgil, Per-
sius, and Statius.   #25

Many of the classic quotations cited in the *Moralium Dogma*
also appeared in other medieval works used by Wittenwiler; and
therefore it is impossible to determine precisely where he found
them. Perhaps he cited many of them from memory, having
come across them constantly in his scholarly reading. As com-
pared to modern scholars, medieval scholars read few books but
read them often, with the result that they could quote from them
with great ease. This was particularly true of the Bible; and
it is probable that many of Wittenwiler's numerous quotations
from and allusions to the Scriptures were from memory. It will
be noted that he was most familiar with, or fond of, the Gospel
of St. Matthew. His quotations from and allusions to Scripture
are listed in Appendix II.   #26

Next to the *Moralium Dogma,* perhaps the two most im-
portant medieval sources for the *Ring* were the *de Cura Rei
Familiaris* of Pseudo-Bernard and the *Secreta Secretorum* of
Pseudo-Aristotle. The former, which was erroneously attributed
to St. Bernard of Clairvaux, supplied most of the information in

Colman's lecture on housekeeping (5016-5200). The latter seems to have supplied many of the thoughts found in Straub's hygiene lecture (4218-4409), which also shows many points in common with the *Regimen Sanitatis Salernitanum*, another popular medieval text.   #27

In general each of Wittenwiler's major sources furnishes the materials for one section of his work. For example, Ovid's *Ars Amatoria*, possibly via Andreas Capellanus, supplies most of the matter for Straub's instruction on that subject in part one of the poem. Pseudo-Bernard and the author of the *Moralium Dogma* supply much of the wisdom in part two, and Vegetius supplies most of the military science in part three. However, odd bits of advice from any of these may appear anywhere in the poem. For example, in part two, when Ochsenkropf describes the ideal husband, his physical qualifications (3661-72) happen to coincide in content and sequence with those given by Vegetius for a young soldier. Because Vegetius describes his soldier's shoulders but not his voice, Wittenwiler's word *gsanch* (3666) is rendered in this translation by "slope of the shoulders" instead of "song" or "voice."   #28

In general, Wittenwiler seems to have comprehended his Latin sources well and translated them rather closely, allowing of course for changes made to suit the rime and meter. However, in some cases he appears to have misquoted his sources deliberately. For example, although most of his rules on housekeeping follow Pseudo-Bernard closely, some do not. Where the source says you should not sell your heritage to a stronger man (*te potentiori*), Wittenwiler says you should guard yourself from an arbiter (*gmainen man*, 5151) who is richer and can do more and is not honorable. Likewise, the source says you should sell cheaply to friend and foe alike, since an enemy can be won over by a service as well as by a sword. Wittenwiler twists this to mean that you should sell cheaply to your friends but dearly to your enemies and thus profit and win an easy revenge (5145-48). Wittenwiler also says you should so write your will that your creditors will be paid before the priests (5170), whereas Pseudo-Bernard had said to remember your friends first. Wittenwiler attributes only one of Colman's precepts to St. Bernard, namely that you should not recommend the pilgrim's staff to your son (5100); but, interestingly enough, this was not in Pseudo-Bernard's work.   #29

Perhaps some of Wittenwiler's deviations from his Latin

sources were not of his own doing; for he may have followed already corrupted versions.   Before the art of printing began to help standardize classic texts, there were almost as many versions as manuscripts, nearly every scribe being guilty of some initiative or oversight.   In any case, it is evident that Wittenwiler preferred to follow Latin texts even when German translations were available.   For example, his hygiene lecture is closer to thé Latin *Secreta Secretorum* than to the Middle High German *Aristotilis Heimlichkeit,* and his lecture on morals is closer to the *Moralium Dogma* than to Wernher of Elmendorf's German translation of that work.   It does not appear that Wittenwiler used any sources written in French, even though his chief Latin sources were written by Frenchmen.   Also, all Greek sources seem to have reached him through Latin translations.   #30

Although pictures were more often inspired by literary works than vice versa, the reverse also took place on occasion. Many of Wittenwiler's descriptions coincide closely with scenes in the graphic arts and may have been influenced by pictures he had seen.   For example, his description of the peasant jousters has an exact counterpart in a somewhat later sketch owned by the University of Erlangen in Germany, which also shows the rustics mounted on nags and packsaddles, armed with rakes, and using baskets as helmets and shields (Fig. 1).   Likewise his riotous dancers agree with a long tradition of pictures on that subject by artists such as Nicolaus Meldemann, Daniel Hopfer, Daniel Kandel, and even Pieter Breughel (See Fig. 2). Peasant banquets were also a specialty of these and other satiric illustrators.   Wittenwiler's reference to the wheel of fortune (2554) or to the fool and ass hitched to the wine cart (3710-14) may have been suggested by drawings or woodcuts, these subjects having been popular in the art of his century.   The allegory about Venus and the Virgin Mary (2286-2396) could have been inspired by some painting, possibly a church mural.   Also, the four-eyed Virgin (2353) may have been suggested by some Janus-like sculpture, for such ingenious figures were not unknown in the Middle Ages.   Thomas Aquinas described such an allegorical figure of Prudence in which the face looking forward symbolized foresight and that looking backwards symbolized memory.   #31

Wittenwiler deserves credit for achieving an amazing degree of literary unity in the *Ring* in view of the fact that he has made his short source, that of the peasant wedding, assimilate more than fourteen times its bulk in extraneous and highly diversified matter.   However serious or tedious his source material, he never lets his readers forget that they are reading an amusing village tale; for the long excursions on religion, health, manners, etc. are presented by the peasants and for the peasants at appropriate points in the poem and are constantly interrupted by clever repartees and comical situations.   Thus one does not feel that the weighty discussions are foreign to the plot.   #32

The unity of the poem owes much to the author's personality, which has imposed itself so strongly on the poem that most passages in it can be immediately recognized as his own, even if seen out of context.   His style is direct and personal and contains many asides to the reader, these consisting chiefly of exclamations, asseverations, and rhetorical questions.   He also shows a condescending familiarity with his characters, whom he calls "my Triefnas," "my Leckspiss," "my little fool," etc.   He seems to speak not only to the reader of the book, as indicated by the use of the word "read," but also to the hearers, as indicated by the word "hear."   Before the invention of printing, books were often intended to be read aloud, since both books and literate people were rare.   #33

The *Ring* gains a certain unity through the repeated appearance of several stylistic devices peculiar to Wittenwiler. One of these is a device by which he avoids describing an action. Instead he lets his characters discuss their plan of action at some length; then he merely states, in a single couplet, that they succeeded in their project.   For example, Rüerenmost describes in detail what he and Henritze should say to Fritzo, yet the fulfillment of the plan is indicated in a terse couplet (3595).   Likewise, old Sir Pütreich devotes many verses to telling how the Nissingers should destroy Lappenhausen; then the successful execution of his strategem is revealed by a single couplet, which even uses the same rime-words as in the previous example (9535).   The same rime-pair is used in the same way to show how Metzi accomplishes her plan to wake Bertschi (7122) and how Laurin succeeds in killing the witches (8807).   In fact the repetition of certain favorite verses and rimes gives the poem a great deal of unity, which, of course, is largely lost in a prose translation.   #34

Wittenwiler has another peculiar device.   Instead of saying a person does something, he says he acts like one who does something. For example, if your wife deceives you, you must act like a man who should hide his shame (2780), you should resemble a man who can deceive you with words (4522), a good husband should act like one who likes good breeding and respectability (3700), a military leader should conduct himself like a man who can play chess (8286), and the Lappenhausers are behaving as one should who, without right or cause, wishes to cause disorder (7180). #35

Wittenwiler also shows a predilection for the number four. For example, the jousters must pay four pennies to redeem their asses (938), Bertschi promises to pay the minstrel fourfold (1377), he can work as much as any four (3831), Metzi knocks down four women (5267), Hächel Schürenprand says she would have taken four men if she had not been given a husband (3775), a daughter should learn as much as four others (5096), a married man needs enough clothes for four people (2858), four guests serve as waiters at the banquet (5536), they serve four eggs (5987), and so on throughout the poem. #36

Judging by medieval standards, the *Ring* is exceedingly well unified with regard to its characters. In spite of the bewildering number of people introduced, the author seldom loses track of them; and a careful reading will show that they are usually mentioned not at random, but only after careful consideration. For example, during the tournament, Neidhart can trounce only five jousters (1176), because two have died after falling from their horses, two have been sent to do penance, and two have been unhorsed in the after-tourney. When the guests bestow their wedding gifts, they do so according to a very elaborate sequence based upon kinship and age (5475); and in the marriage debate Bertschi's kinsmen speak in the same sequence in which they have been introduced (2630 ff). Wittenwiler is also very meticulous in handling his many characters in the confusing battle at the end of the poem, where he commits them individually or in groups always in logical sequence and always against the appropriate enemy. #37

In comparison with the total number of people he keeps in mind, he loses sight of only a very few, as, for example, when he puts Eisengrein on the wrong team in the tournament (1140) and lets Pentza Trinkavil appear at the banquet (5849) and Jäckel Grabinsgaden appear at the dance (6382), even though they both died during the tournament. Likewise, after the brawl he has Eckhart mourn that his son Arnold was killed by a dwarf (6731), whereas Arnold had not been killed by the dwarf Twerg but by Troll (6540), who seems to have been a full grown man. Wittenwiler not only succeeds in keeping his characters in mind, but he also succeeds in giving them consistent personality traits which they maintain throughout the poem. For example, Bertschi is always naive and Henritze is always clever. Because Eisengrein is always offensive (*laidig*, 6449) and raging (*wüetend*, 891), the epithet "snorting man" in v. 136 suggests anger rather than lack of wind. His name is that of the wolf in the Renard Fox cycle, and he is responsible for starting the brawl.   #38

Wittenwiler also enhances the unity of his poem by repeating elements found near the beginning or by making allusions to them later in the poem. Metzi's ugliness, which is so well described in the opening verses, is again mentioned at the marriage debate (3429-33); and her lameness is alluded to in verses 76, 1504, and 3429. Gunterfai blows his bagpipe apart at the tournament (182) and therefore has a new one for the serenade (1374). Kuontz refuses Leckspiss' suggestion that they tie themselves in their saddles during the tournament (336), and Bertschi remembers his warning only after it is too late (616). Krippenkra advises Metzi how to feign virginity in v. 2237, and she successfully does so in v. 7049. Because Bertschi inadvertently slaughters his donkey at the wedding (5373), he has to walk to battle at the end of the poem (8611). Sneck mourns his father's death in v. 6734 and avenges him in verses 9229 ff., and Eckhart mourns his son in verse 6716 and avenges him in verses 9245 ff.   #39

A hasty reading of the *Ring* fails to reveal the laborious care that Wittenwiler took in constructing his work. As a true medieval scholar, he likes to present his ideas in a logical and symmetrical pattern. For example, at the beginning of the poem he introduces his twelve jousters systematically, devoting two couplets to each, the first to describe his name and person and the second to describe his arms. Likewise he allots two couplets to each of the favors that Bertschi requests of his beloved (1892) and one couplet to each gift of the Virgin Mary (2489-96). The entire religious allegory in Metzi's letter consists of a carefully elaborated parallelism between Dame Venus (2286-2324) and the Virgin (2327-96). Naturally such elaborate construction is much less apparent in a prose translation, where the symmetry is entirely lost to both eye and ear. #40

Wittenwiler usually shows great skill in joining his materials to make them flow as an organic whole; and in general the transitions seem inconspicuous and well motivated and more necessary than arbitrary. This is a considerable feat, considering the diversity of his ingredients. However, there are a few exceptions; for even Homer nods. In one case he has failed badly, or, as is more likely, has not tried at all. In discussing the virtue Patience, he says it brings four sacks that will suit anyone who wishes to remain at court (4831 ff). The first of these holds clothes and money. These are obviously not virtues and are not connected with Patience: they are mentioned only so that Dame Richteinschand will have an excuse to bring up the subject of proper conduct at court and thereby give a cue to the next speaker. The other two sacks hold audacity and patience, which are likewise unacceptable as subdivisions of Patience. #41

There are several other apparent discrepancies. For example, we are told that the peasant jousters wear bee-baskets on their heads (165), as depicted in Fig. 1. On the other hand, Eisengrein says that he must hit Neidhart again on his bucket (467). Possibly the word "bucket" was slang for "head," but it is more likely that Wittenwiler was thinking at this point of the buckets often worn in urban Shrovetide tournaments. Unlike a basket, a bucket completely blinded its wearer and therefore made the tournament particularly amusing for the spectators. In like manner there is a discrepancy in the peasants' attitude toward eggs. At the banquet they fight strenuously for four eggs (6019 ff); yet at the dance soon thereafter they donate eggs liberally to the minstrel (6190 ff.). #41a

According to modern standards of composition, Wittenwiler was not very careful in his use of pronouns: quite often one must guess the proper antecedent of a pronoun from the overall context rather than from the syntax of the sentence. For example, the surgeon Krippenkra uses the pronoun "him" (*im*, 2233) to refer to Bertschi, although he has last mentioned the druggist Straub. Likewise, even though he has last spoken of Bertschi, Wittenwiler suddenly uses the pronoun "he" (*er*, 5260) to refer to Ochsenkroph, who was last mentioned some fifteen verses previously. Then, after mentioning Fritzo, he again uses "he" to refer to Ochsenkroph (5272). In the next verse Metzi says "you" to refer to Fritzo, although Ochsenkroph was the last person named. However, we should remember that this peasant marriage scene was so familiar to Wittenwiler's public that they had no difficulty in visualizing the situation. Wittenwiler occasionally changes number in his sentences. For example, if the "bridlers" see any jousters cheat, they should catch them (928) and beat him (933). Also, he makes a peculiar switch in pronouns when he has Bertschi tell himself that you must get up and climb on my sweetheart's house (1482). #42

Some apparent faults in Wittenwiler's style were acceptable in his day. Typical is his habit of letting one word serve as both the object of one verb and the subject of another. For example, he says, "That did not please Zink and (he understood) said" (6867). However, such "double duty" was normal in his day, even if not in ours; and therefore these passages have been translated with the addition of a pronoun subject. All in all, the *Ring* seems to have been a careful piece of workmanship, and most of the errors were due to the copyist. As we shall see, the scribe has omitted several verses. However, Wittenwiler himself seems to have forgotten to mention the gift given by the fourth donor at the wedding (5523-24); for its omission did not disturb the rime scheme, as did the scribe's omission of the verse that should have followed v. 527.   #43

In general, Wittenwiler was both capable and careful in his use of rimes. In keeping with his times, he allowed himself the luxury of assonances; but even these had to meet certain rigid requirements. The vowels had to be pure rimes; and the consonants had to be homo-organic, that is, tenues could rime only with tenues, mediae with mediae, and liquids and nasals with other liquids and nasals.   #44

Like other poets of his era he took certain liberties in forcing his verses to rime. Many of his rime-words remind one of Morgenstern's clever little weasel that sat on the *Kiesel* amid all the *Geriesel* just for the sake of the rime. For example, Wittenwiler says that one father can lead seven children better than seven children can lead one father through a lattice, and it is apparent that the word lattice (*gatter*, 3203) serves only to rime with the word father (*vatter*) as it does elsewhere in the poem (1991). It was no doubt for the sake of rime that Wittenwiler placed Lappenhausen in the valley of Grausen (55), which appears to have been fictitious. Wittenwiler's effort at riming is evident in the disproportionately large number of obscure words and idioms appearing in the rimes. For example, where his source merely said one should not build houses unless compelled to, he says one should not build houses *durch den tod*

(5045), which literally means "for the sake of death." Possibly this was some current idiom, but in any case it is clear that it was added primarily for the sake of the rime. Likewise it is difficult to visualize Eisengrein wearing his coat-of-arms on his *drüssel* (137), since this word appears elsewhere in the *Ring* only in the sense of throat or neck.   #45

Sometimes the rime-word does not detract but merely adds nothing to the thought. Although the whole action of the story takes place in Lappenhausen, Wittenwiler tells us that it was decided in Lappenhausen that the old woman should delouse Bertschi's breeches (5435). Likewise, when Lady Laichdenman is betraying her native town, Wittenwiler names her unnecessarily in v. 9441 just to gain a rime. Sometimes the rime-word gives flavor to the expression without actually contributing any rational meaning. For example, the peasants in the *Ring* often shout "out of the mouth" (*aus dem mund*), which adds nothing to the meaning but only to the feeling, as in our expression "You're lying between your teeth."   #46

Often the rime-word is an aside to the reader requesting him to believe the narrator. Typical examples are: Believe me! (*glaub es mir, daz schült es glauben!*); That's the truth! (*daz ist war*); Take my word for that! (*daz sei euch von mir gesait, so hab dir daz von mir gesait*); as it seems to me (*sam ich es vind, sam ich es spür, sam ich es mein, sam ich mich versich*); I must admit (*daz muoss ich jehen*); in my opinion (*nach den sinnen mein, nach der lere mein*); That's my advice (*daz ist mein rat, so ist mein ler, ist mein sag*). On the other hand he also says: I don't know how (*ich waiss nit wie*). He is likewise fond of assuring the reader of the authenticity of his information. For example: Truth says (*die warheit spricht*); The wise man says (*spricht der weis*); as is said (*sam man spricht*); according to true report (*nach rechter sag*), etc.   #47

Wittenwiler also fills rimes by adding adverbial expressions of time or place, even where these are not needed by or even suitable for the sentence. Typical are: at once (*ze stund*), at this time (*ze diser stund*), at the same time (*zuo der selben stunde, ze den selben stunden*). In most of these expressions the word *stund* can be replaced by its synonyms *frist*, *vart*, or *zeit*, depending upon the need of the rime. He also uses expressions such as "on this street" (*auf diser strass*) and "on this heath" (*auf diser heiden*) when he merely means to say "here." He is particularly fond of word pairs such as night and day

(*nacht und tag*), here and there (*hie und dört*), early and late
(*fruo und spat*), since these can be used in either sequence de-
pending upon the rime. Sometimes his rime-words are re-
dundant, as in the expression *oft und dik* or *oft und vil*, all of
which mean "often," or in the much used rime-pair *sterben* and
verderben, both of which mean to die. #48

Wittenwiler often achieves his rime by altering his normal
word order. For example, instead of saying "with a small kid,"
he says "with a kid. It was small" (5484); and instead of "He
carried a sick duck," he says "He carried a duck. It was sick"
(5492). Sometimes he achieves his rime by use of metonomy.
For example, instead of saying "death" he says "death's maw"
(*des todes schlund*, 4170); instead of "stomach" he says "the
stomach's gate" (*des magens tor*, 4321); and instead of "honor"
he says "appearance of honor" (*der eren schein*, 6800). When
all other devices fail, he can fall back on his last trump, the
rime-pair *so* and *do* or *aldo*, which mean approximately "thus"
and "then" and can be added to almost any rimeless couplet with-
out affecting its meaning. #49

Even allowing for these liberties, which are relatively few in
such a long poem, Wittenwiler must be considered far superior
to most of his contemporaries in his use of rime. Likewise he
is a master of meter, and his verses flow smoothly and in com-
plete accord with the rhythms of the spoken language. His skill
in versification can be observed by comparing his proverbs with
their more usual forms; and it will be seen that in many cases
he actually improves the originals. Even biblical passages flow
smoothly in his verse without much damage to their mean-
ing. #50

A comparison of the *Ring* with other literary works of its
vintage will reveal that many of its humorous motives ap-
peared in other works as well. If the *Ring* was actually written
at the beginning of the fifteenth century, then it is older than
most extant works containing similar humorous elements; and
one might therefore argue that its humor may have been original.
However, such conjecture is without purpose, since it was not
Wittenwiler's goal to be original. Like other humorists of his
day he gladly found his material ready-made in popular tradi-
tion, both oral and written. #51

Such humor was international, being carried from country to
country by journeymen, wandering scholars, merchants, and
pilgrims. It flowed freely through linguistic frontiers and

passed from vernacular to vernacular, being stored away occasionally in some Latin jest-book where it might remain for decades or centuries before being returned to the living stream of oral tradition. The story-teller was less concerned with telling something new than with telling something well. #52

Such traditional humor is generally frowned upon today by sophisticated people, who think that a joke or anecdote is of value only as long as it is new; for, although willing to see a painting or hear a song time after time, they feel that a joke loses through repetition. However, even today there are groups that prefer to hear their favorite jokes retold, provided they are retold "correctly."   #53

I can remember a typical scene from my childhood, which is probably still typical in that area today. The setting is a country store, where a dozen farmers are sitting on cracker barrels around an iron stove, discussing the weather and drinking from a communal bottle of corn-licker. Clearing his throat ceremoniously, one of the men announces, "Now I'll tell one. . . . There was a fella down to Montgomery County an' he had two mules, a white one an' a brown one. Well, one day this here fella gone to town an' . . ." Then follows a longwinded and detailed account telling how the man in question was cruelly deceived by a horse-dealer, or perhaps by his wife.   #54

When the story ends, there is a courteous but unenthusiastic applause, and then an awkward silence. Finally one of the audience can restrain himself no longer. He too clears his throat, spits the results onto the red-hot stove, and says, "Well, that ain't the way I heared it. Hit warn't two mules, hit was two hosses." Noting the look of agreement on the listeners' faces, he then proceeds to repeat the story almost verbatim, except for a few other "corrections" that are likewise irrelevant to the point of the story. Long before the story ends, the listeners are bursting with laughter; and its end is greeted with loud guffaws of approval.   #55

At this point a stranger joins the circle, and the successful narrator is unanimously requested to repeat the story for his benefit. He does so readily, using the same words and gestures, and evokes even more merriment than before, since the old-timers now feel an added sense of superiority in knowing the outcome, apparently unmindful of the fact that the stranger has probably known it too from his cradle.   #56

Wittenwiler uses such traditional humor often in the *Ring*, most conspicuously in his various farces such as the mock-confession, the serenade, the vigil on the roof, and the rendez-vous in the barn, all of which were common property in the Middle Ages. Because these motives were so well known, it was not necessary to make them understandable to an uninitiated public. For example, the mock-confession does not seem convincingly motivated. The peasants pursue Neidhart so fast that two of them fall from their mounts and are killed (657). Thereupon the others, seeing that these have died without confession, fear for their salvation and beg Neidhart to shrive them. We are not told why they think Neidhart a priest, and therefore their action seems poorly motivated. Wittenwiler's contemporaries, on the other hand, were so familiar with the story that they knew Neidhart had ridden out of sight, put on a cowl, and returned in the guise of a priest. This is suggested in v. 829 when Neidhart gets up from the confession like an unordained brother: in other words, without his disguise. The presence of a disguise would be assumed by any reader who had seen this plot presented as a Shrovetide play. #57

Wittenwiler, or his copyist, must have assumed that the farce about Bertschi's serenade was known to the reading public, since he does not go into lurid detail as Chaucer does in his *Canterbury Tales* when the Miller tells the same story. Judging by the abrupt transition between verses 1385 and 1386, it is probable that it was the copyist who omitted the offensive scene. However, in either case, the omission implies that the details were not necessary for the reader. #58

Wittenwiler could also assume that his readers were familiar with the episode about the mirror broken during the dance; for, as we have seen (#17), this motif appeared in the songs of Neidhart and his successors. Wittenwiler's readers naturally expected the brawl to begin at this point, but the poet teased them by saying it was not yet time for the brawl to begin (6245). Instead, it begins only after one of the swains, in good Continental style, scratches a girl's palm to show his erotic desire (6452). Wittenwiler's public was probably familiar with the perennial joke about the man who is cut in two but does not find out until he tries to move; for his presentation of it (9030 ff) is not immediately clear to the uninitiated. #59

The humor of several passages in the *Ring* depends upon the fact that certain coins were known to be worthless. When Bertschi (1347) and his colleagues (4216) pay the minstrel with *hellers,* they are showing their niggardliness; for by Wittenwiler's day these coins had become debased and symbolized worthlessness. The same was true of the *Perner* that Blasindäschen gives as a wedding present (5498); for Bernese pennies had likewise become devalued in northeastern Switzerland. #60

Much of Wittenwiler's humor consists of comical situations (*Situationskomik*) in which the amusement depends upon the discomfort suffered by the person concerned. For example, in the tournament the peasants are bruised and half drowned, Triefnas is dragged under his horse's feet, the jousters are unmercifully beaten by Neidhart, and one of the female spectators falls to her death. Bertschi is shamefully thwarted during his serenade, he is injured by the cow in the barn, and he falls into the fire when he tries to spy on his love from the roof. He skins his donkey instead of his cow, and he is deceived into thinking Metzi a maid. At the banquet one of the guests strangles to death on a fish bone; and in the brawl many of the villagers are maimed or killed.   #61

Thus we see that an important ingredient of this humor is malicious joy (*Schadenfreude*) felt at someone else's discomfort. This type of amusement still exists today, particularly among children and funny-paper readers of all ages. However, it is less popular now among educated adults than it was in the fifteenth century, when cruelty was still fashionable. Such literary sadism is understandable in a society capable of thrashing children and apprentices, maiming unruly peasants, torturing suspects, and burning non-conformists. Wittenwiler even accepted brutality and cruelty as virtues on occasion (4582). Also, we should remember that he wrote his work not only for the pleasure of good people, but also for the harm and heartfelt pain of the wicked (6).   #62

Such malicious joy is closely related to the pleasure derived from ridicule, which reminds the reader of his own superiority. Much of the humor in the *Ring* consists of ridicule at the expense of the peasants, a subject that will be discussed later at some length. Throughout the poem, fear of ridicule is one of the strongest incentives to good conduct and conformity.   #63

Wittenwiler also strives for comic effect through the use of exaggeration, a device much used in popular ballads and epics in his day. This device appears often in the tournament, for example when Leckspiss falls so hard he goes three spans into the ground (438) or when the jousters shout so loudly they can be heard for three leagues (655). In the brawl Dietrich pulls Fesafögili by the beard so hard that his chin falls onto the ground (6490), and Dietrich throws Twerg over Bertschi's roof so that he is never seen again (6596). By the time the regular battle begins, this hyperbole has long since surpassed our willingness to believe. When the heroes advance, the earth trembles under them, they uproot trees and throw them at the giants, and one of the giants replies by throwing a mountain at one of the heroes (9011-17). Their sword-play can be heard for seven miles (9057); they raise a cloud of dust half a mile high and wide (9059), the Torenhofers cannot see the plight of their allies because of the dust over the field (9376). Sneck impales seven of the enemy on his lance and lifts them like chickens on a spit (9236). In general the action of the battle is intensified progressively, as we see by the fact that the warriors first wade in blood up to their heels (8855), then to their knees (9145), and finally up to their belts (9410). However, this otherwise smooth progression is spoiled when, soon after the blood is knee deep, we are told that the field got wet with blood (9180).   #64

Wittenwiler is particularly fond of describing violent signs of emotion. When Bertschi is angry he curls his lip, emits flames from his eyes, foams at the mouth, trembles with rage, loses his color, and stutters (526-32); and when he is in love he eats clay from his sweetheart's house (1288) and gets a nosebleed (1327). As long as he is languishing for love, he nearly starves to death (2610); but, as soon as he knows his love is requited, he eats half a cow (2612), which is the same amount previously eaten by the jousters (1044). The penitent peasants strike themselves on their breasts until their mouths and noses bleed (683), and Leckspiss falls on his knees so hard he almost breaks his legs (699). Much of this exaggeration is in parodies of popular literary clichés.   #65

Wittenwiler does not seem to make much use of understatement. He often says "seldom" (*selten*) when he means "never," but Middle High German poets so consistently used this word in that sense that it was probably understood in that sense and did not suggest irony. However, when he says that a burial did not harm the priest (1233), he is sarcastically inferring that the priest profited unduly. Likewise, when he says that the surgeon was not harmed by the injuries of the jousters

(1241), he means that he, like the druggist (4208), profited from other people's misfortunes.   #66

In addition to his comical situations, social satire, and grotesque hyperbole, Wittenwiler also wrote verses that show he was a born wit, capable of entertaining an intellectually sophisticated public. Among his most successful devices are his unexpected twists, incongruous similes, plays on words, parody, sarcasm, and irony.   #67

One of Wittenwiler's favorite tricks is using a well-known cliché with an unexpected twist. For example, while the peasants in the tournament generally try to speak in an exalted and chivalrous style, Count Burkhart says that Neidhart's insult hurts them in their stomachs (383), whereas we expect him to say it hurts them in their hearts. Bertschi is described as a man "who never forgot himself" (192), whereas the chivalrous cliché would be "who never thought of himself," or "who never forgot his lady." When Bertschi vows to marry Metzi even if he should lose his pants (861), the reader naturally expects him to say his life, as in v. 2660. When Metzi sees the letter tied to the stone, she is surprised in her goiter (1948); and, when she weeps because of having lost her virginity, Bertschi tells her that she is mistaken, not in this matter, but in this bed (7032). When Uotz says it would be better to hear a song than to eat dead fish (5926), it takes the reader a moment to realize that it would be even worse to eat live ones.   #68

Wittenwiler also likes to add an unexpected and humorous twist to an otherwise serious sentence. In describing Leckspiss's contrition, he says he knelt down so sincerely on the field that he might have broken his legs (699). When Bertschi is discovered in the barn, we expect the alarmed neighbors to arm themselves at once, but instead they do so until midnight (1453). Until the reader learns to expect such twists, he often assumes that he has misunderstood such passages.   #69

Wittenwiler also likes incongruous similes. Leckspiss charges against his enemy like a plow (420); and Bertschi rushes back to Lappenhausen like a lead bird (864), which seems to suggest a slow object, unless it should refer to some sort of projectile. Wittenwiler also likes to use a proverb in both a literal and a figurative sense. When the Lappenhausers pursue the Nissingers to their home town, he uses a current figure of speech: "The bell was not yet cast," which meant that the matter was not yet settled. However, he gives this expression a second meaning by saying that the alarm was sounded not by a bell, as in Lappenhausen, but by the resounding strokes of their swords, since their bell was not yet cast (6663).   #70

Wittenwiler also shows a fondness for word-plays. For example, the peasants of Lappenhausen are *esler* (59), which is a play on the words *esel* (ass) and *edel* (noble). The same humor is seen in his word *eselman* (128), which is a play on *esel* and *edelman* (nobleman). The word *rittigmäss* in the same verse is a play on *rittermäss* (competent for knighthood) and *rittig* (feverish). The word *genesen* in v. 3107 can mean either to bear a child or to recover; and the word *versen* in v. 6292 is probably a play on the words *versen* (verses) and *versen* (heels), since Bertschi is running out of verses and is also tired of standing.   #71

Possibly the word *segen* in v. 8231 is a play on the word *segen* meaning scythe and *segen* meaning blessing; for the Switzers are Christians with the privilege of leading the attack against heathens (8206) but are also dairy farmers, as we see by the milk-pail on their banner (7962). The word is used in the first sense in v. 9134 when the Switzers attack the heathen, and it is used in the second sense in v. 9149 when they receive their friends' blessing. Sometimes it is difficult to tell whether or not Wittenwiler means to make a play on words. For example, his word for chess (*schaffzagel*, 8286) literally means "sheep's tail" and is a conscious or unconscious corruption of *schachzabel*. However, since the word appears in this form elsewhere in German literature, it may have been an accepted popular etymology. A similar situation occurs when Hächel Schürenprand says that Fritzo should give Metzi to Bertschi because it is bad to have a wench in the house; since the word for wench (*Mätz* 3770), happens to be the same as Metzi's name.   #72

Wittenwiler was a past-master at parody. Much of the high-flown language in the peasant tournament is parody of stilted commonplaces prevailing in courtly literature; and the peasants' coats-of-arms are parodies on those of the knights. Perhaps his cleverest parody is his description of Metzi (76ff), which is the exact opposite of that of the fair heroines of courtly literature, who usually had thick braids of silken gold, bright eyes, ruby lips, rosy cheeks, teeth like ivory, hands as white as snow, small high round breasts, a straight and slender figure, and narrow and dainty feet. The circumlocutions used by Metzi and the doctor during the seduction scene (2141-80) parody

current medical terminology. As we shall see, the conduct of
the peasants at the banquet is a parody on well known rules of
table-manners; and the song sung by Guggoch (5929) is a
parody on a popular epic beginning, "Knights were sitting in a
hall, listening to marvelous stories told."   #73

A modern public finds that clever parody tends to devalue
its model or at least make it look ridiculous; for example Rai-
mund's parody of Hebbel's drama *Herodes and Mariamne* made
it impossible to present the original on the stage again. In the
Middle Ages, on the other hand, this was not the case. Holy
things could be parodied without losing their sanctity: comical
masses could be held in church without blasphemy and obscene
songs could be written in imitation of prayers. This medieval
attitude is evident in the *Ring* in the love-letters composed by
and for Metzi and Bertschi, since the crudity of those written
by them does not detract from the seriousness of those written
for them. Likewise, the parodistic elements in the mock-con-
fession do not detract from the serious theological lore inter-
spersed in it; and the aubade sung after the wedding night
(7100) loses nothing of its beauty because of the lecherous scene
that precedes it. Also, Wittenwiler's teachings lose none of
their value through the fact that his Christian dogma is taught
by Lastersak (Shame-bag), his art of housekeeping is taught
by Saichinkruog (Piss-in-pot), the code of morals is taught
by Übelgsmak (Evil-smell), and the institution of marriage is
championed by Laichdenman (Deceive-the-husband).   #74

It appears that the brawl immediately following the wedding
dance was at first planned as a parody on certain popular epics,
the struggle between the little man Twerg (Dwarf) and the
large man Dietrich (6574 ff) clearly alluding to the dwarf Laurin
and the hero Dietrich of Bern, the chief protagonists in a popu-
lar poem called "Laurin and the little Rosegarden." Later, after
the fight has passed all bounds of credibility, these legendary
figures actually enter the poem in person. The setting of this
poem had been at Worms on the Rhine, a fact explaining why
Laurin is called a "mannikin from the Rhine" (8689) although
the dwarves had come from the Heuberg in Swabia (7912). The
legendary Dietrich of Bern derived from the historical Gothic
emperor Theodoric the Great, whose capital was at Verona. #75

A similar sense of humor led Wittenwiler (8025-28) to allude
to Gawain and Lancelot, two of the most beloved knights in
German versions of the Arthurian epics. He also mentions

Tristan, the famous lover, and Astolff, one of Charlemagne's paladins in German versions of the *chansons de geste*. Strangely enough, Charlemagne's greatest paladin, Roland, appears in the *Ring* as one of the giants called to the aid of Lappenhausen (7992). Just as King Arthur had twelve knights at his Table Round and Charlemagne had twelve paladins, the heroes of Germanic legends, such as Beowulf and Siegfried, also travelled "with twelve companions." However, the number twelve included the leader; and that explains why Bertschi can arrive "with twelve companions" (107), although there are only eleven others.   #76

Roland's colleagues (7988-94) are a motley group. Goliath comes from the Old Testament, but all the rest come from popular German epics. Egge or Ecke was a celebrated warrior, about whom Guggoch sings at the banquet. Sige is a shortened form of Sigenot, another doughty hero; and Reimprecht appears to be a corruption of Reinfrit, another warrior known to fame. Reimprecht is called "horny" (*hürnin*, 8915) because, like Siegfried in later epics, he was covered by an invulnerable hide of horn. The giant Siren is probably due to a misunderstanding of the fact that Reinfrit once encountered a siren. Wecke may have been another popular hero known to Wittenwiler's public, but it is also possible that he was created to rime with Ecke.   #77

Hildebrand is called a *maister* (8067) because he was Theoderic the Great's legendary weapon-master or armorer. Dietleib of Styria and Wolfdietrich, who appear with him, were heroes in the same cycle of epics. The heathen Mägeron (7985) is probably another form of the name Magog, the colleague of Gog. Wittenwiler may have introduced these fictitious characters purely in a sense of fun, or he may have been ridiculing the type of literature in which they appeared; for during his era it was conventional for scholars to mock such useless and worldly stories.   #78

In many cases Wittenwiler's parody is used sarcastically, usually to ridicule the peasants. For example, when Galgenschwank takes Schürenprand by her snow-white hand (6303), the literary cliché is amusing because it is attributed to a peasant woman, who would naturally have rough and discolored hands. In this case it is doubly sarcastic in that the name Schürenprand (Stir-the-ashes) suggests a Cinderella. As we shall see, most of the peasant-satire in the poem is sarcastic.   #79

Perhaps Wittenwiler's most humorous effect is achieved through his adept use of so-called "romantic irony," a stratagem whereby the author flaunts his literary sovereignty at the expense of his credulous reader. First he wins the reader's credence and tricks him into accepting a world of illusion, then he willfully destroys this illusion with one stroke of his pen. In this cold-water technique Wittenwiler is fully the equal of Tieck, Heine, and other masters.   #80

After reading some three thousand verses, the reader forgets how unrealistic it is for the persons in the story to speak in rime and meter. Therefore it comes as a shock when Henritze, in giving his verdict after the marriage debate, says he will have to give it in prose, since wise matter wants no rime (3520). Obviously it is not the scribe speaking to the villagers, but the author teasing his readers. Likewise, although Dame Laichdenman is speaking to her colleagues, she says she could say a lot more about poverty except that it would make the little book too heavy (3484). It also seems unusual that the peasant woman Fina calls Ofenstek a peasant as a word of opprobrium (2971). In fact the entire marriage debate is ironic in that the peasants would naturally have been unable to discuss such erudite matters. Wittenwiler again destroys his world of illusion during the final battle by saying that a certain Sir Bückel of Ellerpach (8031) would have taken part, except that he was not yet born. This was probably some local celebrity known to Wittenwiler's public.   #81

When Wittenwiler states that he is mixing humor in with his serious matter (37), he may be following the advice *Miscebis interdum seriis iocos,* which St. Martin of Braga gave in his *Formulae Vitae Honestae* (I, v.25). If so, he seems to have overlooked the Spanish bishop's further advice that these jokes should be "temperate and without detriment to dignity or modesty." Possibly the excessive amount of obscenity in the *Ring* explains why it was largely neglected by the scholars of the nineteenth century, an age less tolerant in matters sexual than the fifteenth century had been. On the other hand, several twentieth-century scholars have tried to justify this obscenity on the grounds that fifteenth-century man was innocently unaware that it was improper. However, this argument is untenable; for only social repression makes obscenity amusing. A truly innocent person sees no mirth in biological functions because he does not know that they are wrong. Surely Adam told Eve no off-color jokes before the fall.   #82

That Wittenwiler knew his language and descriptions improper is shown by the fact that even the peasants in the poem realize it. For example, Hüdel scratches her foot in an attempt to hide her social error of breaking wind (6141), and Colman objects to Metzi on the grounds that one would be ashamed to say her name (3434). Her name, Rüerenzumph (Touch-the-penis), has the same connotation as the name Nimindhand (Take-in-hand). Although Dame Laichdenman puts the blame for Metzi's vulgar name on the person who christened her (3466), it was really Wittenwiler who was to blame. Similar humor is seen in the *Canterbury Tales* when Chaucer puts himself "out of blame" for the obscene story told by his churlish Miller.   #83

Whereas all excretory functions are discussed openly, reproductive organs and functions are usually described by displacements and circumlocutions. For example, the male organ is called a "stump" (*stumph*, 2118), a "buddy" (*geselle*, 397), and a "stake" (*stekken*, 2159). The female equivalent is called a "pussy" (*mutz*, 1566), a "nut" (*nüssli*, 2139), or "hers" (*die iren*, 6410). The sex act is called "the thing" (*das dinge*, 5504, 6997), or "fooling' (*geteusch*, 4960). The latter term originally meant "deception," as is suggested by the word *teuscherin* in v. 1323; but this meaning must have been forgotten, since Wittenwiler uses the word to refer to marital relations. The verb for the sex act is displaced by the words "file" (*veilten*, 7095) and "thrash about" (*pollen*, 2180) and by the circumlocution "to help the wife feed the cow" (426). However, it should be remembered that such displacements were so common in Wittenwiler's day that they connoted about as much as the words they displaced. The vulgarity of the *Ring* is well represented by its only illustration, a crude sketch (Fig. 4) of Metz and Bertschi inserted after the preface. Although Metz is drawn in all her hideousness, Bertschi is nevertheless committing an obscene gesture such as is alluded to in v. 6423.   #85

Even though the *Ring* is so free in describing most sexual functions, the scribe appears to have censured a passage concerning menstruation, perhaps more through tabu than propriety. In any case, there seems to be no other way to explain the lack of transition between verses 3100 and 3101. There seem to be several phallic symbols in the *Ring*, for example the three nuts on a grape vine (130) and the three flies in a glass (134) in the jousters' escutcheons, which are reminiscent of the three spices or roots in v. 2142. A calf in a stork's nest, as found in the jousters' crests (162), usually symbolized something difficult to find; but, like the hedgehog on a stump (8042), it may have had an obscene meaning. Such symbolism may seem far fetched, but it is corroborated by many pornographic pictures of the era. Also, these passages must have had comical meanings, and no easier ones can be found. #86

The *Ring* is often called a realistic work; and its standard edition even appears in a series entitled *Realistik des Spätmittelalters*. Likewise, it is often cited in scholarly works describing peasant life in the Middle Ages. However, Wittenwiler says distinctly in his preface that he has included village life only in order to make the work more palatable, man being too inconstant to read serious matter alone. Thus it is clear that its descriptions of the peasants were to entertain the reader rather than to teach him about village life. Obviously, if Wittenwiler had been aiming at realism, he would not have let Metzi immediately show advanced symptoms of pregnancy (2187), nor would he have allowed only two days for the widespread cities of Europe to be notified and to assemble, reach an agreement, and even inform the Lappenhausers of their decision. #87

Wittenwiler's choice of conventional peasant names is further evidence that he is not trying to be realistic; for these names, which typify the various foibles and shortcomings proverbially attributed to the peasantry, would obviously never have been used by actual living peasants. On one occasion the author specifically states that we may judge the peasants in the poem by their names (5312). Because literal English translations of these names would not sound like names, they have been unchanged in this translation, except that their spelling has been standardized where necessary. However, many of them are explained here and there in this discussion, and all of them appear in the alphabetical list in Appendix III. In looking at this list we will see that they ridicule the peasants' weaknesses in about the following order of frequency: lechery, filth and bodily excretions, menial work, ugliness and physical defects, impetuosity, gluttony and intemperance, robbery and theft, low-class dietary habits, quarrelsomeness, dishonesty, and folly. #88

Wittenwiler may not have been aware that he was writing

peasant satire. Perhaps he merely wanted to entertain his bourgeois readers, and that happened to be the kind of humor that appealed to them best. Even before the development of cities, the nobility had formed a stereotyped concept of the peasant embodying all unknightly and uncourtly qualities. As the burghers rose economically and socially, they took over much of the nobility's prejudice against the peasant class, from which most of the burghers themselves had so recently risen. To protect themselves from the economic competition of later migrants from the land, the established townsmen closed their guilds to them and built up habits and tastes as social barriers against them, much as the nobility had previously done against the up-and-coming burghers. As an imaginary contrast of the ideal burgher, the peasant of urban fantasy gradually developed into a stereotyped caricature embodying all possible human faults; and this uncritical concept was handed down from generation to generation of city-dwellers and was continuously reinforced by jokes, stories, and Shrovetide plays repeating the familiar commonplaces. The resulting peasant of bourgeois literature was filthy, flea-ridden, ugly, lecherous, foolish, arrogant, and violent.   #89

Like most peasants in medieval peasant satire, those of Lappenhausen are inordinately dirty. They have never had hot baths (1400), they do not wash their hands before eating (5572), their table cloth is washed but once a year (5557), and their food is probably unclean, being prepared by a cook named Kochunsauber (Cook-filthily). Like true villagers, their lives and thoughts are limited by their manure piles, and three of them have names referring to cow-dung, namely Ochsenkäs (Ox-cheese), Fladenranft (Cow-pie), and Rindtaisch (Cow-dung). The Lappenhausers are generally careless about personal hygiene and go about with unwiped arses (6611); but Twerg seems to be an exception, since he uses his shirt for that purpose (958).   #90

The Lappenhausers indulge in every sort of bodily excretion, be it nasal, oral, urethral, or anal. Since the peasant stereotype in literature had a running nose, it is not surprising that Bertschi Triefnas (Drip-nose) is a hero like a pitcher (112). Knotz behaves as a typical peasant when he blows his nose through his fingers (5961); for, as the old adage goes, the poor man throws away what the rich man puts in his pocket. Peasant satire, particularly in art, often shows the peasant vomitting; and the *Ring* makes use of this tradition on occasions, as when Knotz is struck in the belly (239) and when Burkhart becomes nauseated because Hüdel breaks wind (6158). The latter action, typical of peasants in literature, occurs numerous times in the *Ring,* often maliciously.   #91

The peasants of Lappenhausen are not well housebroken. Kuontz wets his bed (907); and Gunterfai is probably doing so when awakened by Bertschi (1307), since it was believed that dreams about the sea indicated a full bladder. When the men leave the table to relieve themselves, Lady Laichdenman remains behind, having already done so in her seat (6174). Involuntary defecation was a typical symptom of fear, especially in peasant satire, which Wittenwiler uses to show how frightened the peasants are in the tournament (623) and how frightened Schilawink is by the Lappenhauser council (6948).   #92

Although fleas also appeared at court, as Goethe's well tailored one does in Mephisto's song, they nevertheless played a rôle in peasant satire. Lappenhausen does not seem to have lacked these vermin, as we see in the episode about Frau Hüdel (6134), which was popular in Wittenwiler's era and still lives today in various versions. Lice are alluded to in the mock-confession (284) and also in the story about the old crone who claims that Bertschi has proposed to her. This story is difficult to understand, the verdict being given in complicated and pseudo-legalistic syntax. Its gist (5436 ff) is that the woman has a right to Bertschi only if she can still see as well as a wife should. To prove this she must find the lice in his breeches and burn them to death without harming the buttons on the ends of his laces. However, she can not see well enough, with the result that all the lice survive and the buttons are burned so badly that, if they were alive, they would die.   #93

The peasant stereotype was not only filthy but also ugly. As we have seen, Metzi is a paragon of ugliness, having exactly the reverse qualities conventionally attributed to upper-class ladies; and the sketch inserted after the preface does nothing to flatter her (Fig. 4). The other villagers must not be much prettier, if we can judge by their names as Wittenwiler avows (5312). Whereas Metzi and Snatereina have dingy teeth (77, 5518), Fülizan (Foal-tooth) must have protruding ones and therefore be as unattractive as Dame Laichdenman *mit dem blöden reffzan* (with the decayed eye-tooth).   #94

Besides facial ugliness, the Lappenhausers had other physical handicaps. Metzi is lame (76) and Gnepferin probably limps, since her name is related to the verb *gnepfen*, which appears in the *Ring* in the sense of hop or leap (6285). Many of these villagers must be misshapen, if their names are to be believed. The name Twerg means dwarf, Künckelstil (Distaff) suggests a lean man, and Storchenpain (Stork-legs) suggests one with spindle-legs. Ofenstek (Oven-rake) suggests a thin man, although he is actually revealed as too fat (6211), and Schabenloch loses his breeches because he is too lean (6225). Eselpagg (Ass-jaw) probably has large jowls, and Ochsenkropf (Ox-goiter) and Schilawink (Cross-eyed) likewise have names suggesting physical infirmities. #95

Wittenwiler follows bourgeois tradition in attributing unrestrained sexuality to his peasants. Not only does he describe their lecherous behaviour, but he also gives many of them names suggesting it. The name of the heroine, Metzi, signified a country lass. Therefore, for the burghers, it signified a wench or slut, every country girl being assumed to be such. Thus the name had the same connotation as its English cognate Mawkin, which happens also to be a diminutive of the name Matilda or Machthilda. The name Laichdenman means "Deceive-the-husband." As we have seen, the names Rüerenzumph and Nimindhand both have obscene meanings, and the name Stumph is a displacement. The name Fallinstro (Fall-in-straw) is explained in the passage about the old bath-woman who will fall in the grass herself if one can find nothing better (2570). Even more obscene are the names Grabinsgaden, Nagenfleck, Schabenloch, and Fützenpart. #96

Farindkuo (Go-in-cow) is the only name that suggests an act against nature. This act could be alluded to in Heintzo's mock-confession (810), because Neidhart thereupon calls him a heretic and it was customary to accuse heretics of bestiality and other aberrations. However, such an accusation would not be in keeping with the mock-confession tradition, the humor of which usually lay in the discrepancy between the trivial offense and the grave punishment. #97

The name Föllibruoch (Drop-the-trousers) suggests that she causes men to do just that. The upper classes in the Middle Ages often accused the lower orders of gross immodesty; and consequently Wittenwiler lets his peasants expose themselves, for example when Gunterfai sets out without his breeches (1371), when Bertschi takes his off at the wedding (5445), and when Hüdel raises her skirt indecently at the dance (6409). Schabenloch, on the other hand, drops his breeches accidentally (6226). The great emphasis upon sex in the *Ring* is connected with its Shrovetide origins; for, as the Shrovetide plays so often demonstrate, the ancient fertility principle remained a dominant factor in these spring festivities. The burghers' scorn of the sexuality of the lower orders was probably mixed with envy of their freedom and fear of their sexual vigor, which caused them to reproduce at a greater speed than did the ruling classes.   #98

Closely related to the peasants' great sexual vigor was their unrestrained violence, a trait often ridiculed in peasant satire. As previously mentioned, the dances in Neidhart's poems usually ended in a brawl; and the "peasant-brawl" became a well defined genre in satiric literature, a good example of this genre being "Metzi's Wedding," the chief source of the *Ring*. Wittenwiler not only retains the motif of the brawl but also makes many allusions to the peasants' proverbial violence and querulousness. For example, the names Farindwand (Run-into-the-wall), Reuschindhell (Rush-into-Hell), and Snellagödelli (Hurrier) all suggest turbulent natures. Likewise, the name Wüetrich means madman, as the word does in v. 762. As we have seen, Eisengrein, whose name is that of the wolf in the Renard Fox cycle, is constantly referred to as being belligerent; and therefore it is not surprising that he and Schinddennak (Cutthroat) precipitate the fight at the dance. Schürenprant (Stir-the-fire) and Blasindäschen (Blow-in-the-ashes) have names suggesting either menial work or trouble-making. Burkhart's sobriquet *mit dem üeberpain* (with the bump) may indicate a hot temper, since the bump probably suggested a love of fighting. The word is used in verse 6947 to mean the bump the Nissinger messenger will suffer if he does not leave Lappenhausen at once.   #99

That the peasant wedding would end in a brawl was a foregone conclusion, that being the inevitable outcome of most peasant festivities in literature. Therefore Wittenwiler was able to tease his readers by postponing the fight until many verses after the mirror incident where it was expected. When it finally does come, he comments that the peasants' sport has turned into disorder according to their custom (6456). However, the peasants' short tempers have already been revealed on several occasions. The Lappenhausers' council had to be

brought to order with staves and rakes (3043), and the fight
would have begun at the banquet if the peasants had drunk a
bit more (5625). During the tournament Twerg and Troll lose
their tempers and draw their knives, for knife-pulling has al-
ways been a favorite motif in social satire, being traditionally
applied to the lower orders. Even today we make a social dis-
tinction between the expressions "He drew his sword," and
"He pulled a knife": the former suggests everything noble and
brave, whereas the latter suggests everything base and coward-
ly. Perhaps the real distinction is due to the social standing
of the people involved rather than to their motives. In Wit-
tenwiler's day it was not only permissible, but obligatory, for
noblemen to fight to defend their honor. Peasants were ex-
pected to refrain from this activity not because fighting was
wrong, but only because it was wrong for the lower orders, who
had no honor to defend.   #100

The upper classes enjoyed the peasants' brawls because of
their subconscious fear of the peasants' vigor and because of
their realization that, with proper arms and training, the peas-
ants would be able to overthrow the existing social order. The
peasant-tournament tradition amused the upper classes by as-
suring them of the peasants' innate incapability of performing
the intricate art of jousting; for the maintenance of the social
order depended largely upon the nobility's monopoly of heavily
armed cavalry. So that they would not challenge the hegemony
of the ruling classes, the peasants were required by law, tradi-
tion, and economic necessity to walk or else to ride work horses
unsuitable for war. It will be seen that the peasants in the
Ring ride mares (579), mares being unsuitable for war and
therefore "dishonorable." A gentleman would have died rather
than be seen on one. The peasants in the *Ring* also ride asses
(1203); but these beasts were actually rare in northern Europe.
In fact Hagen, the miller's ass, would probably have been the
only one in a town the size of Lappenhausen. Except for carry-
ing grain to the mill, the ass served primarily as an invidious
comparison for men in didactic literature. Wittenwiler's intro-
duction of so many asses in his tournament suggests his discon-
cern for realism and his dependence upon literary sources or
recollections of urban Shrovetide festivities.   #101

Just as the peasants were not to ride steeds, they were for-
bidden to carry arms. Consequently, the sword-bearing peas-
ant was a commonplace in social satire ever since the Neidhart

songs. Actually, bearing arms had been the right of all Germanic freemen, and the medieval nobility of Germany had to import laws and prejudices from the Romance world in order to disarm their own free peasantry. It was precisely in Switzerland, particularly in Schwytz and Appenzell, that the Germanic peasantry best maintained their ancient right to bear arms. The peasants of Canton Schwytz made such good use of this right that they became Europe's most noted mercenary troops. Later the name "Switzer" was used to include all mercenaries from the various cantons of the Helvetian Confederacy. Although Wittenwiler never states the fact, we may assume that he visualized his peasants as freemen; for nowhere in the *Ring* is there any mention of feudal dues or even of seigneurial permission for Bertschi and Metzi to marry. Therefore Strudel is not exaggerating when he says that the Nissingers have the right to wage war (6840), a right enjoyed by all freemen subject only to the Emperor.   #102

Even though the free peasants were entitled to bear arms, the burghers copied the knights in ridiculing and reproaching them for doing so, and Wittenwiler follows this tradition. When the guests arrive for the wedding feast, some of them bring *praite swingen* (5351). The word *swinge* literally meant a flail for beating flax or grain; but in peasant satire, especially when modified by the adjective *prait* (broad), it generally meant a sword as it does in v. 6546. Whereas some of Wittenwiler's peasants illegally brought their swords, others arrived with wooden staves (5354), the weapon conventionally allotted to their social order.   #103

According to medieval theory, only well-born men enjoyed the prerogative of fighting; yet Wittenwiler follows Vegetius in saying that blacksmiths and butchers make good fighting-men (7481). His contemporary, the English translator of the *de Re Militari*, restricts war to men of "noble birth" with "land and fee;" yet he too approves of butchers and blacksmiths. Thus we see that written authority prevailed among scholars, even when it conflicted with popular theory. Wittenwiler also follows Vegetius in stating that weavers and tailors are poor military material (7495); and he confirms this belief by letting the Nissingers, who are mostly butchers and blacksmiths and carry an anvil and a skinning knife as their emblem (8615), defeat the Lappenhausers, who are mostly weavers and tailors and therefore have a spool and tailor's shears on their banner (8582). #103a

In addition to being filthy, ugly, lecherous, and violent, the peasants of literature were also incorrigibly foolish, so much so that the word for peasant became a synonym of that for fool. The names of the villages Lappenhausen, Narrenheim, and Torenhofen all mean "Foolsville," and the personal names Töreleina, Jütz, Kuontz, and Hesseller all mean fool or simpleton. As we have seen, social satire rather than economic function caused so many asses to be in Lappenhausen. #104

Ridicule of peasant dietary habits was a favorite element in the humorous literature of the Middle Ages: the upper-class writers either ridiculed the rustic for eating simple food or reviled him for eating food that was too good for him. According to their own views, the upper classes had an innate right to venison, fish, white bread, and wine, whereas the peasant was divinely ordained to eat turnips, fat pork, and coarse bread of rye, oats, or barley and to drink water, cider, or milk. #105

The *Ring* follows this tradition. The minstrel Gunterfai is always full of turnips and barley (1057); and Fritz and his children are eating turnips when Bertschi falls through their roof (1490). The importance of turnips in peasant satire was enhanced by their carminative and laxative effects, which were so suitable for this kind of literature. The peasant Gumpost has his name from a popular peasant dish made of turnip greens or other kraut prepared with fat pork. This dish is served at the banquet (5711), even if not so named. The humor in this passage is due to the incongruity of serving the lowly kraut with fish, since the latter, as Töreleina has previously mentioned (2905), is a food for lords, in fact even for such lavish lords as the Margrave of Ferrara (3379). #106

Like fish, venison was also restricted to the nobility by custom and by law, a fact that explains why Elsa cannot distinguish between venison and donkey-meat (5686). Since it is customary for the upper classes to ridicule the poor man's love of fat meat, it is not surprising that the guests at the banquet struggle for the greaves, or small pieces of fat, in the kraut (5739). Similar satire is seen in the name Schlinddenspek (Gulp-the-pork) and in the scene in which Leckspiss's wife cuts a slice from the bacon (753). #107

The lowly minstrel Gunterfai was usually full of barley (1058), and barley bread is served at the banquet along with oat and rye bread (5565). Since these were peasant foods, the name Hafenschlek (Gulp-the-oats) well suited a peasant. The author of Wittenwiler's source, "Metzi's Wedding," was no doubt being facetious when he let his lowly peasants eat white bread.   #108

Since literature associated wine with fish, game, and white bread as appropriate for the upper classes, the peasants were expected to be satisfied with less fashionable beverages. Therefore Bertschi serves his guests apple and pear cider and sloeberry water (5994), and one of his guests is named Rüerenmost (Stir-the-cider). Bertschi also serves water (6102) and milk (5998), which were likewise symbols of peasant life and were disdained by noblemen and burghers alike. Although beer was preferable to all of these drinks, it too was less fashionable than wine and more appropriate for a minstrel like Gunterfai (1369).   #109

Although wine is discussed in Straub's hygiene lecture, which is directed at the bourgeois reader, it does not appear at the banquet. The word *win* in v. 5658 refers to the *most* mentioned in v. 5649, which was probably cider as in v. 5682. The minstrel, who had previously drunk beer, is drunk with wine at the dance (6191); yet he is no drunker than the wedding guests. Thus Wittenwiler is again inconsistent: he has followed one tradition in ridiculing the peasants for drinking non-intoxicating beverages and also another tradition in upbraiding them for their drunkenness.   #110

In peasant satire clothing served a function similar to that served by food: the upper classes either scorned the peasants for their simple garb or reviled them for wishing to ape their betters. Already in the thirteenth century the courtly singer Neidhart had made fun of the ostentatious clothing of his village rivals, who were trying to affect the dress of the nobility. By Wittenwiler's day clothing styles had been largely fixed by law and custom, and the burghers felt less resentment and more amusement at the peasants' awkward attempts at elegance. However, vestiges of the older sartorial satire still appear in the *Ring*, even if Wittenwiler may not have recognized their significance.   #111

His peasants come to the wedding wearing a good doublet, two red hose, and a hat (5350). Obviously this passage is not supposed to be taken at face value, since elsewhere in the poem the peasants always wear shirt and breeches, as befitted their social station. Being more conservative than the other classes, the peasants still wore shirts and breeches as their Germanic ancestors had done; and eventually this costume inspired that of the fools in Shrovetide processions and fools-literature. The doublet and hose worn by the nobility were derived from military apparel, namely from jackets of leather or tough cloth reinforced with metal plates and from leather or chain-mail leggings. Later these garments were modified so that they could be worn under armor in battle or without armor as a court costume. Even after they had ceased having military significance, they remained symbolic of the knightly class. Likewise, spurs were a symbol of knighthood and therefore unfitting for the peasant Bertschi, who affects them in the tournament (1065).   #112

The hat mentioned in the above passage from the *Ring* is also a vestige of earlier satire. In the poems of the Neidhart tradition, the peasants were often ridiculed for wearing fancy hats, of which Meier Helmbrecht's bonnet was perhaps the most extreme example. Often the hat was described as blue, a color theoretically forbidden to the peasants. The red hose worn by Wittenwiler's villagers was another item of clothing satire, since the peasants were expected to wear only black or grey.   #113

The hempen sleeve given to Metzi (5512) is comical because of the incongruity between object and material. In the Middle Ages sleeves were worn only by the upper classes and served as a form of conspicuous consumption, often hanging to the ground and being made of silk or satin. Those given to Metzi, on the other hand, were of hemp, which was a rustic and inexpensive stuff. This incongruity is emphasized when the donor assures Metzi that hemp is expensive this year (5514). The gloves given by Snatereina (5517) were humorous because only the upper classes were supposed to wear them, the peasants being expected to wear mittens.   #114

Bertschi violates a popular sumptuary law by wearing *geren* (gores, decorative fringes) on his shirt, since these were forbidden the peasantry. His *geren* are so large that he can carry salt (6131) or even stones large and plentiful enough to repel an assault (9596). Satire is also intended when Twerg trips Harnstain by stepping on the points of his shoes (6567), for moralists often ridiculed people who affected *Schnabelschuhe* or beak-shaped footwear.   #115

Although most of Wittenwiler's social satire was aimed at the peasants, he also ridiculed several other professions, some of whom would scarcely be encountered in a town the size of Lappenhausen. Several of these professions were classified as "dishonorable," which meant being denied human dignity and legal rights. No distinction was made between being morally and legally "dishonorable;" and no amount of good works could remove this stigma, which was visited even beyond the biblical third and fourth generation. This inherited handicap kept dishonorable people beyond the pale of good society and made them a race of pariahs, subject to all sorts of social and economic restrictions. #116

The first dishonorable person to appear in the *Ring* is the minstrel Gunterfai, whose name means counterfeit. The chief cause of the minstrel's low status was his lack of property and his consequent venality. Minstrels supported themselves by singing the praises of the highest bidder, a practice known as *guot umbe ere nemen*, which literally meant to take money for praise but could also be translated as "to sell one's honor for money," since such venality automatically caused a loss of respectability. Moreover, the minstrels were scorned because they usually avoided battle, as those in the *Ring* do during the final conflict (8677). #117

Minstrels were usually vagabonds; for, as soon as they had exhausted their repertoire in one locality, they had to move on to find another patron or public. This fact is alluded to in the term *die farnden leut* (travelling people), which Wittenwiler uses of the minstrels in the battle scene (8675). In the Middle Ages, when respectability largely depended upon the ownership of property, all vagrants were scorned, as indicated by Eisengrein's use of the word vagrant (*herverlauffner buob*, 456) as a word of abuse. Strangely enough, Gunterfai appears to have a house and wife, but perhaps these were included only in order to introduce the motif of the drunkard's dream. In any case, he seems to receive the contempt due to his group. #118

Gunterfai's low social position is cleverly revealed when he calls Bertschi a "mare's son," which is equivalent to our "son-of-a-bitch;" for Bertschi is less offended by the epithet than by the fact that the minstrel has spoken to him with the familiar term of address "Du" rather than the courteous form "Ihr" (1334). Throughout the poem Gunterfai shows his mercenary nature, playing only when paid and agreeing to leave his house without his pants rather than lose a paying customer. His status is equal to his musical instrument; for in Wittenwiler's day the bagpipe, being representative of the peasantry, symbolized folly, lechery, and other peasant-like qualities. Like many minstrels in satiric literature, Gunterfai is a drunkard. As we have seen, he is drunk when Bertschi wakes him, and he is full of wine at the dance. #119

The second of the dishonorable people in the *Ring* is the miller, who is acting in proverbial miller fashion when he offers to buy Eisengrein's donkey for half its value (486), knowing that the unfortunate man will sell if only to be rescued from his wild ride. The miller's dishonesty and unfair business tactics were a favorite theme in medieval literature, Chaucer's dishonest Miller being only one of numerous examples. This prejudice against the miller probably resulted from the fact that the peasants were obligated to grind their grain at their lord's mill, regardless of the service they received, and that they were unable to control the amount that the miller kept as his fee. Wittenwiler again alludes to the miller's dishonesty when he says that one's own chickens seem fatter than the miller's fattening hogs (3376) ; for it is was alleged that the millers fattened their hogs on the grain stolen from the peasants. #120

The third of the dishonorable people in the *Ring* is the bath woman who serves as Bertschi's go-between. In the year 1406 Emperor Wenceslaus granted a charter making bath-attendants an "honorable" profession, supposedly out of gratitude to a bath-maid named Susannah, who had rescued him from captivity. However, no matter whether Wittenwiler wrote before or after this charter, he expressed the prevailing prejudices against bath-attendants by letting his bath-woman be a procuress who could do business with sluts[200] or even service her customer herself if he could do no better elsewhere (2570). The peasant woman Wasserschepferin is probably a bath-attendant too, because her name means "Water-drawer" and she is later referred to as a *wöscherin* or Washerwoman (7096). Her lecherous behavior on the wedding night (7096) is in keeping with what many moralists said about the sexual behavior of such people. Her epithet "scabby" (*reudig,* 5329) probably alluded to the fact that public baths served to spread skin diseases, serving as they did both as baths and as brothels. Because of this latter function, they finally disappeared almost entirely as a result of the scourge of syphilis that swept over Europe at the close of the fifteenth century. #121

The fourth dishonorable person in the *Ring* is Krippenkra, the surgeon who seduces Metzi; for surgeons also served as barbers and bathers. It is no coincidence that Krippenkra knew the old bath-woman who carried Metzi's letter (2564). On the other hand, Straub, the druggist, is not dishonorable, since he represents the physicians, who were not so scorned. However, like other physicians in medieval satire, he is a mercenary character as Bertschi states (4214). Like the surgeon (1241), the physician was also accused of profiting from other people's misfortune (4209).   #122

According to ancient Germanic law, defeat in battle brought an automatic loss of honor; and all captives and their descendants were judged "dishonorable." Consequently serfs were dishonorable, whereas free peasant proprietors were not. Later, under the influence of Romanic civilization, the nobility began to scorn all tillers of the soil equally, regardless of their free or unfree status. This prejudice was inherited by the newly rising bourgeoisie, who lumped all rural commoners together as peasants and considered them "dishonorable" and unworthy of entrance into their guilds. This attitude is indicated in Wittenwiler's sarcastic statement that many "honorable" people attended the two family councils (2640, 3624). Likewise, the word *namhaft*, which is used of Ochsenkropf (3645), was a term applied to "respectable" people worthy of guild membership.   #123

The *Ring* appears to contain a considerable amount of folklore, such as peasant dances, songs, yodels, marriage customs, folk-medicine, superstition, and popular beliefs. However, in view of Wittenwiler's satiric intent, we cannot accept any of this information as a valid picture of the peasantry in his era or area, since much of it shows the influence of antiquated literary sources, conventional beliefs and prejudices, and wishful thinking. The burgher enjoyed the folkways of the peasants, both real and imaginary, because they proved his own cultural superiority. Before the Romantic Movement of the early nineteenth century, the antics of the lower orders served primarily as an object of ridicule rather than of aesthetic or sentimental interest. When Wittenwiler includes the songs of his peasants, he is doing so to entertain his bourgeois reader rather than to record them for posterity; and therefore we cannot put complete faith in his accuracy. Satiric intent is suggested when Henritze maintains that the song he is about to sing is "courtly" (*hübsch*, 6330), for this *Mailehen* was suitable for a village but not for a court.   #124

Similarly we cannot accept all the wedding customs in the *Ring* at their face value, particularly when they are expressly designated as peasant practices. It is probable that in Witten-wiler's day the peasants of Toggenburg still married without benefit of clergy, as all classes of society had done a few centuries earlier. However, Wittenwiler took his passage concerning the absence of the clergy (5276) directly from "Metzi's Wedding," which in turn may have come from some considerably older source. Therefore he may be attributing a custom to the peasantry that was actually obsolete and existed only in the memories and writings of the upper classes. #125

There are several other customs in the *Ring* that may be questioned. In ancient Germanic society it was customary for the groom to give his bride a morning-gift as a compensation for her lost virginity; and wine was served to the newly-weds soon after they were bedded. These customs were practiced by the upper classes and were often mentioned in the courtly epics of the thirteenth century. By Wittenwiler's day, however, the upper classes had dropped these customs entirely; and it is questionable whether or not they really lingered among the peasantry. It is possible that Wittenwiler introduced them into his poem as amusing parodies on courtly poetry (7058, 7136). The same may be true of the *Botenbrot*, or messenger's gift, demanded of Metzi (5222) and given by the Nissingers (7588), for it had once been customary to reward the bringers of good tidings. #126

Wittenwiler's purpose is clearly more satiric than folkloristic when he lets Guggoch sing about Dietrich of Bern (5923), interest in such popular epics being an accepted badge of folly. Latin scholars disdained such entertainment as suitable for the *rustici*, but we should remember that for them that term included not only the peasants but also everyone unable to read Latin. In scholarly Latin writings the name Dietrich of Bern was symbolic of all such worldly and stupid literature. #127

One apparent marriage custom in the *Ring* is unquestionably ridicule. When the villagers go to church with the young men in front of the old and the old women in front of the young (5400), they are going in exactly the wrong sequence. Thus Wittenwiler is not trying to tell us how peasants act, he is merely showing that the Lappenhausers do everything wrong, as their name implies. The custom of assaulting the groom and pulling out his hair and beard (5290) was probably authentic, since it still exists today; but again the author's purpose was to ridicule the peasants' backward and boorish ways. #128

In general the folk songs recorded in the *Ring* seem somewhat more authentic than the marriage customs, for they agree with other popular songs recorded elsewhere in German and Germanic areas. The most convincing customs mentioned by Wittenwiler are those containing no satiric intent. Some of these are survivals of pagan practices, such as the St. John's blessing drunk by Fritzo and Bertschi's representatives (3612) and the dubbing of knights in the battle scene (8637). Before the Church gave it a Christian significance, St. John's blessing was a Germanic ceremony in honor of some pagan deity; and likewise the dubbing of knights was a Germanic practice before the advent of Christianity. #129

The banquet scene in the *Ring* is cultural satire with pedagogic purpose. Wittenwiler based it on the considerably shorter account in *Metzi's Wedding*, which he greatly expanded by letting his peasants violate most of the accepted rules of good table behavior. During the fifteenth century the middle classes were trying to acquire courtly habits in order to distinguish themselves from the lower orders, and great effort was made to learn good manners, especially with regard to eating. For this purpose many books were written giving the rules of polite conduct at the table. #130

Wittenwiler explains the purpose of his banquet scene earlier in the *Ring* when Übelgsmack says that the way to become a courtier is to observe the peasants and do the contrary, as Bertschi will have the chance of doing at his wedding (4862-70). Thus he is following a favorite pedagogical device: in order to make his instructions amusing, convincing, and easy to remember, he gives grotesque examples of how it would appear if people did the opposite. This method was used more than a century later by Friedrich Dedekind in his *Grobianus*, which repeated many of the motifs found in the *Ring*. #131

Most of the social errors committed in the *Ring* are still disapproved of and are too obvious to require explanation. Others are clarified elsewhere in the poem. For example, pears, cheese, and nuts are served first (5633), and cherries, grapes, and figs are served last (6119), whereas Straub had previously said that the sequence should be the reverse (4304-13). On the other hand, some passages in the banquet scene help explain passages elsewhere in the *Ring*. During the marriage debate Töreleina mentions that one person often has to serve another and yawn down his throat (2920); and this thought is clarified in the banquet scene when we learn that servants should not yawn at the guests (5818). Likewise, the humor of Eisengrein's escutcheon, which is nine spoons in one platter (138), is explained when the vulgar peasants at the banquet thrust ten or more hands and spoons into the platter simultaneously (5735-36).   #132

Whereas most of these social shortcomings are self-explanatory, there are some that are no longer recognizable as such. However, these can be revealed by comparing the banquet scene with pertinent passages in popular books on table manners, as Wiessner has done so thoroughly in his commentary. From these parallels we see that Wittenwiler's peasants are violating accepted rules of conduct when they set pitchers on the table (5559), fail to slice the bread for the guests or give them knives (5563), fail to bend the knee and incline the head while serving at table (5585), peel apples from the stem or pears from the head (5641), lift their mugs with both hands (5655), slice bread toward their breasts (5687), share one egg between two people (6078), or stick their pieces of bread back into their egg or platter after having bitten from it. Verse 6185 probably means that the servants wash their own hands, since they should be washing those of the guests. It is safe to assume that every statement in the banquet scene had a purpose, either didactic or humorous, or else it would not have been included.   #133

Wittenwiler claims that he has written his poem in order to instruct (11 ff); and, surely enough, more than half its bulk is devoted to miscellaneous bits of information. However, it still seems hard to believe that he really wished to instruct his bourgeois readers in all this knowledge, for example in the intricate, worldly, and stupid art of courtly love at the beginning of the poem or in the art of war at its close. On the other hand it is easy to believe that he wrote the middle part of the book in earnest, for it instructs in the more important matters of pleasing man and God. As he tells us (24), he considers it to be the most important part of his poem.   #134

The love-lore in the first part of the *Ring* is typical of much literary tradition inherited by the fifteenth-century bourgeoisie from their courtly precursors, who had toyed with it as a social and class ideal but not as an actual norm of life. Medieval marriage was largely a matter of convenience, and romantic courtship remained a fiction. Nevertheless, Wittenwiler appears serious in teaching the art of courting, even if he does so by letting Bertschi court in just the wrong manner. Thus his pedagogical technique is the same as in the banquet scene, even if less obvious.   #135

Although Henritze, following the tradition of Andreas Capellanus and other authorities, warns Bertschi that one must court clandestinely to win a lady's favor (1715), the latter presses his suit openly and thus makes a fool of himself. His serenade deserves its ignominious dénouement, for moralists down to Sebastian Brant inveighed against this stupid and worldly pastime. Likewise, Bertschi's awkward attempt at dictating a letter violates another tenet of courtly love (1863), namely that the lover not be too frank about his carnal desires, it being an accepted fiction that a courtly lover served his lady as an inaccessible ideal.   #136

On the other hand, Henritze's letter (1878-1912), although overly florid for modern tastes, was dead serious and was intended as a model for Wittenwiler's public. This was also true of Henritze's love-song (1758-65), which appears to have been a madrigal and may have been based on two verses from Ovid. Metzi's letter, as written by Krippenkra (2261-2554), is actually a religious allegory following a long tradition popular since Martianus Capella and Boethius. Such allegories usually reveal somewhat more virtuosity than conviction on the part of their authors.   #137

The military science in the third part of Wittenwiler's poem is hardly more convincing than his love-lore. Like Wittenwiler, Vegetius himself had been a scholar rather than a warrior; yet he had succeeded in compiling his sources into an up-to-date and practical handbook. On the other hand, Wittenwiler follows medieval usage in faithfully following his source even when it is unintelligible, archaic, or of no practical value. For example, he tells how the cavalry should hurl their javelins (8406), although this mode of fighting had ended before the age of chivalry, as we see by the fact that Parzival was rebuked for having hurled his javelin at the Red Knight. It seems amazing that Wittenwiler describes all the war machines of antiquity yet does not mention cannons until the end of his poem, and then only negatively (9619). One weapon described by Wittenwiler is obscure, namely when the Torenhofers fight with lead balls firmly fastened with iron chains to their clothes (*chlaider*, 9391). Perhaps he is thinking of some weapon like a mace, the word *chlaider* being an undocumented word or a scribal error for a term meaning helve.   #138

It is hard to decide whether Wittenwiler meant to be serious or humorous in letting Pilian state that, in order to fight a battle, one must have 7100 troops on foot and 719 troops on horse (7412-16). Vegetius had also cited such specific numbers; but

he had been describing the strength of the various components
of a legion, not the number of troops necessary to win a battle,
which number would naturally depend upon the strength of the
enemy rather than upon apriori text-book numbers. Very pos-
sibly Wittenwiler was indulging in the same kind of humor as
Rabelais did later by having Gargantua cite vast but comically
precise numbers. This is indicated by the unusual numbers of
combattants in the final struggle.   #139

The second or chief part of the poem opens with a council of
Bertschi's family. Supposedly they have gathered to decide
whether or not Bertschi should marry Metz, yet actually they
devote most of their time deciding whether or not a man should
marry. Such marriage disputations, which were popular in
medieval literature, concerned scholars and priests, not the peas-
antry or even the bourgeoisie, who generally took marriage for
granted.   #140

The lectures given at Metzi's family council contain the real
meat of Wittenwiler's ragout, and in them he tries to crowd all
the knowledge necessary for a Christian layman. The *Ring* ex-
plains the Trinity, the Ten Commandments, the works of mercy,
the sacraments, the seven capital sins, the commandment of
love, and the importance of fasting and going to mass; and it
also cites in prose the General Confession, the Lord's Prayer,
the Ave Maria, and the Apostles' Creed. It also teaches the
futility of life in this world.   #141

Nevertheless the *Ring* seems most convincing when it teaches
how one should get along in this world, that is, how to stay
healthy, popular, and financially solvent. Saichinkruog's lecture
on housekeeping (5017 ff) sounds strangely modern and middle
class, with all the earmarks of what Max Weber has called the
"Protestant Ethic." It was based closely on the anonymous let-
ter *de Cura et Modo Rei Familiaris*, which, even if no longer at-
tributed to St. Bernard, is still believed to have been written no
later than the thirteenth century.   #142

This letter was purportedly written to a knight, yet its senti-
ments are most unaristocratic. Saichinkruog follows it in warn-
ing against excessive expenditures for hospitality, minstrels,
buildings, and clothes, whereas courtly poets had never tired of
praising unlimited expenditures, especially for minstrels. Sai-
chinkruog also says that one should acquire more every day than
he spends, he should let his wife do the housework and suckle
the baby, and he should work along with his servants. He should
sell his corn and wine cheaper than other people, and he should

let his sons be artisans and merchants. Obviously these sugges-
tions would have offended the sensibilities of an aristocratic
public, for whom all productive labor was repugnant and un-
worthy.   #143

Whereas scholars like Wittenwiler performed a valuable serv-
ice in perpetuating and disseminating ancient knowledge, they
also did a dis-service in perpetuating and disseminating much
misinformation along with it. This is evident in Wittenwiler's
attitude toward medical science. If we may judge by the red
line drawn through his verses, it would seem that Wittenwiler
really believed that a concoction of lily leaves, tree gall, and sloe-
berry would cause an abortion (2216), as was stated in certain
Latin writings. On the other hand he was skeptical of the
"bogus drugs" that Straub gives Bertschi to increase his sexual
potency on his wedding night (5499) ; but no doubt he questions
them not because they are unproved but because they are not
vouched for in ancient texts.   #144

Many statements made in Straub's health lecture were equally
unfounded; yet Wittenwiler accepted them because they were
attributed to Hippocrates, Galen, and other ancient medical
authorities. Scholars like Wittenwiler considered it subversive
to question authority and unethical to experiment in medical
matters. Therefore they thought that those who did so were
quacks and no better than barbers and surgeons. It is ironic
that our modern medical science owes most of its knowledge to
the empirical method.   #145

Throughout the *Ring* there are other bits of misinformation
without which the world might have been better off. Like
Chaucer before him, Wittenwiler seems to have been serious in
his astrological information (7442-7519) and could assume that
his public knew that Tuesday is the days of Mars (7484), as
the Latin and French words *dies Martis* and *Mardi* show. It is
possible, however, that Wittenwiler did not really believe in
"judicial astrology" but merely used astrological symbols for
literary purposes. Nevertheless, Dame Laichdenman's predic-
tions (7469 ff.), which are based upon astrology, all come true
(9661) ; and this would suggest that he had faith in the horo-
scope. Even if he did not personally believe in the horoscope,
his discussion of astrology surely contributed toward furthering
this pseudo-science, which was to reach such unfortunate pro-
portions during the Renaissance. It is not by chance that the
Nissingers and Lappenhausers are the children of Mars and

Venus, the god and goddess of the irascible and the concupiscent passions.   #146

Wittenwiler also helps to perpetuate uncritical prejudices against the Jews. The Jews are cowards and weaklings (7895), and they are a race of money-lenders and pawnbrokers who would be grieved to see the peasants' extravagant trappings (176). You are still a Jew if you have not been properly baptized and have no religious fervor (306), you will be lost like a Jew's soul if you do not confess sincerely (4097), and you should not follow the wicked Jewish multitude by rendering verdicts without mercy (4605).   #146a

Wittenwiler seems to have believed in witches, in fact he could hardly have done otherwise as long as the Bible attested their existence by saying, "Thou shalt not suffer a witch to live" (Exodus 22:18). However, he does not associate them with heresy and devil-cult, as people in the succeeding centuries did with such tragic results. Nevertheless he did believe in magic for evil purposes, as we can see in his reference to spell-casters who damage people's cattle (2923). His witches seem drawn from popular superstition, probably from former Germanic deities such as the Valkyries, who had been sent to Hell by the Christian missionaries. In any case, like the dwarves they dwelled on the Heuberg in Swabia (7889). The "Wild Man" (8719), who fights against both witches and dwarves, was also a figure from popular superstition, probably originally an elemental spirit.   #147

Some of the misinformation in the *Ring* is harmless yet shows the uncritical attitude typical of the Middle Ages. For example, it follows both popular and learned belief in saying that falcons kill their victim by crushing it with their breasts (8793), whereas they actually strike it with their fists. Wittenwiler is indulging in a typically medieval mental activity when he debates whether it is better for a child to be in Hell (Limbus Infantum) or to remain unborn. This useless scholastic argument is finally decided, after a venomous debate, through a reference to Judas, whom medieval legend had turned into a second Aedipus, who killed his father and married his mother (3305).   #148

Perhaps the most controversial question about the *Ring* concerns the author's real intent. Although he states in his preface that his purpose is didactic, many scholars have doubted his seriousness in view of his delight in horse-play, slap-stick, and pornography. To them it appears that he wrote for entertainment and claimed his pedagogical purpose only as a disguise.

One scholar has even maintained that the poem was written by two authors, of whom one wrote the serious parts and the other the humorous. However, this argument is untenable in view of the structural and stylistic unity of the poem.   #149

As hard as it is for a modern reader to believe, especially after a single reading, the *Ring* is an entirely serious work. It begins with a pious dedication to the Trinity, the Virgin, and the Heavenly Hosts (1-4) and it ends with an equally pious invocation to God the Father and Son (9697-99). Both of them are compiled of popular formulas found in many other serious works of the time. Moreover, even the humorous parts of the poem often have serious moral lessons in them. As the poet states in his preface, he intended to distinguish between his serious and jocular verses by indicating them with a red or green line respectively (39). Unfortunately the scribe of our manuscript must have failed often in this task, since many of the passages marked red could not possibly have been meant to be serious: for example, the ludicrous description of Metzi (76-96), and many episodes in the tournament (325-340, 401-404, 515-519, etc.). Likewise, some passages now marked green appear to be quite serious. In view of their inconsistency and because of technical difficulties, these colors are not indicated in this translation. Anyone interested in them can find them listed on pp. 344-45 of Wiessner's edition.   #150

Wittenwiler tells us that man is too inconstant to hear serious matter without any jest, and that that is why he has mixed humor with his teaching (32 ff). However, he has not really mixed his serious and humorous elements but rather juxtaposed them. That is to say, he has not blended them like red and white wine but mixed them like red and white bricks; and the resulting juxtaposition is disturbing to a modern reader. Nevertheless, we should remember that medieval man was less disturbed by such contrast and contradiction.   #151

The *Ring* is contradictory in many ways. Just as it is difficult to determine whether the author was serious or frivolous, it is also hard to determine whether he was religious or sceptical, pious or blasphemous, idealistic or practical, peace-loving or warlike, for or against marriage, friendly or hostile toward the peasantry, or optimistic or pessimistic. Modern man tries to be consistent and wishes to be either or, whereas medieval man was satisfied with being both and. Of course there are still many people who endorse contradictions, as is shown by the success of certain politicians who run on the platform of Democracy, Christianity, and White Supremacy; but these are usually disapproved of in intellectual circles. Naturally there were voices in the Middle Ages that cried out against the inconsistencies of the time; yet learned men like Wittenwiler could still preach and teach contradictions that we would find intellectually tabu today. #152

To understand Wittenwiler's striking discrepancies, we should remember that he was a product of a tradition-directed society, a type of society that tends to accept all tradition as sacrosanct, even if contradictory. As such, his duty was to perpetuate and disseminate the knowledge of the age, not to question it. His was the receptive mind of Famulus Wagner, not the questioning mind of Doctor Faust. #153

Wittenwiler's Alemannic ancestors had had an aristocratic value-system suitable for a warlike and conquering race. Eventually they received, and nominally accepted, an almost completely opposite set of values from the Christian missionaries. For the next thousand years they tried to reconcile these contradictory values, but without success. Instead of blending them or choosing between them, they retained them largely intact with all the piety due to what has been handed down from time immemorial. #154

During this millenium the native pagan values enjoyed certain advantages over the foreign Christian ones. Firstly, being the values of the ruling element, they were admired and emulated by all classes; and naturally the ruling element had to preserve them in order to maintain their own hegemony. Christianity had entered the Roman world stealthily through the servants' entrance, taking root first among the lowly and dispossessed. In Northern Europe, on the other hand, the process was largely reversed: Christianity entered via the king's court, and conversions were usually by royal decree. #155

This was the natural result of the Germanic social system; for, when a Germanic chieftain swore allegiance to a new liegelord, his new allegiance was automatically binding for all of his retainers and their retinues. Consequently, when he swore allegiance to the God of the Christians, his retainers were ipso facto Christians, regardless of whether or not they had been personally convinced. Many tribes were converted by force, others were merely persuaded that the God of the victors must be a useful god. Therefore the tribesmen could accept Him without any profound inner conversion. #156

Another advantage enjoyed by the pagan values was that they

were more practical in a lawless age of private warfare, in which a tribe or individual that had really accepted Christ's message would have been easily defeated and destroyed by one that clung to the warlike code of the ancient Germanic peoples. Moreover, the Christian religion had already been largely diluted and altered before reaching Northern Europe, having absorbed much Greek philosophy and pagan usage that distracted from its ethical teachings. During the period of the conversions, much energy was wasted in dogmatic controversy and political struggles between the Unitarians and the Trinitarians. The East Germanic tribes that overran Southern Europe embraced the former, or Arian, faith and therefore had difficulty in endearing themselves to their Roman Catholic subjects.   #157

Moreover, the New Testament, which contains the core of the Christian religion, was disseminated along with the Old, which contained many passages contradicting Christ's message and justifying certain acts and attitudes of the pagan Teutons. As we shall see, Wittenwiler himself cites the Old Testament on several occasions to justify attitudes at variance with the teachings of Jesus.   #158

Ancient Germanic society was based on a moral code of merit and reward, merit consisting chiefly of military service to a leader who rewarded with support and protection in time of peace and with a share of the spoils in time of war. Perhaps the major incentive to combat was not wealth (*guot*) in the form of booty and ransom so much as fame (*êre*); for fame brought not only social prestige but also a chance of further success. In a lawless society a man's personal security depended largely upon his reputation; for without a good reputation he would find neither leader nor followers.   #159

The relationship between leader and follower was designated as *treuwa*, which at first meant a pact or truce but later acquired the ethical value of loyalty. If a follower failed to fight for his leader or if a leader failed to protect or reward his follower, then he was guilty of breaking his *treuwa* and thereby lost his good name. When the Christian missionaries reached Northern Europe, they tried to adapt the native moral code to their own needs. The new God was explained as a King of kings, a super liege-lord to whom all Christians owed their *treuwa*. He in turn rewarded them with his favor (*huld*) in the form of victories and spoil. The missionaries explained that God's rewards are also given in the next world; but in general they seem to have found it necessary to assure their converts that God also rewarded his loyal vassals with tangible rewards in this world. The *treuwa* between man and God long remained a strictly *do ut des* relationship. #160

It is amazing how many of these ancient attitudes survived to Wittenwiler's day and are recorded in the *Ring*, often in the same terms used by the pagan Germanic peoples. For example, he says that *treuw* is a key to *er* and that if anyone loses the latter he will be worth nothing (4714). He also uses the old feudal term *huld* to designate the favor God grants in return for our services (786). God, like Wotan before him, is a king of battles and ordains who will have the luck to rob and ransom his enemy (8414). He is very rich (*überreich*, 836; *reich*, 1330 *et passim*), and service is rendered to Him in return for His favor. You should love God because it will profit you (4027), and you should please Him so He will help you withstand your enemies (8123). You should do good works so you will live and die happy (4493), and you should share your wealth with the poor so that it will follow you to your grave (5066). You should hear mass daily because it is useful (4049); and, if you have virtue, your purse will be filled (4435). Apparently Wittenwiler would have found it incomprehensible that virtue could be its own reward: the categorical imperative was still more than three centuries from the Germanic mind. #161

Like the minstrels of old, Wittenwiler is obsessed with the concept of *êre*, the word appearing literally scores of times in the *Ring*. It is used most often in its original sense of fame or renown such as won in battle or tournament; and in this sense it often appears along with *guot*, the other great incentive to effort. This is especially true in the third part of the poem, which treats of war and therefore retains many ancient Germanic values undiluted. In the second part of the poem, which shows stronger bourgeois tendencies, *êre* includes not only military fame but also admiration or respect won through wealth, good clothes, decorous behavior, etc. But even here the word connotes a utility, not a virtue. For example, Scheissindpluomen says that a good wife will guard your "house and *er* and other wealth" (2804), and Töreleina says that house and yard are an *er* (2909). Because Wittenwiler uses the word *êre* in a strictly utilitarian sense, it is seldom rendered in this translation as "honor," since the latter word now usually suggests moral overtones. Instead it is rendered as glory, fame, reputation, respect, public approval, etc., as the case may require. #162

The opposite of *êre* is *schande* or *laster* (reproach), which is won through defeat, ridicule, or non-conformity to certain standards. Like *er*, it is not a moral quality, but merely the disapproval of society. *Schand* and *laster* are won by the jousters when they are defeated (324) or by an old man who does not want to learn (3216). On the other hand, the jousters hope to conquer and thereby win *êre* by tying themselves in their saddles (334), even though this was against the rules of jousting. After tying himself into his saddle (606), Bertschi suffers *schanden* not because he has cheated, but because he is dragged under his horse's hooves. After being seduced, Metzi can even maintain her *êre* by concealing her folly (2243).   #163

Thus we see that *êre* was not a moral virtue nor *schande* a vice. However, Wittenwiler occasionally follows clerical tradition by trying to equate *schande* and *laster* with sin, or rather by saying that sin brings one *schande* and *laster*, or, in other words, the disapproval of society. For example, the penitent jousters beg Neidhart, who is disguised as a confessor, to forgive them their wickedness and save them from *schanden* (663). Leckspiss begs God to free him from his sin so that he will not die *lästerleich* (695), and later he trembles with *scham* because of his sins (735). Haintzo's sin (785) was also a *schand* (800). The equivalence of sin and shame is seen when Eckhart mourns that his son has died shamefully and without confession, injured in honor and soul (6732).   #164

Wittenwiler's contradictory attitude toward *êre* is typical of his attitude toward most spiritual values. Throughout the poem he uses *êre* as the reward people will win by conducting themselves bravely, diligently, or cleverly, as the case may be; yet on three occasions he preaches against it. In Metzi's allegorical letter, the glass crown worn by Venus symbolizes ephemeral honor (*zergäncleich er*, 2424), the General Confession (4081 ff) denounces vainglory (*üppig er*), and his *memento mori* warns that worldly *er* rages like the wild sea (4108). Likewise, a father can jeopardize his soul in pursuit of *er* (3140). Throughout the poem he makes it clear that a disconcern for *êre* is a sign of depravity. Dogs know no *er* (2850), and Colman objects to Metzi on the grounds that she cares nothing for it (3432). The same may be assumed of Erenfluoch, whose name means "Curse-honor;" and Eisengrein, as a true peasant, regrets his disgrace less than his injured hand (520).   #165

In spite of this emphasis upon public acclaim and approval, Wittenwiler also follows classic Latin sources by saying you should not mind if other people do not respect you (4793); and he follows church sources by saying you should have no regard for praise (4122). Thus we see that Wittenwiler reflects the views of his sources, be they Germanic, classic, or patristic, without attempting to reconcile them. As we shall see, this inconsistency also appears in his use of other words, for example *recht, from,* and *tugend.* #166

Before the advent of Christianity, the basic meaning of the word *recht* had been the relationship of an individual or group to society as a whole. One's *recht* depended upon his birth, unless he had lost it through a misdeed, expulsion from his group, or defeat in battle. Since *recht* was interpreted and enforced by the ruling classes, any change in the status quo was considered a violation of *recht.* It was clearly recognized that each group had its own *recht,* even at the expense of other groups; and the chief function of most law codes was to maintain the rights of the privileged groups. There was a *recht* for kings and one for subjects, one for freemen and one for serfs, one for men and one for women. #167

Wittenwiler sometimes uses the word *recht* in the primitive sense, for example when Fritzo provides a dowry for his daughter in accordance with his family's *recht* or social station (5471). Such *recht,* in turn, determined one's rights and duties toward society. It is the *recht* or duty of Bertschi's servant to help him up when he is unhorsed (228), and it is the *recht* or privilege of the Emperor to enslave his captives (8480). Likewise, old people have a *recht* freeing them from military service (8530), and the Switzers have the privilege of leading the attack as one of their ancient rights (8207). Not only did each individual have his own *recht,* but each tribe had its own *recht,* which did not have to be extended to people outside of the tribe. One's *recht* was valid only as far as he and his clan could enforce it through threat of revenge. #168

The Christian missionaries were quick to utilize the Teutons' respect for *recht,* and they made it clear that converts had to accept the *recht* of their new celestial Liege-Lord. This was done, in so far as the new law did not differ too much from the old; and thus God and *recht* became linked together in the public mind and one fought "with God and right" when he defended himself against an aggressor (6819). Wittenwiler, himself averse to war, warns that four soldiers can scarcely win enough booty in battle to enable one to fight "for God and right" (8449).

In any case, if we cannot reconcile two enemies, it is our duty to help the weaker if he has *recht* (7827).   #169

As we have seen, each group of society had enjoyed a different *recht*. Christianity, on the other hand, gradually introduced the novel idea that God's *recht* was the same for all classes. Naturally such an innovation was not readily accepted, even in theory, since the leaders of the Church hierarchy were recruited largely from aristocratic and therefore reactionary elements. Nevertheless, by Wittenwiler's day the new attitude had progressed so far that even captives could demand certain rights (8489). However, he makes it clear that it is up to the whim of the captor to decide what is the prisoner's *recht*, even if he thinks it is a noose (8493). All conduct in war became regulated, at least theoretically, by a law of war, which Wittenwiler calls *des streites recht* (7546).   #170

Because each social class had its own *recht*, it also had its own set of moral values and virtues. The highest virtues in Germanic society were courage and prowess, as they were in Roman days when *virtus* was still immediately associated with *vir*. Wittenwiler denotes these martial qualities on several occasions with the words *frümkait* and *tugend*, which literally meant "usefulness" and "ability or adequacy." By his day the bourgeoisie, which derived from the lower classes, had developed a new set of virtues more in keeping with their own needs, chief among these being diligence, thrift, and self-control. However, by a usual quirk in the development of language, these middle-class virtues were also denoted by *frümkait* and *tugend*, these two words having meanwhile taken on a general meaning of "excellence." It is probably in this sense that Riffian uses these two words in explaining the inequality of man (7228-35). He uses the adjectives *from* and *tugendhaft* as synonyms and contrasts them with *ungeschlacht*, which had originally meant "ill-born" but had gradually acquired the meaning of "ill-behaved," the two traits being associated in the medieval mind. He then contrasts the noun *tugend* with *bosshait*, which had originally meant weakness but had gradually taken on the meaning of wickedness. Thus, in the semantic development of these words we can follow the gradual change from a *Herrenmoral* to a *Sklavenmoral* as an ideal.   #171

Thus it is not always possible to determine what quality Wittenwiler meant when he used these words. In the first and third parts of the *Ring*, which concern jousting and fighting, they generally retain their older meanings, whereas in the middle part they can usually be translated as hardworking, well behaved, or virtuous. For example, in v. 31 the word *frümkait* denotes the prowess and courage of a warrior, whereas in v. 3683 it denotes the diligence, modesty, temperance, and honesty desired in a peasant husband. In v. 9283 the expression *fromen diet* is a military term denoting combat soldiers. Although Wittenwiler often uses *tugend* in its original meaning of prowess, he follows the clerical attitude of the *Moralium Dogma* by saying that fortitude, in the sense of strength, is not a *tugend*, in which case *tugend* is a moral virtue and is contrasted with *vermugend* or power (4745-47). #172

Wittenwiler shows similar inconsistency in his attitude toward the peasantry. The Germanic peoples had divided society into two major strata, the free and the unfree, the latter of whom were bondsmen without any social or political rights. Christianity, on the other hand, recognized the innate dignity of every individual, regardless of his social class. Naturally it was difficult for the Germanic ruling classes to accept this subversive innovation, which would have spelled the end of their social order. Therefore the new view never made much headway except among clerics, and even they were more interested in equality before God and Death, rather than in this world. Today it is generally accepted that all people are equal before Death. This must not have been the case in Wittenwiler's day, or he would have found it unnecessary to stress the fact as he did (4173). The ancient Germanic warriors had allowed only free men to enter Valhalla, and it must have been difficult for their descendants to accept the Christian idea of a desegregated Heaven. #173

The question of social inequality was very prominent in Wittenwiler's day, and many preachers and writers stressed the theoretical equality of man. One of their favorite arguments was that we are all Adam's children, as Lienhart mentions in the *Ring* (7222). However, it was the Old Testament itself that furnished the rebuttal to this claim, as we see in Riffian's answer about Noah's unequal sons (7237). This argument was taken very seriously, even though it had been brilliantly discredited some two centuries earlier by Eike of Repgau, the author of the *Sachsenspiegel*, who cited the Bible to prove that Ham's descendants had gone to Africa and therefore could not have been the ancestors of the European serfs. #174

Wittenwiler's attitude toward the peasantry is ambiguous. Early in the *Ring* he assures his reader that a plowman who wisely supports himself with honest work is truly blessed (46); yet later on he states that the representatives of the cities should have known that peasants do only what they have to and that they should be treated with violence (7867). Both of these arguments were popular literary commonplaces in his day, the first being championed by moralists and preachers, and the second by landlords and burghers. Wittenwiler seems to have endorsed both views firmly, without any feeling of contradiction. Thus he performs the kind of mental gymnastics which George Orwell has described as *doublethink,* that is, "the power of holding two contradictory beliefs in one's mind simultaneously, and accepting both of them."   #175

Wittenwiler makes use of another popular commonplace when he says that true nobility depends upon virtue rather than birth (4422); yet his description of village life suggests doubt that any peasant could ever be virtuous, as does his contention that the right way to be courtly is to observe a peasant and do the opposite (4865). In other words, for Wittenwiler, the peasant was by definition the opposite of the knight: that is to say, the peasant was merely an ideal "contrast-type." Even if we assume that Wittenwiler's peasant-satire was a concession to his bourgeois readers, his success in it indicates that he too found the lower classes comical.   #176

Wittenwiler's attitude toward farm work is particularly contradictory; for, although he claims to respect the farmer's honest toil (46), he nevertheless follows bourgeois tradition in ridiculing all rustic field work. The coats-of-arms and weapons of the peasant jousters are comical not only because they are out of place in a tournament but also because they represent farm work. Such scorn is revealed in many of the names in the *Ring* which, although merely denoting honest toil, are listed right along with names denoting grievous physical and moral faults. For example, the name Schollentrit, which was always used disparagingly in bourgeois literature, merely meant clodhopper or plowman. The name Schlegel (mallet) has the same condescending humor as the nickname *mit dem phlegel* (with the flail). Other nicknames in the *Ring* denoting farm work are *vom stadel* (from the barn), *von dem kerssenpaum* (from the cherrytree), *vom hag* (from the hedge or outlying enclosure), *von dem gatter* (from the lattice or picket fence), *mit dem kruog* (with the jug), and *mit der gäss* (with the goat), the last two of which may also have obscene significance. The name Gredul means a girl of all work, and the names Schüerenprand (Stir-the-fire) and Blasindäschen (Blow-in-the-ashes) suggest either menial work or trouble-making. The two lists of farm labors made by the jousters (1270) and by Bertschi (3832) are probably sarcastic, as is the fact that the villagers can strut about and joust only on holidays (65) and Sundays (105). Although Wittenwiler follows the nobility in ridiculing the manual labor of the peasants, he nevertheless recommends hard work for his bourgeois readers, and more especially for their wives (5089). #177

The ancient Germans had looked upon warfare as a normal and praiseworthy activity; yet they eventually accepted Christianity, although a religion of peace. To do so, they had to make certain mental reservations, such as that war is permissible when God is on your side, which, of course, He always is. Although generally opposed to war as being destructive, Wittenwiler nevertheless cites the Old Testament to justify it by letting Strudel tell how God ordered Moses and Joshua to fight against false hosts (6834). Even though he generally seems to side with the older generation in the *Ring* who oppose war, his description of the battle shows a lively interest in warfare, as if strong atavistic urges were trying to break through the veneer of his clerical training. Had he been entirely opposed to war, perhaps he would not have seen fit to disseminate so much military information from the Roman historian Vegetius. #178

To medieval man, a militaristic Christian priest was no contradiction, and many crusaders were both clergymen and warriors. Also, it was not unusual for ecclesiastical lords to wage wars against each other and harry each other's domains. The English paraphrase of Vegetius' work, *Knyghthode and Bataile*, which appeared shortly after the *Ring*, was written by a priest who showed considerable enthusiasm for the art of war. As Wittenwiler mentions in his preface (25), the very purpose of the third part of the *Ring* is to teach the art of war. Whereas Wittenwiler takes the Church's stand against the Germanic custom of trial by combat (7343), he nevertheless admits that the just man more often wins than not because he knows he is in the right (7347). #179

In listing the gifts of the Virgin Mary, Wittenwiler quotes Matthew 5:39 by saying that, if anyone strikes you, you should turn your other cheek (2489). However, he later says that head for head and foot for foot is a just retribution (4586), an attitude that hearkens back to ancient Germanic law and also to Exodus 21:24. In one respect the Germanic law was more advanced than the Hebrew, since the offender could pay with a compensation instead of with life or limb. Such a compensation was called a *buosse,* as in the *Ring* (4586), a word related to the English word "booty." Until one paid his *schuld* or debt with a *buosse,* he was liable to the vengeance of the wronged party's kindred. The *Ring* does not seem to distinguish between *schuld* in the sense of financial obligation to a person and *schuld* in the sense of guilt or offense against God; for not only debt but also guilt could be ended by a money payment, as in the case of the peasants after their mock-confession (873). Likewise, the word *buosse* seems to have connoted only a payment, without the implication of penitence often found in the modern German word *Busse.* Although Wittenwiler professes to teach Christ's point of view, he often praises revenge. He even seems to agree with Sneck, who says that one should get revenge promptly before a third party can intervene and make peace, lest one lose his honor (6746-57).   #180

Wittenwiler also shows considerable inconsistency in his attitude toward God; for his poem reveals both deep piety and inexcusable blasphemy. As we have seen in the case of his parody, he was not in the least disturbed by the juxtaposition of the sublime and the ridiculous; and in similar manner he could treat divine matters both seriously and humorously. His peasants constantly make pious invocations, but usually in a comical context. In the tournament Grabinsgaden praises God when he falls in the brook and thereby drowns his lice (267). In the mock-confession Neidhart asks Leckspiss to confess everything for the sake of God "who hath created hay and straw" (709); and, when the two dupes go to buy their indulgences, he says, "May the Devil take you and God give you both pain" (825). When Metzi is sitting naked in the hayloft, Bertschi nearly bursts for her love and exclaims, "Holy Christ! Locked up bread how sweet you are!" (1558), and Krippenkra tells Metzi she should submit to him so as not to die in her sins (2147). At the banquet Burkhart invokes God to cause good weather until he garners his spoonful of food (5748), and Galgenschwank thanks God when Farindwand chokes to death on a fishbone (5908).   #181

One could argue, to be sure, that Wittenwiler disapproved

of such levity and therefore put these words into the mouths of his foolish and sinful peasants, just as he blamed Metzi's shameful name upon the person who named her. The Lappenhausers are consistently godless. They neglect to thank God before or after their banquet (6183); and they also take the Lord's name in vain, for example when they say *poks switz* (1457), which means God's sweat or blood, and when they use a corruption of *in nomine domini* (321). When rightfully refused confession (8571), they swear by "the old God" (8574), which appears to have been a blasphemous oath.   #182

However, Wittenwiler elsewhere treats divine matters in a way that would appear frivolous in the twentieth century. Like other medieval writers, he saw nothing wrong in using the same epithets for divine or worldly persons. For example, the word supreme (*obrest*) is used of the Holy Trinity (10), God (2261), Venus (2288), and the Virgin Mary (2548). Likewise, he seems to have seen no discrepancy in ending Bertschi's perfectly serious love-letter with the pious request that both Jesus and Venus protect his lady-love (1910), or in opening Metzi's letter with the hope that God's grace and her service be granted to Bertschi (2271-74). This would suggest that he also saw no disrespect when Engelmar, upon giving Metz and Bertschi a dog as a wedding present, says he hopes that God and the dog will keep them from harm (5477).   #183

In describing his lady-love (1783 ff), Bertschi uses terminology like that conventionally used of the Virgin Mary. Such terminology was largely based upon the Song of Songs, which, ironically enough, had originally been a secular love song. Such contradiction is understandable in an age in which portraits of successful courtesans often had the same physionomy as portraits of the Virgin Mary and in which pious miracle plays often contained pornographic interludes. Thus, Wittenwiler was merely a child of his times when he dedicated his filth-laden poem to the Trinity and the Virgin Mother (v. 2).   #184

Wittenwiler appears more consistent in his attitude toward the clergy than in his attitude toward God. Like most of his contemporaries, he acknowledges the sanctity of the clerical order yet disapproves of the behavior of its incumbents. This was the usual view of moralistic writers, clergymen themselves, who liked to contrast the conduct of most clerics with that of Christ, who had actually wrought as he taught. Wittenwiler follows popular tradition by alluding to the three chief vices attributed to the clergy, namely their greed, gluttony, and incontinence. He satirizes the clergy's proverbial greed by saying that Jützi's death was of no harm to the priest (1233), and thus he suggests that priests wrongfully profited from burials. He is also sarcastic in having Töreleina say that preachers have rosy cheeks and fat faces in spite of abstaining from beef (2904); since the preaching orders, particularly the Dominicans, were often accused of failing to observe their dietary restrictions. Colman follows tradition in saying that a daughter is in danger of being seduced by her priest (3155); for medieval fathers and husbands resented the clergy's access to otherwise well guarded women. Wittenwiler does not explain why the Lappenhausers hate their sexton (7566), but this may have resulted from his function in helping collect the tithes.   #185

In spite of the clergy's misconduct, Wittenwiler does not question the sanctity of their office. Following the Church-inspired code of chivalry, he states that people should help clergymen along with widows, orphans, and paupers (4610) and that one should confess to his own priest at least once every year (4054). He also states that people should not give aid to anyone trying to free himself from the priesthood (7815); and he claims that one of the causes of wars is that we do not wish to pay our tithes to our priest (7368).   #186

On the other hand Wittenwiler also defends the rights of the laity. He states that, however holy ordination may be, one's soul does not suffer without it (4013); and he has Gumpost say that one should never advise anyone to become a monk (2693). In writing their wills, people should remember their creditors before the priests (5170). Wittenwiler also seems to side with the villagers when they remind their priest that marriage is older than monks and priests and is therefore not a Church concern (5430).   #187

Whereas Wittenwiler censures the clergy and defends the laity, he never attacks the Church or its dogma. Of course such docility could have resulted from caution as well as conviction, especially if he was really an advocate at the episcopal court at Constance at the time that John Huss was tried and convicted of such intellectual independance. As we have seen, Huss was censored for believing it possible for a Christian to confess to another laymen; and therefore we may safely assume that Wittenwiler must have preached this same error at an earlier date, when the practise was widespread and not attacked by the

Church. In any case, his theology was strictly orthodox and con-
formed to accepted medieval beliefs. The creed cited by Bertschi
(p. 51) seems to be a free paraphrase of the Apostles' Creed
which includes later innovations introduced by the medieval
Church without authority in Scripture. For example, it includes
the harrowing of Hell, which was based upon the apocryphal
Gospel of Nicodemus and was ultimately derived from the
Greek belief in Hades. For the *Limbus Patrium* Wittenwiler
uses the word *vorhelle* (p. 51) whereas for the *Limbus In-
fantium*, which he mentions in connection with the unborn Judas
Iscariot, he uses the word *helle* (3251). The belief that unborn
children could be punished was first preached by St. Augustine
and long troubled medieval theologians. Wittenwiler's version
of the Apostles' Creed also put more emphasis upon good works
than appeared in the older and authentic version. It will also
be noted that his Lord's Prayer lacks a doxology (p. 50).   #188

Wittenwiler is quite inconsistent in his attitude toward the
sanctity of marriage. In general he seems to agree with Neid-
hart, who says that Bertschi can serve his wife without sin
(847), and with Übelgsmak, who maintains that a woman can
be chaste even though she has marital relations (4960). Dame
Laichdenman likewise claims that even married people can at-
tain salvation, as was the case with St. Eustace (3410), the
hero of a popular medieval hagiography. However, Wittenwiler
does not entirely free himself of the view that marriage, while
permissible, is less holy than celibacy. This is implied when
Metzi's fictitious confessor says you should take a wife if you
cannot do without a woman (2491). This opinion, which de-
rives from I Corinthians 7:9, was popular in the Middle Ages,
being endorsed, for example, by Thomas Aquinas in his *Catena
Aurea*. Henritze reveals the same attitude by saying a man
should marry if he does not[197] want to serve God chastely like an
angel (3524 ff.) ; and in this he expressly contradicts the view
expressed by Übelgsmak. Henritze's view, like the violent mi-
sogynism expressed by Krippenkra (2103 ff.) and Nagenflek
(2840), was to be expected in an age intellectually dominated
by celibates, who had to strengthen themselves against the
temptations of the flesh. For this reason, when Dame Laich-
denman says that beautiful hair injures men in their *gebett*
(3462), I believe that she means it distracts men in their prayers
rather than harms them in their beds.[199]   #189

As we have seen, Wittenwiler seems to be inconsistent in

many of his beliefs and attitudes. However, it may be argued that it was not he but only his *Ring* that was inconsistent. Since the days of Rousseau and Goethe, people have assumed that all true works of literature must be parts of a great confession and that a great poet must write what his muse dictates. Such, however, was not the case in the Middle Ages. Authors wrote to instruct or entertain; and their works did not have to be of a personal or subjective nature. We have no assurance that the author of the *Ackermann aus Böhmen* (*Plowman from Bohemia*) had really lost a beloved wife: he might just as well have been a celibate trying to solve a deep problem in an entertaining work.   #190

Literary historians often try to assess the personalities, beliefs, and social class of medieval writers from their remaining works. This is a questionable practice, especially in the case of poets who are known through only one or two works. For example, if we knew Hartmann von Aue only through his *Erec* and *Iwein*, we would find him a worldly and courtly poet. On the other hand, if we knew him only as the author of *Gregorius*, we would consider him an ascetic and monkish writer. In reality, his choice of matter and attitude was probably determined less by the command of a muse than by the whim of a patron. As he himself says in his *Iwein*, he wrote what people wished to hear. Today such motivation is expected to produce "best-sellers" but not great works of art.   #191

Therefore, in assessing the *Ring*, we must remember that it need not always represent the poet's personal point of view. Today an author is held responsible for the speech of his characters, but that was not the case in the Middle Ages. Chaucer, for example, frankly denied responsibility for the vulgar story told by his Miller, and he would probably have disclaimed the views expressed by his worldly Wife of Bath. The conflicting beliefs in the *Ring* are usually expressed by different speakers, and the poet does not imply which, if any, is his spokesman. #192

Most critics of the *Ring* have assumed that Wittenwiler favored marriage because he let the women, who champion it, win the marriage debate. However, their victory is necessary, or there would have been no wedding and consequently no plot. Actually, the women's arguments are more specious than those of the men. Moreover, the tragic end of the *Ring* seems to confirm the futility of all worldly life, even including marriage. One might even contend that Bertschi's despairing words (9684-

86) express the author's true feelings.   #193

At this point the author seems to throw off his fool's mask and reveal the seriousness of his work. Up to this point he has allowed his readers to enjoy his peasant-satire, which was the type of humor dearest to their hearts; but now he makes it clear that the fools of his story represent not only the peasantry but all of mankind. All life is a great fools' procession advancing through its inexorable folly to its inevitable doom. Nothing in this life is abiding but God's love. Our only hope is to flee the folly of this world and prepare ourselves for a new and better life in the world to come.

The poet has taken off his fool's mask and put on a hermit's cowl. But is that his rightful garb, or is it only another disguise? The answer to this question remains his own secret. #194

CONTROVERSIAL POINTS

The following paragraphs serve to justify my treatment of certain words in the *Ring* wherein I differ from other students of this poem. Being the first to translate it, I am the first who has had to commit himself with regard to all of its riddles. Wiessner has explained many of its words, some in pages 331 to 339 of his edition and many more in his commentary; yet he has left many problems unsolved. Also, as will be shown, I cannot accept all of his solutions. #195

Perhaps the chief cause of my disagreement with other students of the *Ring* is my attempt to get to the values intended by Wittenwiler; for most critics have tended to render his words by their modern derivatives. For example, his words, "An hübschichait und mannes zucht, An tugend und an frümchät" (vv. 30-31) are "modernized" by Günther Müller as "an edlen Sitten, Mannes Zucht, an lauterem und tüchtigem Sinn." (*Deutsche Dichtung*, p. 73). I contend that such values developed in Europe only later and that a closer rendition would be "in courtly behavior, manly training, virtue, and courage," and that even "virtue" would not coincide with its present meaning. #196

Sometimes I differ from other critics because I do not try to make the *Ring* a consistent work. An example can be seen in Fehrenbach's paraphrase of Henritze's verdict on marriage. Where Henritze says a man should marry if he wishes to have children ". . . noch got will dienen sam ein engel keuschechleich," Fehrenbach (p. 4) says ". . . and wants to live chastely . . ." I translate this exactly the opposite as "does not want . . .," believing *noch* to be used as in the modern German expression "weder . . . noch." Wittenwiler uses the word in this sense, always at the beginning of a verse, numerous times, including vv. 3280, 3489, 3688, 3690, 3692, 3696, 3728, 3991, 4103, and 4659, to name but a few in the first half of the poem. In every case the sense is negative. Because Wittenwiler elsewhere contends that marital relations can be chaste, Fehrenbach (p. 170 ff) wishes to prove him invariably favorable to marriage. In general Fehrenbach's interpretation of the *Ring* can be summarized thus: The *Ring* "was written while Europe was still truly Christian" (p. 42), i.e., before Luther and his accomplices corrupted it. Therefore Wittenwiler was a good Christian and believed and felt in all matters as a good (twentieth-century?) Catholic should. Consequently he "can in no real sense be called a *Bauernfeind*. Rather he is the peasant's friend, trying to explain and correct their way of thinking in order to raise them socially, spiritually, intellectually, morally and so to help them remove the obloquy associated with the mere mention of their name." (p. 59) #197

Sometimes my translations differ from those conventionally used for *MHG* words because I go back to Wittenwiler's original Latin thought. For example, I translate *nöten* in v. 4584 as "coerce" because Wittenwiler used it to render *cohercens* in the phrase "Severitas est virtus debito supplicio cohercens iniuriam." (*Das Moralium Dogma des Guillaume de Conches*, ed. John Holmberg, Uppsala, 1929, p. 12, vv. 25-26). #198

In some cases my disagreement with accepted explanations is due to an attempt to get back to the spirit of the times. Where the *MS* says that women's beautiful hair harms men *an dem gebett* (v. 3462), Wiessner and all other scholars I have questioned believe this to mean "in the bridal bed;" yet I find it more likely that it harms men in their prayer. First of all, to say "in bed," Wittenwiler would probably have used the preposition *in* as in v. 7032 or *auf* as in v. 1632. Secondly, long hair was symbolic of carnal temptation. Lady Venus lets her hair hang down (v. 2297), whereas the Virgin Mary wears hers bound up chastely (v. 2352); and female figures often have luxurious hair in allegories, for example in Dürer's picture of the temptations of St. Anthony. #199

Wittenwiler says that his lecherous bath-woman can do business with *schloern* (v. 2566). Wiessner explains this as "veils," but this does not make sense. The word is obviously *Schlôre*, "unstetes, unordentliches

Frauenzimmer" (*Schweizerisches Idiotikon*, IX, 640), since bath-women conventionally served as procuresses, as this one does (v. 2567).   #200

Wittenwiler states that the peasant-jousters' *chlainet* is a calf in a stork's nest (v. 162), which they carry jointly in Metzi's honor. Wiessner explains this as a banner, but it is actually a crest in the sense of the decoration knights wore on the top of their helmets. Such crests were often a bunch of plumes or a replica of the coat-of-arms; but in mock-tournaments they were often comical. In the illustrations to the courtly romance *Freydal* (ed. Q. von Leitner, Wien, 1880), we see fantastic crests such as stuffed birds, stuffed dogs, and even stuffed monkeys sitting on cushions, creatures almost as grotesque as Wittenwiler's calf. It is not surprising that the calf falls out of its nest when Leckspiss charges against Neidhart (v. 422). The crest in the sketch of the Peasant Tournament (Fig. 1.) is more modest, being only a shoe.   #201

After the peasants are tired of dancing, they stand on one foot so that they may rest all the better when they lie down without stepping . . . *sam ein fauler mag* (v. 6284). Wiessner takes *mag* to be a noun and gets "like a lazy poppy," but I think it a verb and get "as a lazy person likes to." #202

Perhaps I differ from Wiessner most in the matter of emendations. Before editing the *Ring*, he himself said, in speaking of emendations proposed by earlier scholars, "In many places it is the task of the editor to protect the Meiningen MS against such conjectures" (Wiessner, "der Dichter . . .," p. 152). Therefore I am taking the liberty of protecting the MS from some of Wiessner's own emendations, examples of which follow here.   #203

In v. 2180 he changes *pollen* to read *nollen*; but this is not necessary since the former fits the context just as well. It is the same word as *bolens* (shooting) in v. 8699, which is cited in Schmeller's *Bayerisches Wörterbuch* (IV, 232). The *Schweizerisches Idiotikon* (IV, 1177) gives not only the meaning of "shooting," but also: c) "sich (lärmend, wild, ausgelassen) herumwälzen,—werfen, treiben," which fits our context adequately. #204

On two occasions Wiessner changes the word "blew" (*blies, bliesend*) to read "struck" (*biess*, v. 186, *biessend*, v. 8679) because he thinks the instrument involved to be a cymbal. However, since the *beki* was really a bagpipe, the emendations were erroneous (See G. F. Jones, "Wittenwiler's *Becki* and the Medieval Bagpipe," *JEGP*, 48, April, 1949, pp. 209-28). #205

In v. 2646 Wiessner changes *mit der seynen* to read *nit der seynen*, which makes no sense. I think *der seynen* a displacement for the genitalia like *die iren* in v. 6410, since possessive pronouns are often used in this sense (Cf. the juvenile joke, "Have you ever seen Mars?" "No, but I've seen Pa's."). The pronoun *sein* is sometimes used irregularly in the *Ring*, for example in v. 2568 it means "their." In both of these cases the irregular use of *sein* may be due to the need of the rime.   #206

After the ass Hagen runs away with his rider, he is caught by means of the miller's *zange* (v. 494). Wiessner changes this to *sange*, meaning a sheaf of grain. However, it is unlikely that the ass would be tempted by such a lure after his mad chase; and it is more likely that he was caught by means of some implement. The word *zange* normally meant tongs, and it is possible that the miller used tongs in his work. On the other hand, the word *zange* could also designate a straight shaft: for example, *Freydal* (p. xxxix) uses the word *stechzange* to designate the blunt lance used in a mock tournament. Therefore Wittenwiler's *zange* may have been some object related to the miller's *spiess* mentioned in v. 6532. In any case, there is no need to emend the text.   #207

This also holds of *reichen* in v. 5124, which Wiessner has replaced by *teichen*. Again the original form is just as intelligible, since the adverb *hintersich* can be humorous or ironic for "not at all" (*Deutsches Wörterbuch*, IV, 1495, i) *hinter sich*, "spottende oder scherzhafte verneinung und weigerung"). Moreover, Wittenwiler uses the verb *reichen* elsewhere (v. 3025), but not *teichen.* I think the change of *seyir* into *ghei* in v. 2863 is far-fetched and unnecessary. A less forced explanation would be that it is an elaborate spelling or an error for MHG *sêr*, meaning physical and mental pain and hardship.   #208

Wiessner changes *schleicht* in v. 4175 to read *schlecht*, although the former, in the sense of take or drag away (*DWb* IX, 569, II, trans.), would well portray Death's action. Likewise, there is no reason to replace *nikket* in v. 5939 with *jukket*, since the former, in the sense of "he lowered his head," is quite suitable (Cf. "Er dehnte sich in den Schultern"). The same gesture is made for a similar reason in v. 5948. Wiessner's emendation *mosts* in v. 5646 is unnecessary, since the original verse was intelligible in the sense of "and saw there was not enough of it." Wittenwiler often uses pronouns with only implied antecedents.					#209

In v. 3262, *wie nach* (how nearly) is just as good as *vil nach* (very nearly); and in v. 2553, the word *stat*, meaning estate, condition, way of life, or dignity, is just as satisfactory as the emendation *stab*, and it rimes better. Likewise, the comparative adverb *mächticleicher* in v. 6124 is just as good as the positive *mächticleichen*.					#210

Some of Wiessner's emendations do not change the meaning of the text and therefore serve no purpose. For example, *Waisst nicht noch* in v. 5125 would have the same meaning as the emendation *Waisst nicht auch*. This also holds of *iren* (v. 7830), *den* (645), and *zerprosten* (for *zerborsten*) in v. 699.					#211

In v. 5717, *verzettet halb* (half spilled) gives the same meaning as the emendation *verzettents halb* (they spilled half); and in v. 3211 the word *partt* (beard) means about the same as its emendation *palch* (fellow) and fits the rime even better.

Sometimes Wiessner "corrects" Wittenwiler in points where the latter may have intentionally made errors for the sake of the rime. For example, the poet may have meant to write *Flander* in v. 1083 without an *n* to rime with *enander*, even if he failed to do so in v. 1163. Wiessner also attempts to standardize Wittenwiler's use of *do* and *da* in the sense of "there;" and as a result he makes numerous emendations. For example he always changes *do mit* to read *da mit*, although Wittenwiler was consistent with the former usage. On many occasions he changes *do* to read *des*, where the former word would do just as well. In vv. 8667-68 he changes the rime pair *gesinder-rinder* to read *gsind-rind*, although the plural *rinder* is used elsewhere, as in v. 3030. Wittenwiler usually uses the plural *gesinde*, but the form may have fluctuated, or else he may have forced it to fit his rime in this case.					#213

The above mentioned couplet brings up an important matter which explains literally hundreds of Wiessner's emendations, namely his determination to make Wittenwiler's verses flow in regular iambics and trochees, that is, in regularly alternating stressed and unstressed syllables. In the above mentioned couplet, Wiessner has not only dropped the plural endings but has also dropped the *e* in the prefix *ge*. Apparently his purpose was to make the meter come out thus: *Dáz die déupin únd ir gsínd Gelígin níder sám die rínd.* I doubt that Wittenwiler and his public were as concerned with regular alternation as Wiessner supposes. German court poets at the turn of the thirteenth century had followed Romance usage in alternating accented and unaccented syllables, although this was actually foreign to the genius of the Germanic languages. In these languages the speed and rhythm of normal speech depends almost entirely upon the stressed accents, it being of little importance whether the intervals between them are left blank or are filled with one or two or even more unaccented syllables. This fact was clear to the ancient Germanic scops, who developed a system of alliterative verse based on the nature of their own language and not upon that of the Latins. The duration of their staves or verses depended upon a fixed number of stressed syllables, between which they could place unaccented syllables almost at will.					#214

In spite of the metric innovations at court and cloister, the poetry of the people largely continued to fit their natural speech patterns, as many folk songs still do. Although most of Wittenwiler's verses show a regular alternation of stressed and unstressed syllables, the Meininger MS nevertheless has numerous irregular verses, some with as many as three successive unstressed syllables, as in v. 674. Wiessner has modified nearly all of these so as to make them fit the ideal pattern, although there is no proof that the poet or his public thought it necessary. As we have seen, he changed the verse *Dáz die déupin und ir gesínder* to read *Dáz die déupin únd ir gsind*, although the original verse better fits normal speech patterns. In like manner, to cite only one of many such verses, he changes *álles, das màn genémen mág* to read *álles, dás man gnémen mág* (v. 9529), which also requires an unnatural accentuation.   #215

Wiessner is able to achieve his desired meter in most cases by merely dropping the *e* in prefixes, particularly in *ge* as in the case of *gesind*, or by contracting *dar über, dar an*, and *in dem* to *drüber, dran*, and *im*, etc. These emendations, which greatly predominate, do not affect the translation and therefore do not really come into the scope of this discussion. However, in some cases Wiessner has added or deleted words that contribute something to the meaning. For example, he deletes the word *ob* in v. 96 and *sin* in v. 199; he adds the word *allem* in v. 267 and *rechter* in v. 381; and he changes *Marien* to *Marjen* in v. 701. In v. 438 the original words *Drey spang tieff* could have been spoken emphatically and received an entire stress on each and therefore not need to be replaced by *Dreier spange tieff* (Cf. Wolfram von Eschenbach's stress on *Cóndwír ámúrs* in *Parzival*, 187, v. 21).   #216

Whereas it is justifiable to standardize the orthography in an edition for the convenience of the reader, it is undesirable to give the work a metrical regularity not intended by the original poet, especially not if it in any way alters its meaning.   #217

This translation differs from Wiessner's edition not only in regard to vocabulary and emendations but also in regard to punctuation; since punctuation, being absent in the MS, must be conjectured from the context. For example, I think that couplet 3864-65 should be included in the same quotation marks as verse 3863: that is to say, I think Wittenwiler meant to attribute both sayings to Solomon, to whom both Proverbs and Wisdom were ascribed. Likewise, I believe that v. 6360 and v. 6361 are the titles of two different songs. The first is a typical opening of a "summer song" and suggests a note of joy; whereas the second is an *Abschiedslied* and suggests sadness. The two titles are probably listed together just for the sake of the rime.   #218

APPENDIX II

QUOTATIONS FROM AND ALLUSIONS TO SCRIPTURE

(All references to Vulgate. Deviations in King James Version indicated by *KJ*)

Ring verse		*Ring* verse	
45	Psalms 127:2 (*KJ* 128:2)	2491	I Corinthians 7:9
787	Job 3:1-3	2493	Matthew 19:21
847	I Corinthians 7:28	2495	Matthew 5:44
1559	Proverbs 9:17	2516	John 19:34
1973	Psalms 125:4 (*KJ* 126:5)	2519	Luke 22:44
2076	Proverbs 5:3-4	2537	Matthew 16:26
2196	Solomon's Song 2:5	2735	I Thessalonians 5:21
2489	Matthew 5:39	2839	Leviticus 15:19-27

Ring verse		*Ring* verse	
2844	Jude I:16, 18	3997	Matthew 25:35-36
2875	Genesis 5:5	4028	Matthew 22:37, 39
2889	Proverbs 31:10	4101	2 Corinthians 5:1 ff.
3089	Matthew 6:24	4144	Luke 22:44
3091	I Corinthians 7:32-33		
3172	I Corinthians 13:11	4166	Genesis 3:19
3221	Genesis 3:3	4430	Ecclesiastes 9:16
3234	Ecclesiastes 5:2 (*KJ* 5:3)	4472	3 Kings 3:5-14 (*KJ* I Kings)
3257	Matthew 26:24; Mark 14:21	4586	Exodus 21:24
3473	Deuteronomy 22:28-29	4692	Matthew 7:12
3477	Ecclesiastes 5:11 (*KJ* 5:12)	4911	Matthew 23:12
3837	Matthew 4:4	4915	Proverbs 27:2
3858	Luke 12:31	5152	Ecclesiasticus 8:15 (not in KJ)
3863	Liber Sapientiae 1:4 (not in *KJ*)	7011	Genesis 2:24
3864	Proverbs 1:7, 9:10; Psalms 110:10	7237	Genesis 9:20-27
3869	Matthew 13:57	7306	Isaiah 14:12
3978	Hebrews 11:6	7463	Ecclesiastes 10:16
3980	James 2:17	9684	Ecclesiasticus 10:12
3985	Exodus 20:1-17; Deuteronomy 5:6-12	9698	Exodus 17:6; Numbers 20:8
		9699	John 2:9

APPENDIX III

RING BIBLIOGRAPHY

*Recommended. **Highly recommended. This bibliography attempts to list all studies of *Ring* except derivative accounts in regular histories of German literature. It does not aim to make invidious comparisons between the works listed; for many of those not recommended were valuable in their day but have since been superseded. Evaluations are of course subjective and aim only to help the laymen read first things first.

ZfdA = *Zeitschrift für deutsches Altertum*
ZfdPh = *Zeitschrift für deutsche Philologie*

Editions

1. *Der Ring von Heinrich Wittenweiler*, ed. Ludwig Bechstein, *Bibliothek des literarischen Vereins Stuttgart*, XXIII (Stuttgart, 1851). Superseded by Item 2.

2. **Heinrich Wittenwilers Ring*, ed. Edmund Wiessner, *Deutsche Literatur: Reihe IV, Realistik des Spätmittelalters*, III (Leipzig, 1931). An admirable edition. Language standardized, but with original forms retained in footnotes. Possibly too many emendations. Inadequate glossary supplemented by Item 54.

Special Studies.

3. Alewyn, Richard: "Naturalismus bei Neidhart von Reuental," *ZfdPh*, 56 (1931), Pp. 68-69. Only brief mention of *Ring*.
4. Baechtold, Jacob: "Heinrich Wittenwiler," *Germania*, 20 (1875), Pp. 66-68. Proves Wittenwiler was Swiss. Cites Item 40.
5. *Baechtold, Jacob: *Geschichte der deutschen Literatur in der Schweiz* (Frauenfeld, 1892), Pp. 182-90. Excellent resumé of plot. Criticism still valid, factual evidence partially obsolete. Somewhat superseded by Item 13.
6. Bleisch, Ernst: *Zum Ring Heinrich Wittenweilers*, Diss. Halle (Halle, 1891). First complete work devoted to *Ring*. Still of interest, although now obsolete. See Item 46 below.
7. Boesch, Bruno: "Phantasie und Wirklichkeitsfreude in Wittenwilers Ring," *ZfdPh*, 67 (1942).
8. Brauns, Wilhelm: "Heinrich Wittenwiler, Das Gedicht von der Bauernhochzeit und Hermann von Sachsenheim," *ZfdA*, 73 (1936), Pp. 57-75. Believes "Metzenhochzeit" influenced by *Ring*, instead of vice-versa. See Items 49 & 55.
9. Brill, Richard: *Die Schule Neidharts, Palaestra*, 37, (Berlin, 1908), Pp. 198-201. Considers *Ring* the most important product of peasant-satire tradition after Neidhart. Shows influence of latter.
10. *Edelmann, Heinrich: "Zur örtlichen und zeitlichen Bestimmung von Wittenweilers Ring," *Mitteilungen zur Vaterländischen Geschichte*, 39 (St. Gallen, 1934), Pp. 1-21. Convincingly locates setting of *Ring*.
11. Ehrismann, Gustav: "Heinrich Wittenwilers Ring," *ZfdPh*, 56 (1931), 470-72. Favorable review of Item 2.
12. Ehrismann, Gustav: *Geschichte der deutschen Literatur bis zum Ausgang des Mittelalters* (München, 1935), II, 2,2, Pp. 484-86. Very brief account.
13. **Ermattinger, Emil: *Dichtung und Geistesleben der deutschen Schweiz* (München, 1933), Pp. 76-86. Brief but excellent account.
14. Fehr, Hans: *Das Recht in der Dichtung* (Bern, 1931), Pp. 260-68. Shows traces of popular and canon law in *Ring*.
15. **Fehrenbach, C. G.: *Marriage in Wittenwiler's Ring*, Cath. U. of America diss. (Washington, 1941), Cath. U. of America *Studies in German*, XV. Excellent preface (vii-xii) and introductory chapter (Pp. 3-24) giving current scholarship about MS, language, and author of poem. Remainder of volume gives information of interest but sometimes shows bias and smacks of religious pamphlet. Satiric passages often accepted as folkloristic fact.
16. Fränkel, L.: "Heinrich Wittenweiler," *Allgemeine deutsche Biographie*, 43 (1898), Pp. 610-16. Obsolete.
17. Frey, Adolf: *Schweizer Dichter* (Leipzig, 1919), Pp. 24-28. Compares Wittenwiler with Rabelais and Cervantes.
18. *Friedrich, Walter: *Die Wurzeln der Komik in Wittenwilers Ring*, Diss. München (München, 1942). Specialized study of comic and *Humor* in medieval German literature in general and in *Ring* in particular.
19. Gervinus, G. G.: *Geschichte der deutschen Dichtung* (Leipzig, 1853), II, 183-84. Earliest evaluation of *Ring* except for Adalbert v. Keller's introduction to Item 1. Still partially valid.
20. Götze, Alfred: "Heinrich Wittenweiler's Ring," *Literaturblatt für germanische und romanische Philologie*, 53 (1932), P. 296. Favorable review of Item 2. Suggestions subsequently incorporated into Item 54.
21. Götze, Alfred: *Ibid.*, 58 (1937), Pp. 237-38. Favorable review of Item 54.
22. Gusinde, Konrad: *Neidhart mit dem Veilchen, Germanistische Abhandlungen*, XVII, Pp. 92-97. Comparison of mock-confession in *Ring* with poems in Neidhart-tradition.

23. Hagelstange, Alfred: *Süddeutsches Bauernleben im Mittelalter* (Leipzig, 1898), Pp. 59-69, 77, 81-86, 244-60. Accepts *Ring* as true picture of peasant life without allowing for satiric intent and literary tradition.

24. Hügli, Hilda: *Der deutsche Bauer im Mittelalter*, Diss. Bern (Bern, 1929), Pp. 124-41. Relates peasant life in *Ring* to that in contemporary works. Interesting observations, with some inaccuracies.

25. Jones, George F.: "The Tournaments of Tottenham and Lappenhausen," *PMLA*, 66 (1951), Pp. 1123-1140. Discusses intent of peasant-tournament tradition. Serves primarily to explain English poem in terms of better understood *Ring*.

26. *Jones, George F.: "Heinrich Wittenwiler—Nobleman or Burgher?" *Monatshefte*, 45 (1953), Pp. 65-75. Maintains that Wittenwiler has not been definitely identified and that he wrote as a burgher.

26a. *Jungbluth, G.: "Heinrich Wittenwiler," in W. Stammler, *Die deutsche Literatur des Mittelalters—Verfasserlexikon* (Berlin, 1953), IV, 1037-41. Most recent evaluation of poem.

27. **Keller, Martha: *Beiträge zu Wittenwilers Ring*, Diss. Zurich (Strassburg, 1935). Written simultaneously with, and therefore partially duplicates, Item 54. Miss Keller, herself a North-Swiss, shows keen insight into *Ring* and its author.

28. Koebner, Richard: *Die Eheauffassung des ausgehenden Mittelalters*, Diss. Berlin (Berlin, 1911), Pp. 59-65. Not available to reviewer.

29. **Kraft, Walter C.: *The Phonology of Wittenwiler's Ring*, Berkeley Diss., 1951, microfilm. Only linguistic study devoted to *Ring*. Proves that *Ring* was written in High Alemannic dialect and later copied by Bavarian scribe.

30. **Martini, Fritz: "Heinrich Wittenwilers 'Ring'," *Deutsche Vierteljahrschrift*, 20 (1942), Pp. 20-35. Discusses Wittenwiler's intent. Finds his "real" world to be fictitious contrast to ideal he is teaching, except for occasions when it gets out of hand and exists for its own purpose. Discusses Wittenwiler's *Humor* with results contrary to those in Item 18. Wittenwiler recognizes positive value of life in this world, provided one lives rationally and listens to instruction. His apparent other-worldly religiosity stems more from convention than conviction.

31. *Martini, Fritz: *Das Bauerntum im deutschen Schrifttum von den Anfängen bis zum 16. Jahrhundert* (Halle, 1944), Pp. 179-95. Maintains that peasants in *Ring* stem more from literary tradition than from observation and are allegorical symbols of human folly. Difficult literary style for non-Germans.

32. Mayser, Eugen: "Briefe im mittelhochdeutschen Epos," *ZfdPh*, 59 (1934-35), Pp. 145-47. Discusses love-letters in *Ring*.

33. Müller, Günther: "Der Ring. Bilder aus der schweizerischen Renaissance-dichtung I," *Schweizerische Rundschau*, 27 (1927), Pp. 782-94. This and following two items treat *Ring* as a product of the Renaissance, rather than of the waning Middle Ages.

34. Müller, Günther: *Deutsche Dichtung von der Renaissance bis zum Ausgang des Barock, Handbuch der Literaturwissenschaft* (Leipzig, 1927), Pp. 73-74.

35. Müller, Günther: *Deutsches Dichten und Denken vom Mittelalter zur Neuzeit* (Berlin, Leipzig, 1934), *Sammlung Göschen*, Pp. 103-05.

36. Nadler, Josef: "Wittenweiler?" *Euphorion*, 27 (1926), Pp. 172-84. Maintains that *Ring* was written by two authors and finds allusions to current political events. Principle thesis discredited by Item 50.

37. Nadler, Josef: *Literaturgeschichte der deutschen Schweiz* (Leipzig, 1932), Pp. 74-79, 508. Repeats thesis of Item 36 without reference to rebuttal in Item 50.

38. Nordmeyer, H.: "Heinrich Wittenwilers Ring," *MLN*, 48 (1933), Pp. 415-16. Favorable review of Item 2.

39. Pfeiffer-Belli, W.: *Mönche und Ritter, Bürger und Bauern im deutschen Epos des Spätmittelalters* (Frankfurt, 1934), Pp. 46-59, 78-79, 115 ff.

40. Scherrer, Gustaf: *Kleine Toggenburger Chroniken* (St. Gall, 1874), Pp. 112-132. Cites several documents bearing name of Heinrich Wittenwil used in Items 40, 52, and elsewhere.

41. Schultz, Alwin: *Deutsches Leben im XIV. und XV. Jahrhundert, Grosse Ausgabe* (Wien, 1892), Pp. 163-69. Excellent illustrations suitable for *Ring*. However, accompanying text shows naive acceptance of items of social satire as factual evidence of real peasant life.

42. **Singer, Samuel: *Literaturgeschichte der deutschen Schweiz im Mittelalter* (Bern, 1916), Pp. 28-30, 52. Brief but excellent description of *Ring*. Reveals keen insight.

43. Singer, Samuel: *Neidhart-Studien* (Tübingen, 1920), Pp. 26 f., 41-45. Relates *Ring* to Neidhart tradition.

44. Singer, Samuel: *Schweizerdeutsch. Die Schweiz im deutschen Geistesleben*, ed. H. Maync, Vol. 58, (Frauenfeld & Leipzig, 1928), Pp. 86-88. Linguistic comments, superseded by Item 29.

45. Singer, Samuel: *Die mittelalterliche Literatur der Schweiz, Ibid.* Vols. 66 & 67, Pp. 125-29, 187, 201. Interesting comparison of Wittenwiler and Rabelais.

46. Strauch, Phillip: "Epos," *Jahresberichte für neuere deutsche Literaturgeschichte*, II, (1891), II, 3, P. 159. Unfavorable criticism of Item 6.

47. Uhland, Ludwig: "Zur schwäbischen Sagenkunde: 2. Dietrich von Bern," *Germania*, I (1856), Pp. 329-335, also in *Schriften zur Geschichte der deutschen Dichtung und Sage* (J. G. Cotta, Stuttgart, 1873), VIII, Pp. 368-375. Meritorious in its time, but now obsolete.

48. Wielandt, F.: "Der 'Ring' und Meister Heinrich von Wittenwil," *Bodenseebuch*, (1934), Pp. 19 ff. Calls attention to advocate of Constance as possible author of *Ring*.

49. **Wiessner, Edmund: "Das Gedicht von der Bauernhochzeit und Heinrich Wittenwilers 'Ring'," *ZfdA*, 50 (1908), Pp. 245-79. Convincing evidence that Wittenwiler's chief source was "Metzi's Wedding," which in turn was based on the shorter "Mair Betz." His comparisons give insight into Wittenwiler's method of using his source material. See Items 8 and 35.

50. *Wiessner, Edmund: "Heinrich Wittenwiler: Der Dichter des 'Ringes'," *ZfdA*, 64 (1927), Pp. 145-60. Crushing refutation of Item 36. Valuable observations and resumé of *Ring*.

51. *Wiessner, Edmund: "Neidhart und das Bauernturnier in Heinrich Wittenwilers Ring," *Festschrift für Max H. Jellinek* (Wien & Leipzig, 1928), Pp. 191-208. Valuable information on "Neidhart-tradition" and "mock-tournament" tradition.

52. Wiessner, Edmund: "Urkundliche Zeugnisse über Heinrich von Wittenwil," *Festgabe für Samuel Singer*, ed. H. Maync (Tübingen, 1930), Pp. 98-114. Documentary evidence gathered to prove Wittenwiler's identity. See Items 26 and 56.

53. **Wiessner, Edmund: Introduction to Edition (Item 2). Best single interpretation and explanation of *Ring*. Very compact.

54. **Wiessner, Edmund: *Kommentar zu Heinrich Wittenwilers Ring, Deutsche Literatur, Reihe IV, Realistik des Spätmittelalters*, Sup. to Vol. III (Leipzig, 1936). The definitive study as of its date, compilation of all previous scholarship and of Wiessner's own contributions. Numerous German and Latin parallels, but no French or English ones. Very compact and not easily accessible to laymen, particularly in regard to bibliographical references.

55. Wiessner, Edmund: " 'Metzen Hochzeit' und Heinrich Wittenwilers 'Ring'," *ZfdA*, 74 (1937), Pp. 65-72. Crushing rebuttal of Item 8.

56. Wiessner, Edmund: "Heinrich Wittenwiler," *ZfdA*, 84 (1952), Pp. 159-171. Gives linguistic and other evidence against advocate of Constance (See Item 48) as author of *Ring*.

APPENDIX IV

INDEX AND NAME-LIST

*Engeldrauden. v. 2644.
**Engelmar, a name common in peasant satire. v. 2630.
ére. #162 ff.
**Erenfluoch (Curse-honor). v. 2644.
**Eselpagg (Donkey-fight? Donkey-jaw?). v. 6698, #95.
Eustace, a married saint. v. 3410, #189.
exaggeration, hyperbole. #64.
Fach, Vach (Catch), name of cat. v. 5480.
**Fallinstro (Fall-in-straw). v. 5336.
**Farindkuo (Enter-cow). v. 2630, #97.
**Farindwand (Run-into-the-wall). v. 5341.
*Feina, dim. of Josephina. v. 2646.
Ferrara, home of lavish margrave. v. 3379, #6.
**Fesafögili (Steal-fowl). v. 2633.
Fettringen, place name. v. 6959.
fish, a food for lords. v. 2906, #106.
**Fladenranft (Cow-pie). v. 6630, #90.
Flanders, home of wild boars. vv. 1083, 1163. cf. v. 6389.
fleas. #93.
**Fleugenschäss (Fly-shit). v. 7158.
fly, instead of grasshopper in Aesop's fable. v. 5007.
folklore. #124 ff.
**Föllipruoch (Drop-the-trousers). v. 2643, #98.
**Fülizan (Foal's tooth?, Decayed tooth?, lecherous person? Cf. "colt's
   tooth). v. 6698, #94.
**Füllenmagen (Fill-the-belly). v. 3705.
**Fützenpart (Vulva-beard). v. 7158, #96.
Fützenswil (Vulva-town), place name, play on Bütschwil? v. 6964.
Gadubri, a real or fictitious place name. v. 6961.
**Gaggsimachs (Stutterer?, Defecator?). v. 7154.
Gaigenhofen, place name. v. 6960.
**Galgenschwank (Gallows-bird). v. 5315.
gall. earth-gall, v. 2225; honey out of gall, v. 2076.
Gawain, knight of the Round Table. v. 8025, #76.
*Geri. v. 1150.
*Gerwig. v. 5317.
gifts of the Holy Ghost. v. 2273.
Giggenfist (Chicken-fart), said to dwarf Laurin. v. 8878.
Glarus, Swiss Canton. v. 5300, #4.
gloves, a gift, v. 7579; symbol of nobility, #114.
**Gnaist (Skinflint). v. 7153.
**Gnepferin (One who hops or limps). v. 5330, #95.
Golias, a giant. v. 7988, #77.
**Grabinsgaden (Dig in the chamber, i.e. vulva). v. 148, #96.
**Grämpler (Retailer). v. 7155.
Grausen, fictitious valley. v. 55, #45.
**Gredul, Gredel, dim. of Margaret, a girl of all work. vv. 2644, 5327, #177.
Greeks, as cowards. v. 7895.
green and red lines. #150a.
Gretzingen, place name. v. 8631.
**Gugginsnest (Peek-in-the-nest), a chicken-thief? a peeking-Tom? v. 5320.
**Guggoch (Fool? Cuckold?). v. 5334.
**Gumpost (Cumpost, a peasant dish). v. 2631, #106.
**Gumprecht, a common peasant name. v. 7156.
gunpowder, a clue to age of Ring. #5.
**Gunterfai (Counterfeit, imitation). v. 181.
**Hächel (a witch?). v. 3762. Hächel, the leader of the witches. v. 7995.
**Hafenschlek (Gulp-the-oats). v. 2635, #108.
Hagen, the miller's ass, named after grim hero of Nibelungenlied. v. 493,
   #101.
Haini (dim. of Henry) von Gretzingen, a warrior. v. 8633.
*Haintzo (dim. of Henry). v. 127.

Mayday, maypole, #11.
memento mori, vv. 4098 ff, 4158 ff.
**Metz, Metzi, Metzli, v. 75, #96.
"Metzi's Wedding," a source of *Ring*, #9.
Metzendorf, Mätzendorf, fictitious village, v. 8037. See Metz.
miller, dishonest, #120.
milk pail, escutcheon of Switzers, v. 7965.
minstrels, #117, 118.
mirror broken at dance, v. 5634, #17, 100.
mock-confession, vv. 658 ff.
mock-tournament, vv. 105 ff.
Montalban, home of Gawain, v. 8025.
**Nabelreiber (Navel-rubber), v. 1645.
**Nagenflek (Gnaw-the-spot, i.e. vulva), v. 2635, #96.
Narrenheim (Foolsville), #19.
Necker, river near Lappenhausen, v. 5912, #4.
Neidhart, peasant-hating squire, v. 158, #15, 16, 20.
*Nickel, Niggel (dim. of Nicholas), v. 2633.
Nidrentor (Lowgate), comical place name. v. 7275.
Nienderthaim (Nowhere-home), comical place name. v. 7272.
**Niemandsknecht (No one's servant), v. 7154.
**Nimindhand (Take-in-hand), v. 3627. Cf. Rüerenzumph.
Nissingen (Peasant-land), a village, v. 5305.
Nissfeld, fictitious battle-field, v. 7582.
Noah's unequal children, vv. 7236 ff., #174.
Nürggel, derogatory name given to Laurin, v. 8688.
obscenity, #82-86.
**Ochsenkäs (Ox-cheese), v. 7137, #90.
**Ochsenkropf (Ox-goiter), v. 3619, #95.
Ofen, a place name, v. 6961.
**Ofenstek (Oven-rake), 2636, #95.
*Öttel (dim. of Otto?), v. 5491.
**Packenflaisch (Grab-the-meat), v. 6692.
Packenzan, Paggenzan (Seize-the-tooth?), fictitious Swiss hero. v. 8160.
**Palstersak (Mattress-cover?), v. 5332.
parody, #73.
Pelsabuk, name of Devil, Beelzebub? v. 7906.
peasant satire, #89 ff.
*Pentz(a), dim. of Benedict, v. 144.
**Pesmenstil (Broom-stick), v. 5520.
*Peter, v. 7159.
Peuschendorf, place name, v. 7641. Identity not certain.
**Pfefferäss (Fast-as-pepper), v. 5328.
*Pilian (a cheap coin), v. 7153.
*Popphart, v. 5345. Perhaps a personal allusion.
Praettigau, a region near Toggenburg, v. 5300.
Prussia, a land without grapes, v. 2882.
**Pütreich (Lard-belly), v. 6697.
puns #71, 72.
red and green lines, #150.
recht, #167.
Reimprecht, a giant, v. 7988, #77.
Renard Fox, v. 5209.
**Reuschindhell (Rush-into-hell), v. 5340.
**Richteinschand (Cause-a-scandal), v. 3628.
**Riffian (Ruffian, villain, procurer), v. 7169. Cf. 2595.
rimes in *Ring*, #44 ff.
**Rindtaisch (Cowdung), v. 6693, #90.
Rivoglio wine (Rainvail), v. 3713.
Roland, a giant, v. 7988, #76.
"romantic" irony, #80, 81.
*Rüefli, dim. of Rudolf, v. 152.

Uri (Aurach), one of original Cantons.
*Walter, v. 7262.
**Wasserschepferin (Water-drawer, Bath-attendant), v. 5329, #121.
Wecke, Wegge, a giant, v. 7988, #77.
wild man, v. 8719, #147.
witches, #147.
Wittenwiler, #1.
works of mercy, the six, vv. 3997 ff.
**Wüetrich (Madman), v. 6696.
*Zink, Zingg, v. 6694.

FOREWORD TO "COLKELBIE SOW"

Like Wittenwiler's *Ring*, the Middle Scots poem "Colkelbie Sow" survives in only one manuscript, and that one a copy. However, unlike the *Ring*, it has received almost no scholarly attention even though it has had two very satisfactory editions. While making the following translation in the winter of 1952-53, I was unaware that anything had been written about the poem except for a few brief and largely unfavorable comments and conjectures made by various historians of Scottish literature. However, upon finishing my study, I learned that the poem had been included the previous summer in an unpublished Edinburgh dissertation by Earl F. Guy titled *Some Comic and Burlesque Poems in Two Sixteenth Century Scottish Manuscript Anthologies*. Since Dr. Guy intended to publish, I agreed to give him priority by withholding my own study. Nevertheless, he was advised not to let me see his dissertation in the meanwhile.

After waiting some three years, I decided to proceed independently. Now, having at last acquired a microfilm of Dr. Guy's work, I discover that there is very little duplication of effort, other than lexicographical, since his annotations to "Colkelbie Sow" are not extensive. Only about one tenth of his pages are devoted to this poem, and these include a complete text. Moreover, he has treated the work largely as a "comic and burlesque" poem, whereas I treat it as a religious allegory in comic disguise. My deviations from Dr. Guy's glossary are summarized at the end of the notes to my exposition.

I am publishing this translation along with Wittenwiler's *Ring* because the two works have many traits in common and because much that is obscure in the Scottish poem can be clarified through comparison with the longer and less obscure Swiss work. This is particularly true of the serious intent professed by the two authors in their prefaces. Studied in a vacuum, the shorter poem does not appear to be serious, whereas the serious intent of the *Ring* can not be questioned. Therefore, in view of the similarities in the two poems, the presence of serious intent in the one confirms the possibility or even probability of serious intent in the other. Likewise, many items of social satire that are briefly reflected in "Colkelbie Sow" appear in greater detail and clarity in the *Ring*.

The following translation appears as originally written, except for many valuable criticisms and suggestions made in the summer of 1953 by Professors Francis Lee Utley and Bartlett Jere Whiting, to whom I am most indebted for their generous aid.

PROHEMIUM

Here begins Colkelbie Sow

When most royal, revered, high, praiseworthy crowned Kings in majesty, elegant princes, dukes, marquises, chivalrous earls, barons, and knights, and gentlemen of high genealogy, such as shield bearers and squires full courtly, are gathered and seated at a royal court with famous folk of high nobility, on such occasions their honorable talk at table before amiable lords and ladies is often singing and tales of solace (where melody is the mirthful mistress): martial deeds done in ancient days, chronicles, gests, stories, and much more. Minstrels among musicians merrily move hearts into heavenly harmony. So it seems well that it should always be truly thus. What is the world without pleasure or play but suffering? So let us make some sport and recreation in order to comfort this company.   P. 20*

Would my lords like to ask who will begin it, who first exhibit it, or who first become involved in it? Who, with your judicious correction, but I who have begun this matter now? For what profits a beginning without an end? It is like a blossoming tree, whose fruit fails. Mindful of this, every man, whatever his station be, should ever pay heed not to begin by blossoming and then decrease. If, as life grows longer, one's good fame then ends, what shall be said but that at his ending he declined from a fair sapling to a withered tree? The life is gone, the lasting praise is lost; the beginning, they say, was but a boast.   P. 34

Wherefore, you men most honorable in all respects, who would enjoy eternal memory, conduct yourselves that first your God will be pleased, and win fame and respect when you die. And if anyone will not, according to his goodly power and considering his station, go profess himself a martyr or suffer reproach, may he be likened to a fair blossom faded on a faulty tree. This simile would apply to me if I should begin to sport and not draw a moral conclusion. Then all of you would quickly say, "Look at him over there, who set out to tell a jest and left it in a mess."   P. 46

Therefore I will tell you out of my imagination some entertainment to please this company. But for the love of God and His apostle Peter, pardon the foolish appearance of this mad

---

* Verse 20 of the Prohemium.

meter. Since its meaning is fantastic to understand, let the letter and language be similar. Since all the world changes so many faces, I trust I will add event upon event. And so let us see which episode you think most foolish (the most foolish way of doing a thing sometimes contains wisdom) so that it will be discreet sport without cruel invidious comparison. Personal malice and all such thing being removed, the most foolish matter is sometimes proved to be the wisest. Wherefore, knowing my own insufficiency to be accounted a prudent practitioner, I propose, not as a presumptuous manner of doing it, but rather as sport, to rejoice my own spirit and that of my lords who will deign to listen. Now I begin with the conclusion.

The prohemium ends and the first part follows.

PART ONE

Here I tell you a story. Once there was a merry man called
Colkelbie. He had a simple black sow and he sold her without
delay for three pence, as you will see later. And verily, as I
heard, he spent the money thus. The first penny of the three
he gave for a girl, the second fell in a ford, and the third he hid
in a hoard. Now which of the three pennies do you think was
best bestowed? The lost penny was recovered and the girl
pleased for a time; but the penny that was hidden did the least
good, I believe; for in an old proverb we sing, "Little good comes
of gathering where miserly avarice burns, hiding treasures into
corners, without knowing for whom and letting honor go astray."
It is great trouble to acquire wealth, and it is fear to keep it
and more vexation to lose it. I find these three perverse prop-
erties in parsimonious hoarding and avaricious gain, where
moderation is not mistress but a gathering for greediness. It
seems to me the hidden penny was the worst bestowed of the
three, for it was not at man's use. So let go the world's goods
with moderation and mirth.   I 37

Yet there is more of this story. The penny lost in the stream
was found and recovered; and he who found it bought with the
same penny for his profit a little pig from Colkelbie's sow. A
harlot lived nearby, and she wanted to give a banquet; but she
had no substance at all. Therefore she stole this poor pig to
furnish a great feast, without any food except this beast. I 50

And yet she called to her board an apostate friar, a wayward
pardoner, a professional palmer, a witch, a weaver, a scoundrel,
a sponger, a fond fool, a ferryman, a carter, a carrier, a hog-
gelder, a liar, a sieve-stealer, a talebearer, a scandalmonger, a
false flatterer, a vagrant falconer, an ill-favored miller, a bear-
keeper, a brawler, an ape-leader, a cursed customs collector, a
gossiper, a tinker, and many others at that time of every wicked
order, with a foolish flowering at first, an old monk, a lecher, a
drunken loiterer, a double tongued counselor, a cheat, a trick-
ster, a hangman, a gambler, a ruffian, a torturer, a deceiver, a
gossiper, a false necromancer, a jester, a juggler, a widow who
loves only for money, a murderer, a paragon of evil women (sour
in all their appearance), with a troublesome neighbor, a lunatic,
a schismatic, a heretic, a pickpocket, a money-changer, a Lollard,
a usurer, a vagabond minstrel, a hypocrit in Holy Church, a
barn-burner in the dark, a mariner on sea and sand who takes

charge of life and property and knows neither course nor tide yet is presumptuous in pride, doing nothing expertly in knowing compass or chart, a scamp, a scorner, a scold, a bawd, a procuress, a worthless graybeard, a ribald, a ruffian, a murderer of loyal men, a ravisher of women, and with them two learned men: Sir Usury and Sir Simony. Still many more stood around in a great crowd for lack of room.   I 107

Now I would like to ask who at this feast got the best share of this pig? I think the folk fared best who were standing far outside of the door, away from this cursed company and indecorous feast. Yet there is more of this story: the poor pig gave a roar when, to kill him, they pained him so sorely that the wretched pig squealed until the swine thereabout rushed forth in a great troop. I do not care now to discuss or to make heraldic descriptions of the diverse natures, temperaments, and colors of all animals: which ones the law permits us to eat or which ones should be no man's food (nor of the fowls of the air), how some fare with closed feet and some with cloven hoofs (nor of the fishes with their scales). All this I set aside now.   I 130

Let us get back to Colkelbie's sow; for, to say the truth, swine are loving animals, contrary to the nature of dogs. For, if dogs brawl at the door, they all set upon the sorry hound that is always lying on the ground. And he that cries most and roars is overthrown, beaten, and most damaged. All the remainder pull at him, some by his legs and some by his ears. They are loving to men, but not to each other; for woe is to him who falls down. But this is not so with swine: if one of them is overthrown so that his cry may be heard, all the rest that hear come as best they can to rescue him if they may.   I 150

So they did this day, in such fashion that I never heard of sows' sons winning such great glory for ever. On account of Stiftapill all the flock rushed out with a roar. When they heard this pig they came grunting up very grimly. Many a long-toothed boar and many a shoat came forth, and many a great aged hog grunted and gambolled: Wrotok and Writhneb, Hoggy ever on the tidal flats, with the spotted Hoglyn, Suelly, Suattis, Swankyn, Baymell bred in the bog, hog hopped over hog, Madge of the mill hill, Grom Gym of the glen, the filthy sow and the dirty, Red Kit that often roared, Patypull of the Pappourtis and Knutknot of the Kuppourtis, the grey, the grisly, and the grim. Hurlheckill hobbled with him, Sigill Wrigill our sow, great

Boar Tusky the gruesome, many a shoat and many a young sow
came to keep the pig from being killed. I 179

With bristling backs there ran out far more than I can count,
with such a din and dither, a tumult and hirdy-girdy, that the
fools were frightened and the harlot was hurt there with Boar
Tusky's tooth. And to say the very truth, in that cruel affray
the little pig got away; and every boar and every beast trampled
on the fools at the feast. Some were mocked, maimed, and
marred; and thus they were scared from the food. Isn't this
a foolish incident? Yet it became a far worse one. I 195

A new trouble and noise arose with a clamor so that, to define
the incident, it might be called a tempest; for all the swine's
owners said, "Upon my word! How the fools are carrying on!"
And they see so cursed a company, hearing their own swine cry
in conflict with these rascals, afraid the fools had caught them
in order to steal them away. Then din and confusion arose.
Stock-horns blew vigorously. Many a one issued out: Gilby
on his gray mare, and Fergy on his fair sow held Hodge Higgin
by the hand, and Symie who was sunburned, with his lad Lowry
and his gossip Glowry. I 215

Fergy passed to the front, and Finny followed him closely.
Thurlgill grabbed for a club so fiercely he flew into a puddle
until Downy pulled him back. Then Rany of the Red Ravine
with Gregory the tenant, for the love of his sweetheart, lightly
jumped at a brook; he failed and fell in. And Hodge was so
hasty that he splashed past him, until Toby the carrier pulled
him to land with a sheep crook. The shepherds pushed on to
land, and Fergy Flitsy rushed in front, leader of that main
attack, a tar bucket on his back, with his lad Luddroun and his
hound Hunddroun. Many a shepherd was with him from brooks,
banks, and streams. Their banner, of two crooked ramhorns,
was borne on a birch stick, with Barmybeard their standard-
bearer and his cousin Cachcran. I 241

Their minstrel Dick Doyt went in front with a flute. Then
Doby Drymouth danced "The sun shone in the south;" and,
when they looked upon a meadow, they saw another crowd.
Then they all fled very much afraid, with the master shepherd
Fergy Flitsy out in front, although it was little to his advantage:
his feet made such a din that he lacked breath for running. I 253

"How!" quoth Hobby. "Listen to me! We need not flee any
further. Those folk are our own friends, I know by their ban-
ner." They had never been half so happy and gladly turned

around and knew by their array that they were all cowherds who
had issued forth to the hue and cry.   And their banner was
borne past: the tail of Crumhorn the cow fastened on a long
flail.   In addition, I trust, their captain was called Colyn
Cuckow; and Davy Doyt of the dale was their mad minstrel.
He blew on a pipe that he had made of a bored elder tree.   Beside
him Waytscath danced a dandy.   I 273

He saw the third fellowship that they very well knew: the
swineherds in a crowd. And Sweirbum with his snout was captain
of them there.   And his banner was borne unfurled on a shovel:
a spotted many colored pigskin tied high with flail straps.   Who
bore it but Botgy?   And Clarus, tall and awkward, played on a
bagpipe.   Haggyshead and Helly, Ballybrass and Belly danced
and his son likewise.   I 288

Then all assembled with a game, and all the minstrels blew
their bagpipes up at once and played on that occasion.   Shep-
herds, cowherds, and swineherds rushed out to dance merrily.
A master swineherd Swanky and his cousin Copyn Cull, foul
with crammed bellies, led the dance and began, "Play us 'Pretty
Sweetheart'!"   Some trotted "Tras and Trenass," some clumsily
danced the "Base," some "Perdowy," some "Trolly Lolly," some
"Cock, crow thou until day," "Taysbank and Ternway," some
"Lincoln," some "Lindsay," some "Lovely sweetheart, dawns it
not day?"   Some sing "By yon woodside," some "Late, late in
the evening," some "Handsome Martin with a jeer," some
"Lulalow, little cock."   Some bowed, some scraped, some curtsied,
some stooped.   Some danced "Most make revelry," some "Simon
sons of Whinefell," some "Master Peter of Conyate," and some
others dressed fancifully to dance at leisure: some "Overfoot,"
some "Orleance," some "Rusty bully" with a bow and every note
in other's neck.   I 320

Some were accustomed to consider the dances of Cyprus and
Bohemia, some very eagerly the steps of Portugal and Navarre.
Some imitated the way of Spain, some of Italy, some of Germany.
Some sang forthwith the dances of Naples, some others those
of Aragon.   Some contrived the dances of the Khan of Tartary,
and some all those of the Sultan of Syria, some of Prester John of
great India, some as the Ethiopians do.   I 333

Some danced and some refused.   Some had many more dances,
with all the dances of Asia, some of Africa's antiquity and prin-
cipally of Carthage.   There pressed in Perry Pull and, with their
bellies very full, Master Myngeis the Mangeis, Master Tyngeis la

Tangeis, Master Totis la Toutis, and rugged Rottis the Routis, Master Nykkis la Nakkis and Sir Jakkis la Jakkis, the Hary-hurlerehusty, and Calby the cursed rascal. Many lads and many louts, knobby-kneed bastards, rascals, rogues, brawlers, and knaves crowded in and danced in droves. With them Towis the Mowis and Harry with the red hose.   I 354

Then, all arrayed in a ring, they danced "My dear darling." And all agreed in a troop to the manner of Europe; for they believed so firmly that they were experienced and well proved in the Orient as is briefly related here. They included the simple manner of the islands in the ocean and of the mainland of France, and how the Emperor dances, and of the Swiss in Swabia long ago, and also of the Rhine River, of the broad island of Britain, of Ireland and Argyle, Burgundy and Brabant, Hainault and Holland, Flanders, Frisia, and also Brandenburg and Brunswick, Dithmarsch and Bavaria, Prussia, Poland, and Pomerania, Lübeck, Lund, and Lüneburg, Marstrand and Mecklenburg, the seventy-seven Hanseatic cities and all their boundaries with them, Reval and Russia, Sclavia and Gotland, Denmark and Norway.   I 383

All their dances and play they performed in their mad pantomime; and they failed in their dancing. Because their minstrels were confused, their instruments fell in tone. And all their plain poor thoughts could not perform any of the dances, except for such things as appertain to herdsmen and their manners; for they had heard speak of good men but understood little of that and rushed forth headlong. A Copyn Cull could lead them; and so they thought they danced well and did it without knowledge and merely pranced and, when they had all finished, it was a chattering out of tune. Then they began to quarrel until Horlorhusty shouted, "Cease this brawling and uproar! Remember why you came here!" Every knave and every rogue understood Horlorhust to be a wise and commendable man; and thus they ended their dancing. And thus concluding, they went to their masters just as quickly to rescue the poor pig.   I 411

All have met loyally together. By then there were assembled on earth as many as they wanted. Lord God, how loud they cried! They defied the fools very often and rushed together against them at once, and there was a breaking of bones! Behold how high was higher. They chased with a fresh courage and fell on the aforementioned sots and overthrew all the idiots, both the swine and the men.   I 423

By this you may well know that folly is no wisdom; for a crowd in disorder seldom has the palm of victory, unless God and good wit guide them. And all this great brawling, babbling, and other things were for a pig, as you heard said; yet he escaped unslain. Now judge as you wish about this; for this is but a fantasy and a little point of poetry, and sport to make us merry. And yet this is a strange tale.   I 437

But afterward this pig grew into a mighty boar. Lo! Such is the glory of the world: now low, now high, we see nothing stable in this world of variance. Yet a new adventure and fortune occurred. When this pig was a boar, he grew matchless in strength so as to fight for vainglory with antelope or elephant, tiger, leopard, or panther, bull, wolf, or wild bear, with the awful unicorn or any beast that was born; for he fought bravely with Wade and with mad Meleager. He battled at close quarters with adventurous Hercules and he was hunted in the plain in front of the Goddess Diana; yet he escaped unharmed and killed hounds in the chase. The rich king of Sidon and all his knights were afraid of this boar. Formerly he lived there and gave strange battle to Eglamour of Artois. The ugly dragon never prospered so well while this bold boar was alive, nor the dragon in the Holy land either, as I understand.   I 470

Isn't it a strange fact that this pig was first so poor and that in so many dangers he escaped with good fortune? You may understand by this narration that much often comes of little. I consider it unwise to scorn a small foe while he has grace to ride or walk at liberty and in freedom, or, for love of pennies, to let honor perish. And thus ends the tale of the penny that was spent, that grew to such great fame. Parsimonious spending harms wellborn people. Thus I have told you a tale to give you entertainment; for excessive meditation may sometimes cause melancholy. Therefore, to make us merrier, my fantasy fared thus. And I beg your pardon for all this hirdy-girdy and confusion.   I 494

The end

PART TWO

Because of these mocking meters and mad matter, your high reverence, I again humbly request that all the hearers pardon with patience my mischievous noises, foolishness, and carelessness. And to make amend for my aforesaid simple story, in recompense for it, I shall now write of the second penny, the expenditure for the girl, how it did thrive that was half lost for a while.   II 8

A year later, while walking for his pleasure by a river, Colkelbie saw an old blind man come with a pretty maid. I believe she was not more than twelve years of age; but, to tell the truth, she was not like an earthly creature, so wonderfully fair she was, so well nurtured as if she had been reared in a cloister or court, as daughter to king or queen. Innocently she knelt before this rough man, this aforementioned Colkelbie. Yet, to tell the very truth of it, he was a man of both substance and wisdom; and he said, "Daughter, have God's blessing and mine." The old man asked, "Le pour amour divin, charité;" and he said, "Father, come to my house."   II 23

He took him home and gave him fair alms and intently inquired where he had got that fair innocent goodly maid, and to say whether she were his daughter or kin. He said, "Truly, she is neither, by my faith; but a palmer, a respectable man he was, an alien who had come from beyond the sea with his own wife, a blessed creature, lodged with me, although I am poor; and through the will of God, so as it was, they were visited with sudden sore sickness and died of it both within an hour. This little maid, this tender creature was their daughter and remained with me, who leads me now, since I myself cannot see."   II 38

Colkelbie said, "I believe it is so. But no matter from what country those people came, it seems that they were of very powerful family, to judge by the demeanor of this innocent daughter. But, good Father, if only you would agree to let the maid remain here with me for the sake of her good name. I would advise you otherwise, except that you will have a boy of mine to lead you."   II 46

The blind man said, "Three sons I have at home; and, were I there, I would crave no more guiding. The maid has been with me for a long time; if you take her, I should be better off." II 50

Colkelbie said, "I had three round pennies. The first was

once lost in a stream and found, and it bought a pig, which some call a gryce, which grew to high fame and praise. So marvelously many men report of him: he was the cause of many wonderful deeds, as his legend bears witness, let him look who wishes. The second I have here in my fist, and one lies in a hoard. This is the story about them. Indeed, I hold these two pennies together. The said second penny I shall give you for this young maid, if both you and she wish, with my favors to come in time also." They agreed, and thus I let them go. II 65

This Colkelbie reared her in his house; she grew so fair and very virtuous, so gentle in all her actions and docile and sober in service and amiable, that all who saw her loved her as their life, and especially this Colkelbie's wife, a praiseworthy woman in her house. They called her by name Bellamorous. Between her and her husband Colkelbie they had a son called Flannislie. Gallant he was and good in all his behavior, and of all men by far the best archer in any land, right praiseworthy and wise, big of bones and a man strong in strategy. And, as his father and mother often noticed, he studied this young lass attentively in his thoughts with steadfast contemplation, her most pleasing perfect pure person, her fresh figure beautiful with respect to form and face, given to all good, full of God's grace, so that, of all bounty and beauty that could be, she had enough worthy components. He loved her so well that there was no other; but, with consent of friends, father, and mother, he wedded her to wife, know ye, for ever. This amiable innocent girl was called Adria by name. To tell the very beginning of it, this occurred in France before it became very strong, plenished, and populous where the city of Paris is now situated. II 94

This Colkelbie lived there where the incident occurred of the pig, fools, and all that was told before, until one time that the high king of France rode, to inspect the boundaries of his realm, to the place there where Colkelbie dwelled, a man of provisions who dealt with such things because no one could grow grain. That powerful king lodged at his inn; and on the next day they proclaimed a great shooting match, where Flannislie won the victory over all. The king saw him to be so big a man and strong and goodly too that, to delay you no longer, he made him a squire for his body. And in his wars he conducted himself so well he was made a knight at court with inherited rank. II 109

And then he sent for his fair true lady, Dame Adria, whom the king appointed to attend upon the queen in her chamber.

Best beloved and most perfect was she because of her demeanor and beauty and goodness above all the rest of the ladies who were there. And Flannislie bore himself so well in wars that the king later made him a royal earl and gave him by seal, inheritable for ever, a corner of a separate country as it lay, then found uninhabited, which he furnished with people and policy and named after himself and his lady: this is to say, Flannislie and Adria. His whole earldom he called Flandria, "flan" from the first syllable of Flannislie, and "dria" taken from Adria the generous, the which famous earldom of Flanders has ever been a fief of France and the Twelve Peers to this day.   II 128

Thus great grace came from the second penny, and, with your correction, I call this a tale. I did not read this in authentic history, I learned it from a very old woman, my great grandmother. Men called her Gurgunnald. She knew the lives of many old ancestors, notable gests of peace and wars in history, fresh in her mind and recent of memory, notwithstanding that she was well set in old age. Her age, I believe, held and saw some seven score of winters. But to tell the truth, I believe there was not a tooth in her head! Therefore she ate gruel most greedily; and her lack of teeth so impaired her faculties that few could understand her mumbling mouth, save me, who was experienced therein from youth. Then I would say she had great grace of God.   II 145

"Why so, my son?" quoth she, and made a nod.

"Madame," quoth I, "for there are many women who never thrive because of their abundant speech. And I would exchange, if it might be at my judgment, all the teeth in their head for a good tongue. Then they would not be named, as you are now, scolds, and bawds, and thereby be injured and disgraced."

Then she got angry and said, "By St. John, you frivolous boy, you intend much sorrow and will do more if you remain alive."

"Madame," quoth I, "I do it in your interest."   II 156

Then she would try to beat me angrily, but it was well for me she could not run or rise. And I would up and whisk away full wild. Then she would coax, "Come in again, my child; and you will have, see, standing there on the shelf, wheat bread and cream preserved for myself." Then she set me to learn little at the school, to be neither a wise man nor a fool. And often with punishment she made me report on her stories.   II 166

And, in short, to draw a moral conclusion, she said, "My son, by this tale you should learn five bits of wisdom. And the first of them all is to consider the folly of fools. Put together they increase and multiply. They may never more bear fruit in felicity: their ignorance requires that it not be so. My son, you will comprehend proof and evidence from the aforementioned fools that they had a poor pig in their possession and firmly determined to kill the same and make a feast of it. And afterwards they were overthrown, most and least, by miserable swine, being afraid of their grunting, until the pig broke from them with a start. And later the knaves overcame them with a cry. Therefore, for the first bit of advice, keep yourself from such foolish folly and fellowship.   II 183

"The second is, if you will learn it, my son: always assume that poverty may prevail, if it be righteous, against men of great power who are not wise but wrongful in their deeds, in case at times they vex you when you are in want. Son, as an example, witness this pig that was caught in the fools' assault and was to be killed but was certainly recovered again to such great grace, as is previously mentioned. Therefore, my son, do not leave your good cause at the appearance of dangers and peril; for, if you are just, God will be your judge in all perils and deliver you well. And, once the danger is passed, you will be as safe as you ever were, and stronger in nature to venture again in righteousness. But whosoever will cowardly hide his face in defence of his just action, when, because of such foul emotion, he trusts himself to safety, he shall be at once suppressed where the righteous shall go free from all fear. Never disdain your good cause for fear of all perils, doubt, harm, or danger. If that should be so, never would martyrdom fortify faith or win the see of Rome. Whoever keeps himself safest will slip soonest without good cause or Grace. God be your guide.   II 210

"If you wish to know the third bit of advice, my son, wherever you see great wisdom in virtuous men, though they be poor, especially old or young, do not scorn them, son, and behold why: This maid, this little girl, this poor Adria was left, when young, fatherless and also motherless in a foreign land; and yet the Holy Ghost lifted her up to great honor because of her wisdom and, in like manner, her lord, Earl Flannislie. Let whoever would have oppressed them because of their poverty remember now, in such eminence as they are, what they may do to their opponents. They may well requite and overthrow them entirely. Never despise wise virtue in poor people.   II 224

"The fourth bit of wisdom is: Never let your penny or the

world's riches be your master, my son; for a little thing well
spent may increase to high honor, respect, and great riches, as
did these two pennies well spent on the pig and the poor damsel.
I don't need to be more loquacious about them; you already know
how they prospered.   Therefore do not esteem pennies as overly
precious, but allow them to be spent in prospering and service-
able fashion.   In truth, sometimes you may spend a penny that
may well profit you till your life's end.   Therefore, my son,
if you hope to endure, spend with moderation for luck, wisdom,
and moderation.   II 238

"The fifth bit of wisdom is, my son, never set your heart to
storing up treasure while suffering honor to pass by; for you
little know how soon you may slide from it slyly, or it slip from
you.   And, in any case, while it is lying in the hoard, it neither
serves the world nor multiplies; and, if you die, it is unknown to
men.   What joy do you have then in avarice?   II 246

"For which reason this man, this worthy Colkelbie, who in
all his life had only three pennies, saw two thrive well, the third
did not.   Forthwith he brought out that penny and avowed to
God with solemn word that he would never contemplate gather-
ing a treasure.   Just so, my son, I charge you to do it: Dispense
honorably and do not spare God's goods.   How little do you
know who may at some other time enjoy your wife and money-
bags after your day."   Thus Gurgunnald, my great grandmother,
instructed me; if I have misspoken in anthing, I will make
amends.   II 258

Here ends the second part.

PART THREE

And now, with your high lordships' pardon and your reverend worships' correction, I would like to tell you here of the third hidden penny. As I have told you, two bore fruit. This Colkelbie, considering well the fact that Grace never grew out of miserly avarice and having in his heart the whole experience of how the two pennies increased in value, thought he would test the third penny, which had been hidden until then and had brought no fruit or profit during that time, and allow it to go out into the world and bear fruit. And, whereas some folk might say I pass over the question of how a penny should bear fruit contrary to nature, since gold, silver and all kinds of metal refined by people vanish and do not increase, some would claim my ignorant language is lies.   III 16

But, before I wade further in this wilderness, I will clear the fact from such doubt: as long as the ore is in a natural state and not refined or forged by man's care, for so long the force of the four elements, and especially of the earth, gives it nutrition for increasing, just like herbs, stone, or tree until they are cut from their original stock and are divided from the firm ground in which they were first rooted. Then, so separated, they may not by nature bear fruit and flourish as before. Just like a beheaded man: he may do no more unless his soul, only through the Grace of God, bears fruit in spiritual joy.   III 30

So the metal, cut off by man, does not bear fruit naturally, unless human reason and God-given wisdom find the means to exalt and multiply the money in greater fame and might than ever it did while it lay in the earth. Because, as long as it lay in the ground, it was unrefined and never found as fruit. And, when it was recovered by man's wit, it was always welcome throughout the world and set in a chest and diminished a little, used and handled by men. Yet, where a mite thereof is lost, man's wit brings again a thousand pounds refined out of rough ores. The moral is that, if anyone have a talent, let him use it wisely, since often ten may grow from it.   III 46

And in short, my long legend, if anyone listens, the Gospel attests the truth of it: God's own word that took a poor penny from a foolish man who had no more at that time, and gave it to the wise man who had ten pennies counted out. But why was that? Because the foolish man would not dispose of his penny wisely but left it unused and hid it. And he that had ten used

them well. Therefore God took a penny from the unvirtuous
man and gave it to the good man who had ten. Just so, if one
has knowledge and does not use it, not pursuing its fruit closely,
but refusing it, God will give it to him who has far more. I do
not intend to gloss all day vaingloriously or to lengthen legends
that are prolix.   III 61

Therefore I turn to my first text as to explain the third
penny which was hidden until then and subsequently brought
out and managed. Grace did it as follows here, if anyone wishes
to take note of it, experienced through the ideas of Colkelbie.
As from a seed sown in the earth and dead, many fruits flourish
vivified like martyrs killed, whose merits rise as saints in
Heaven, whom sinners disappoint.   III 70

And hearken how there dwelt beside this Colkelbie a man who
was rich in wealth and cattle, where Bodyvincant Castle now
stands in the plain. Men called his wealthy neighbor Blen-
blowane. A worthy wife he had wedded, and she was called
Susan, by whom he got a son; and Colkelbie was the godfather
of the same. And he called him Colkalb as his first name. With
the said third penny Colkelbie bought twenty-four hen's eggs,
and with them he visited his godson, to remember him with a
baptismal present, as will be shown hereafter.   III 82

Susan got angry at this (as women, who know all tricks,
are often passionate for a while), and disdained this gift, this
simple thing, and said, "Gossip, take home your poor present.
Do you mean to mock my son and me? I will have no more of
it. Therefore, take it away."

He said, "I shall keep them for my godson," and he took
them home to the place where he lived and charged his henwife
to care for them and make them multiply. Then, to set them,
she took her best brood hen who was called Lady Peckle Pes,
whose lord and lover was young Cockrell. She set her on these
eggs so that in a short time she had twenty-four chickens from
them, twelve male and twelve female, according to famous
chronicles. And what they were with their names, we shall
hear: III 98

The first one, if you look, was that same Chantecleer of whom
Chaucer treats in his book, and his lady Partlot, sister and
wife, which was no life of sin at that time because folk lived
by natural laws then. The second brother was called Cock
Cademan; he took to wife his fair true sister Toppok. Cock
Crawdon was the third and his wife Coppok. And to account

for the fourth, correctly, Cock Lykouris and little Henpen his
pretty paramour. The fifth lord was Lyricok in hall, and they
called his lady Kekilcrouss. Red Kittilcok that sat on a red
cabbage head and Fekelfaw, fairest of the flock, was the sixth,
and Cock Rusty the seventh, Dame Strange his wife, who had a
stout voice. Cocky the eighth, his lady was called Lerok. Cock
Nolus the ninth espoused his sister Erok, Cock Coby the tenth,
and Sprutok his favorite; Cock Obenar the eleventh, they called
his mate Dame Julian. The twelfth was Cock Jawbert, and
Lady Wagtail his joy and all his heart.   III 120

So great a supply came from these brothers and their sisters
that I cannot say the fiftieth part myself, because they were so
fruitful. And at Shrovetide some were so belligerent that they
would bravely win for their master forty florins in the field with
bill and spurs. This Colkelbie sold some of this number, some
old, some young, some eggs in the shell, and bought therewith
other wares. And so it turned out that he increased this penny,
which was not idle for fifteen years, to more than a thousand
pounds.   III 131

Then one time he called his godson to himself before his
father and mother and all of his friends and said, "Colkalb,
my son, you will receive all these goods; for by rights they are
yours from your baptismal gift, kept through divine Grace,
from the twenty-four hen's eggs which I gave you, although your
mother, my son, would not receive them." Then he told all
the story, as you have heard it. Afterwards this Colkalb grew
to such great wealth through this penny that he became the
mightiest man in any realm. And this was accomplished then by
the penny which, first hidden in a treasure and not applied to vir-
tue and later brought forth, multiplied so greatly. Therefore, my
son, never in your life think to store up the world's wealth avari-
ciously, and do not give up hope of God's Grace.   III 147

The third penny this was, and the last story, as my grand-
mother, old Gurgunnald, told me. I claim no other authority
for this truth expressed in confusion, which seems to be an old
wives' tale. Subject to your correction, I now definitely conclude
thus. God, who redeemed us with His own blessed blood, may
He deign to save both you and me, through the humble merits
of His only Son. Amen.

Here ends the third and last part

EXPOSITION

The anonymous Middle Scots poem "Colkelbie Sow" was first mentioned in Gavin Douglas' "Palice of Honour," which appeared in 1501.[1] However, it must have been written somewhat earlier, since Douglas lists it along with several works which he assumed to be well known. Although preserved in a popular anthology and often mentioned in literary histories, the poem has remained a stepchild of scholarship, perhaps because most critics have not known what to make of this "very singular performance," as David Irving so aptly described it.[2] Whereas Guy says it is "not an allegory,"[3] I believe that this is just what it is.

Like Wittenwiler before him, the Colkelbie author assures us that his purpose is both to entertain and to instruct; yet, in view of his "mokking meteris and mad matere" (II 1),[4] it is as hard to believe in his sincerity as in that of the Swiss poet. One might argue that he was merely following a literary convention, for poets had acknowledged this dual function ever since Horace proclaimed it in his "Art of Poetry."[5] However, a careful study of CS will convince the reader that its author was really serious.

Medieval scholars were accustomed to interpret Scripture on three levels, namely those of the *littera* or vocabulary and syntax, the *sensus* or apparent meaning, and the *sententia* or deeper significance.[6] Likewise, when writing serious works, they usually wrote them to be interpreted on these same three levels. At the moment we will ignore the *littera* of CS, which is discussed in the notes wherever controversial, and concentrate on the *sensus* and *sententia*.

The *sensus* of CS is the simple narrative itself, the story of the three pennies and the adventures they produce. It is the "solasing" the poet promises for the entertainment of his audience (P 48).[4] On the other hand, the *sententia*, or "sentence," as he calls it (P 51), is the deeper moral of the story, the chief purpose and unifying factor of the whole poem.

This "sentence" is summed up in Christ's parable of the talents,[7] to which our poet alludes in Part Three (48-59), a parable teaching that we should not leave our "pennyis" buried and unused. We must realize, however, that he understood this parable on two different levels, that is, both literally and figuratively.

On the literal level he understood this "sentence" to mean that we should not hoard our wealth, but rather let it go with moderation (I 36). To prove his point, he cites the popular medieval adage that it is trouble to acquire wealth, fear to keep it, and anguish to lose it (I 25-27). He may have borrowed this idea from Robert of Brunne's *Handlyng Synne*, which expresses it similarly; but direct borrowing is not necessary since the idea was common property.[8] Perhaps its original source, like so much of the wisdom in *CS*, was in Ecclesiastes.[9]

The literal or worldly interpretation of this "sentence" can be further interpreted from what we may call an "aristocratic" or a "bourgeois" point of view. Courtly poets objected to hoarding chiefly on the grounds that it kept one from winning praise and fame, both of which depended to a large extent upon largesse, particularly to poets; and bourgeois poets objected on the grounds that buried treasure did not prosper.

Our poet subscribes to the aristocratic view on several occasions. He states that little good comes of gathering avariciously if it causes us to lose "wirchep" (I 24); and he considers it unwise to let honor perish for the sake of pennies (I 480). Since parsimonious spending harms people of gentle blood (I 485), we should never lose honor by gathering a treasure (II 240) but rather spend it in a praiseworthy or praise-winning manner (II 254).

The close relationship between generosity and good birth is suggested in the Latin word *generosus*, which covered both concepts. A similar correlation can be seen in the word *fre* as used of Adria in Part Two (126), since it meant both freeborn and generous, that is, both *liber* and *liberalis*. Liberality was a favorite theme in courtly poetry. Our poet also follows courtly tradition when he calls avarice "wrechit" (I 21, III 6), since "wretches" were originally exiles without the means of being generous. In the Middle Ages, particularly in courtly epics, gifts seem to have been judged more by their value than by the sacrifice entailed. The widow's mite was not a popular theme, at least not among minstrels.

According to the "bourgeois" interpretation of this "sentence," it means that we should not bury our treasure, because it will never multiply so long as it stays hidden (II 244). Proof of this fact furnishes the matter of Part Three of our poem; for the third penny, which had not prospered while hidden in a hoard, increased to the value of a thousand pounds as soon as it was invested. On this level the poem seems to point to a philosophy of life that Max Weber has anachronistically called the "Protestant Ethic." In this connection it is significant that Colkelbie recognizes that divine Grace caused this increase (III 136) and that he does not keep this wealth for himself but merely serves as steward for his godson (III 134).

Still on the literal level, and found in both the aristocratic and bourgeois interpretations, is the fear that a stranger will inherit your wealth when you die. This idea, although also found in Greek antiquity, seems to have derived chiefly from Ecclesiastes.[10] This dog-in-the-manger attitude was not only pardoned but even extolled by both secular and clerical writers; and it was considered a praiseworthy reason for marriage, as Wittenwiler and many other medieval poets avowed.[11] The Colkelbie poet says it is useless to save when you do not know for whom (I 23); and he advises you to spend in a praiseworthy and praise-winning way, since you little know who may enjoy your wife and goods after your day (II 255).

On a higher and more important level the talents in Christ's parable represented the word of God, which one should not fail to put to fruitful use; and this spiritual interpretation was generally accepted by the Church Fathers.[12] That our poet understood the parable thus is shown when he says that, if anyone uses a virtue wisely, ten will grow from it (III 45) and that God will take knowledge away from any man who has it but refuses to use it for fruitful ends (III 57). This "glossing" is further evidence that the author was serious in his preface. Having the knowledge, he would sin if he refused to use it by teaching a moral lesson.

In his prologue to his tale about the cock and the fox, Chaucer's Nun's Priest says, "But he that holden this tale a folye, As of a fox, or of a cok and hen, Taketh the moralite, goode men. For seint Paul seith that al that writen is, To oure doctrine it is ywrite, ywis; Taketh the fruyt, and lat the chaf be stille."[13] It is to be noted that the Colkelbie poet alludes to this tale (III 100); and it is safe to assume that he read it on a spiritual level, as Chaucer advised, and that he too believed the "fruit" of his story to be more important than the "chaff." In any case, he uses the words "fruit" and "fructify" on many occasions.[14]

A secondary and closely related moral taught by the author of CS is that you should never begin something without finishing it. To illustrate this point, he refers to the story of the

barren fig-tree cursed by Jesus[15] and says that it would apply
to him if he were to begin to sport but not "conclude" (P 44).
This story too can be interpreted on two levels,[16] as our author
so subtly does by selecting the word "conclude" instead of the
word "finish." On the literal level he means that he would be
reproved if he refused to tell his tale after suggesting the
story-telling.

However, the word "conclude" also had a theological mean-
ing of "to draw a moral conclusion,"[17] as in verse II 166. There-
fore, on a profounder level, he means that it would be wrong for
him to entertain his audience without profiting them with some
spiritual value. If he did so, he would be like a tree that blos-
soms but bears no fruit (P 26) or like a fair sapling that
withers and falls (P 32), the first image coming from the story
of the withered fig-tree and the second coming from the Epistle
of Jude.[18] This interpretation explains one of the categories
of fools attending the harlot's banquet, namely those who are
evil although they at first blossomed (I 70).

Two levels of comprehension can also be found in our poet's
reference to cloven-footed animals and fish without scales (I 120-
29). On one level, this is merely a comical allusion to the Old
Testament,[19] which forbids us to eat such unclean creatures.
However, medieval man detected deeper meaning in these pas-
sages and, ignoring them as dietary laws, continued to eat
pork and eels. The allegorical meaning of these two laws,
which was already known to Hrabanus Maurus,[20] still appears
in a note to the Douay Bible, which states: "The dividing of the
hoof and chewing of the cud, signify discretion between good
and evil, and meditating on the law of God; and where either
of these is wanting a man is unclean. In like manner fishes were
reputed unclean that had not fins and scales; that is, souls that
did not raise themselves up by prayer and cover themselves with
the scales of virtue." It is apparent that our author did not
make this allusion at random or only in a spirit of fun; for the
"unclean" animals are clearly related to those people who re-
ceive the word of God but do not follow up its fruit.

Some similar meaning is probably to be found in the com-
parison our poet makes between hogs, which aid one another,
and dogs, which do not. This is indicated by the surprising
fact that the innocent looking verse "ffor wo is him (the dog)
that has royne" (I 144) is a paraphrase of Ecclesiastes 4:10,
Vae soli, quia, cum ceciderit, non habet sublevantem se, which

was generally assumed to refer to Christ as the lifter of fallen people. Possibly this is a bit of scholarly horseplay, but a serious purpose is more likely.

Esoteric meaning may be suggested in the reference to the dragon that our boar fights in the Holy Land (I 470) and even in the name of Bodyvincant Castle (III 73), which suggests some idea like mortification of the flesh.[21] Whether or not the entire poem is a single and consistent allegory, I cannot say; but a more speculative mind than mine may well prove it to be so. In any case, it is evident that our poet, like the Nun's Priest, considered the "fruit" more important than the "chaff," the "sentence" more important than the "solasing."

In speaking of metal that has been taken from the ground, our poet says that it can multiply only if managed by human wisdom, and then only if this is the gift of God (III 33); and throughout the poem he emphasizes the necessity of divine Grace. A multitude in negligence seldom has the palm of victory unless God and good wit guide them (I 428); and he who keeps himself safest falls soonest unless he has a good cause and Grace (II 210). Colkelbie's gift to his godson prospered because it was stored through "grace devyne" (III 136), and therefore we should never lose hope of God's Grace. Adria's success is due to her being full of God's Grace (II 84); and the poet, as a child, sarcastically assured his (great-) grandmother that she has the Grace of God (II 145). His argument, however, is not very clear.

Grace is generally the cause of success; and therefore it comes as a surprise when the author, in speaking of Adria's success in becoming countess of Flanders, says, "Off the second penney thus come grit grace" (II 129). This would suggest that the penny was the cause rather than the result of Grace. If so, then in the sentence "grace it did," which is said of the third penny (III 64), the word "grace" may be the object instead of the subject. In this case, the word could not refer to divine Grace in these two passages.

Unlike Wittenwiler, the author of *CS* includes little purely utilitarian information. Instead, most of his teaching is of an edifying nature or else serves to confirm the truth of his maxims. For example, he tells us how metals can increase in their natural state even though this appears to be contrary to nature (III 19); but he does so only in order to win our credence for his argument against hoarding. This belief was accepted as a geological fact in the Middle Ages.[22]

Nevertheless, some of the conclusions drawn in *CS* do help us to conduct ourselves properly in this world. For example, the five bits of wisdom propounded by Gurgunnald (II 168-246) serve to help us get along with other men. However, nearly all of this wisdom is based on Scripture, in fact most of it is from the Book of Proverbs; and it is no coincidence that this advice, like that in its chief source, is given by an older person to a young one whom he addresses as "My son." The first maxim, "fra sic fulich foly and fellowschip keip the" (II 182), echoes Prov. 14:7 and 9:6; and the statement that fools "ryss and multeply" (II 170) suggests Prov. 29:16. The second bit of advice, "Presume nevir bot povert may prewaill, Be it rytwiss againis men of grit availl That ar not wyiss bot wranguss in their deidis" (II 185) recalls ideas repeated in Prov. 10. The expression, "the richtouss frome all feir shall go fre" (II 204) suggests Prov. 1:33 (*timore malorum sublato*).

The statement, "Quho that surest dois keip him sonest dois slyd" (II 209) echoes Matth. 16:25; and the New Testament is also reflected in the fifth "wit" in the maxim, "set nevir thy harte to mak an hurd suffering honor by start" (II 240), which suggests Matth. 6:19, 21 and Luke 12:34. The third "wit," that we should not despise people because they are poor or old or young, suggests Eccl. 4:13-14. However, in spite of these minor verbal parallels elsewhere, Gurgunnald's five "wits" derive chiefly from the thought and the spirit of the Book of Proverbs. Although our poet quotes the Bible only approximately and probably from memory, he could very likely expect his public to catch the allusions.

Perhaps the only secular lesson stressed by our poet concerns the proper place of fame, a subject that he mentions on numerous occasions. Like the court poets, he recognizes the desire for fame as a most praiseworthy incentive to effort. In his preface he advises his honorable audience, if they desire to have eternal fame, to conduct themselves such that they will please God and also obtain fame and praise (*wirschep*, P 38) when they die. As we have seen, he advises the reader not to let *wirschep* go astray through greedy hoarding (I 24); and he tells us that a little thing well spent may increase to high honor, *wirschep*, and great riches (II 228). Even the swine that rescue the little pig obtain *wirschep* (I 154); and the little pig in turn grows up to win great *priss* (I 485), which must mean about the same thing, since we are told later on that the pig increased to high *wirschep and pryss* (II 54).

Even though these last two references were jocular, the fact remains that our author considered praise and fame of positive value. On one occasion he ironically says that a person who first flourishes and then decreases will lose his lasting fame (*loss lesting*, P 33); yet he does not appear to imply that all fame is ephemeral, as so many other medieval writers did.[23] To the contrary, he seems to believe in the possibility of "eternall memoriall" (P 36).

Whereas the serious matter of the *Ring* and *CS* differ right sharply, their humor has much in common. Like Wittenwiler, the poet of *CS* loved exaggeration, grotesque name-lists, incongruous and unmotivated actions, comical situations provoking malicious joy, parody, and moral and social satire.

Typical of his exaggeration is the fact that old Gurgunnald is seven score years of age (II 137), which is precisely twice the proverbial three score years and ten. Likewise typical are the incredible number of fools who intend to dine on the one little pig, the impossible number of dances performed by the herdsmen, and the unlikely number of adventures experienced by the pig after it became a boar.

This exaggeration is related to his love of grotesque name-lists, such as those of the fools, the swine, the herdsmen and their dances, and the antagonists of the boar. The humor of these lists depends not only upon their absurdity but also upon the author's linguistic virtuosity; for he not only forces the names of the fools to alliterate but also puts many of them into sizable groups ending with the same rime. Virtuosity is also shown in the names themselves; for the author seems to have exhausted all sources, both clerical and popular. The names of the swine are of particular interest. Unfortunately they are so obscure that any attempt at translating would depend too much upon conjecture. Moreover, it is impossible to distinguish which words in the list are proper names and which are nouns, verbs, or adjectives. For example, *Rowch rumple* (I 180) could mean "headlong," or "with rough or bristling backs" (like the boars of classical literature), or else it could be the name of a hog.

Our poet also loves incongruous behavior. Just as Wittenwiler's peasants dally until midnight before giving chase to the thief in the barn, our poet's angry herdsmen interrupt their mad pursuit just as soon as a bagpiper strikes up a dance tune (I 285).

As in the *Ring*, the comical situations often end in discomfort for their participants. The fools are trampled by the swine, the harlot is gored (I 185), and the fools and swine are both beaten by the herdsmen with a breaking of bones (I 438). Likewise, one of the swineherds falls into a puddle (I 219) and another falls into a pond (I 224), just as several of Wittenwiler's peasants fall into a brook (v. 248) and one falls into a millstream (v. 6527). There also seems to be a touch of malicious joy in the way the poet, as a child, teased his toothless old (great-) grandmother, even though the text does not seem to make sense as it now stands (II 149-52).

Critics of *CS* have generally agreed that the poem contains some contemporary allusions which were clear to the poet's public.[24] If this is the case, these probably appear chiefly in the names of the herdsmen and dancers that have no particular intrinsic humor; for example, the name Colyne (I 267) could possibly have been a dig at some member of the Campbell clan,[25] and the dancers or masks named in verses I 341 and I 346 may have been nicknames of people known to our poet's public. In this case, the work may even have been an "occasional poem" written to be read at some court or cloister feast, as the Prohemium suggests. However, we may detect some irony here, since the company concerned would not have been quite so exalted. There is romantic irony in the words "this is the caiss of them" (II 59), which Colkelbie says of the three pennies, provided that it means "This is the story about them;" because Colkelbie is a person in the story, not the narrator.

Like the *Ring*, *CS* abounds in literary parody, especially in the adventures of the boar, and perhaps in the courtly behavior of the poultry in Part Three. Among the boar's antagonists we find Meleager, Hercules, Diana, Wade, Eglamour of Artois, the rich king of Sidon, and the dragon of the Holy Land. Meleager was the leader of the Calydonian boar hunt, and Wade was a Germanic hero known in German epics as Wate. This comical juxtaposition of Greek and Nordic hero was probably suggested by Chaucer, who mentioned them both in his tale of Troilus and Criseyde.[26] Both the rich king of Sidon and Sir Eglamour are taken from the courtly romance of Sir Eglamour of Artois.[27] Perhaps the erroneous spelling "Artherus" was influenced by the name "Arthur," since early Arthurian legends

had the king fight a boar. Arthur also fought wild boars, prob-
ably through scribal error, in the "Awntyrs of Arthur."[28]

It is obviously in fun that our poet alludes to these epics;
yet, as in Wittenwiler's case, he is following an ancient clerical
tradition inspired by contempt of and resentment at these
worldly poems that distracted men from contemplating their
salvation.[28a] In other words, these works had more *sensus* than
sententia. The dragon of the Holy Land may allude to some
obscure romance; or else it could have referred to the great red
dragon in Revelation[29] or to any one of several dragons men-
tioned in the Old Testament. Thus it may belong to either
level of comprehension.

Although Part Two appears to be a clever parody on courtly
romances, it probably is not; for, as Janet M. Smith says, it
"seems hardly amusing enough for that."[30] Miss Smith (p. 88)
suggests that this story "seems like some ill-remembered or de-
liberately mangled scrap of French romance," and this is likely
true. However, the names Flannislie and Adria may have been
a later addition added to explain the etymology of *Flandria*.
Because of the Latin spelling (in contrast to *fflanderis* in I 373),
it is probable that this motif stemmed from some scholarly
rather than popular tradition, since learned etymologies had
been a hobby of scholars since the days of Bishop Isidore of
Seville. Flannislie's success at court recalls, in both plot and
language, the success of Arcite-Philostrate at the court of
Theseus in Chaucer's Knight's Tale.[30a]

The humor in Part Three, as in the Nun's Priest's tale, lies
largely in the quaint incongruity of using aristocratic termi-
nology in describing the love-life of the henyard. This episode
also shows the influence of Henryson's "The Cock and the Fox"[31]
and other medieval beast epics often used for didactic purposes.
The reference to the chickens' incest is probably a frivolous
allusion to Scripture.[32]

Moral satire supplies a large part of the humor in *CS*, es-
pecially in the list of fools. It will be seen that these fools include
not only foolish people, but also criminals such as murderers,
robbers, thieves, pickpockets, rapers, and arsonists and also
immoral and indecorous people such as lechers, drinkers, gam-
blers, cheaters, deceivers, hypocrites, flatterers, renegade clerics,
and their ilk. Some of these, such as witches, necromancers,
and scorners, had been conventional villains since the Old
Testament.[33]

Also, as in the *Ring*, there is a good deal of professional satire in the list of fools. Conspicuous among the professional groups pilloried are all kinds of wandering entertainers such as minstrels, jesters, jugglers, bear- and ape-leaders and others who competed with preachers for the attention of the public.[34] Likewise we find professional beggars and certain questionable groups such as hangmen, torturers, userers, harlots, customs-collectors, and tinkers.[35]

However, there also seems to be some satire against perfectly upright yet scorned groups such as weavers, millers, carters, carriers, and ferrymen.[36] This is particularly true of the shepherds, cowherds, and swineherds who drive the fools away; for herdsmen of all kinds, being without property, were held to be "dishonorable."[37] Medieval man drew no aesthetic distinction between shepherds and swineherds as we do today; in fact our pastoral term "swain" originally meant a swineherd.

Like Wittenwiler, the author of *CS* followed many conventions of the peasant-satire tradition, particularly in Part One verses 207 to 298, which express humor similar to that in the contemporary songs "Christis Kirk on the Grene" and "Peblis to the Play."[38] For example, Gilby rides a gray mare, although mares were "dishonorable." To us, or rather to our grandparents, the "old gray mare" suggested the patient animal that brought the loyal village doctor out to the farm in fair weather or foul; but to medieval man it suggested the scorned work-horse and its equally scorned owner.

It was also customary to ridicule the peasants for being sunburned, as Symy is, since sunburn implied field work rather than expensive leisure class sports as it does today. Dietary satire can be detected in the peasant name Haggishead, which represented a typical peasant dish; and clothing satire can be found in the red hose worn by Harry.

Our poet also ridicules the peasants' rustic pursuits, just as Wittenwiler does. Fergy Flitsy has a tar-bucket on his back; and Toby *carior* has a name that suggests hard work and also appears among the fools at the feast (*cariar*, I 58). The shepherds' banner has two crooked ram horns, the cowherds' banner is Crumhorn the cow's tail on a flail, and the swineherds' banner is a spotted pig skin; and these suggest the banners carried in the *Ring*.[39] Like Wittenwiler, our poet also ridicules the boors for using bagpipes.[40]

In view of the satiric intent of these passages, I think that

Gregory the bowman is a tenant rather than an archer,[41] for lack of property was a reason for scorn. Social satire is probably suggested in the name *hoge*, whether it meant Hodge or Hogg. In England, "Hodge was so common a rural name that it became a generic term for a rustic," and Hogg was "a nickname derived from the name of the animal."[42] The name Clarus would have been more suitable for an illustrious knight than for a lowly herdsman.

The ridicule of dancing, on the other hand, was moral rather than social satire; for our poet, like Wittenwiler before him, followed clerical tradition in opposing this sinful pastime.[43] The pagan origin of the shepherds' dances is suggested by the word *gamyn* (I 289), which was sometimes used to denote games derived from ancient fertility rites, and perhaps by the word *muting* (I 385).[44] Likewise, a vestige of the *Lebensrute* may be seen in the birch branch to which the shepherds' banner is attached (I 239).[45]

Although early commentators on *CS* thought the poem displayed rustic customs,[46] this is not the case; and the peasants are scarcely more Scottish than the fools at the feast. Apparently the fools are supposed to be recognized as abstract ideas, as is obvious in the case of two personifications: Sir Usury and Sir Simony (I 105). The author quickly forgets his dancers' social status and lets them affect the dances of the court. In doing so, he is surely recalling mummers' dances, probably those danced at Shrovetide.

According to James Murdoch (p. 70), *haryhurlere* is "the name of a performer in the masque"; and, if this is so, the same may be true of the quaint names preceding it (I 341-46). Mummings or masks, which were popular at the royal court of Scotland, would easily explain the horse-play and the fanciful dances. Anna J. Mill (p. 53) describes a "maske" at the court of Scotland in 1594 in which actors represented three Turks, three Knights of Malta, and three Amazons. There should have been three Moors and also "such beastes as lyon, elephant, hart, unicorne, and the griphon, together with camel, hydre, crocadile, and dragon (carrying their riders)." Such a mask would explain not only the Khan of Tartary, the Sultan of Syria, and Prester John, but also the beasts that fought our famous boar. Perhaps even these fights were inspired directly by a mask and only indirectly by literature.

Such influence is quite apparent in William Dunbar's allegory, "The Dance," which uses similar satire and echoes *CS* in both vocabulary and style.[47] Dunbar's dream occurs "Off Februar the fyiftene nycht" (v. 1) and is in observance of "the feist of Fasternis evin" (v. 8). The Colkelbie author mentions "schriftis evin" only in connection with cock-fighting;[48] but it is safe to assume that he had that date in mind during his entire description of his exotic dances. Dunbar's dance is called for by "Mahoun" (v. 27), who suggests the masks of the Khan of Tartary, the Sultan of Syria, and Prester John.

A comparison of *CS* with the *Ring* will show certain similarities in both form and intent. In regard to form, we see that both works begin with a preface in which the poet explains his end and apologizes for his means and that both are divided into three clearly separated parts. On the other hand, there are also sharp differences. Although ten times as long as the Scottish poem, the *Ring* is far better unified in both composition and style. However heterogeneous his matter, Wittenwiler succeeded in assimilating it and giving it a certain inner coherence; and all of his verses flow in the idiom of the common man. All his matter fits into the framework of a single action, which takes place in one spot and during only a few days. The Colkelbie author, to the contrary, joined his three disparate parts into a single frame by a tour de force, namely by associating them with the three pennies obtained from the sale of Colkelbie's sow, which gives its name to the poem but never appears again after the fifth verse. With his three parts thus linked, he did not bother to give them a common setting in time or place, or even a common style.

Part One, if we may judge by the names of the swine and their owners, should take place in the Scottish Lowlands; yet in Part Two we suddenly discover that the action in Part One, like the action of Part Two, had actually occurred in the region where Paris now stands (II 95). Part One lasts long enough for the little pig to become a famous boar, Part Two lasts long enough for Flannislie to work his way from archer to earl, and Part Three lasts long enough for the godson's gift to increase to a thousand pounds and for him to grow up to be the mightiest man in any realm. In other words, the poet was not overly concerned with the three classic unities. Even the individual episodes are inconsistent. For example, in Part One we learn that Colkelbie is a "man of substance" (v. 20); yet later on in the same episode we discover that he never got but three pennies (v. 248).

With his three parts nominally linked, our poet did not bother to give them a common style. Instead, he wrote his first part in a type of doggerel sometimes called Skeltonics, which seems to have been an offshoot of the alliterative verse once popular in Germanic lands. Although this type of verse had subsequently lost its alliteration and added end-rime, it retained its emphasis upon stressed syllables as the ancient alliterative verse had done. The remainder of his story is written in rather rough heroic couplets of a type sometimes known as rime-royal. As comical as this juxtaposition of styles may appear to us today, it is probable that the author was perfectly serious in writing Parts Two and Three and that he thought them an elegant display of poetic talent.

The Prohemium begins with a dedication in "aureate" language, a stilted style embellished with numerous high-sounding foreign words, mostly from Latin. Many of these words were not actually incorporated into the Scots vernacular and were intelligible only to people familiar with Latin. The basic word-list in Part One is in the vernacular, which was Northern English with its heavy admixture of Scandinavian; but even it was so overlarded with French and Latin terms that it could not claim to be popular in style as was Wittenwiler's *Ring*. Parts Two and Three, at least in their narrative sections, are written in the style and vocabulary of the courtly romances, in which French words abound. Their moralizing sections are more like sermons and take on much of their thought from the Vulgate, expressing this thought in Latin loan-words which may also have been obscure to the common man. Parts Two and Three are both strongly influenced by Chaucer's style and vocabulary.

Typical of the pseudo-Latin words in *CS* are *mortificat* and *vivificat* (written *vinificat* in the MS!) in verses III 66, 67, which are "aureate" constructions like *magnificat* in verse 2 of the Prohemium. They appear in an allusion to John 12:24, "nisi granum frumenti cadens in terram mortuum fuerit." The word *mortificat* is coined from the past participle of *mortificare*; yet it means no more than "dead." It is preferred, however, because it is impressive and also rimes with *vivificat*, which is of similar coinage. The spelling *vinificat* was probably a scribal error; but it could also have been an abstruse allusion to Christ's turning water into wine (John 2:9), since the two passages were often "glossed" similarly.   There are also many interesting loan-translations from Latin, for example "with recent mynd" (P 28) and "recent of memorye," (II 136), which were probably based on *recentis animi,* and "dowble toungit" (I 74), which was probably based on *bilinguis,* as used in Ecclesiasticus 6:3.

So far, no critic of *CS* has made any mention of Scriptural influences, except for casual reference to the self-evident parable of the talents.   This is regrettable; because, as we have seen, the language of the poem can hardly be understood without reference to Scripture.   Even such a minor point as the association of India and Ethiopia (I 332-33) stems from Scriptural tradition based on Esther 1:1.   But such tangible influences are less important than the general influence of Scripture upon the mood of the poem.   Notwithstanding his love of the Book of Proverbs, the author of *CS* seems most influenced by the Book of Ecclesiastes.   Like the author of this book, he seems resigned to the world despite its vanity.   As he tells us (II 164), his great granddame taught him to be neither a wise man nor a fool; and this seems to allude to Eccl. 2:19.   The general tone of *carpe diem* found in Ecclesiastes appears early in his Prohemium (18 ff.) and again at the very end of Part One (489), when he tells us that excessive study is a weariness of the flesh (Eccl. 12:12, "frequensque meditatio carnis adflictio est").

Likewise, no critic has yet tried to fit *CS* into the general course of European literature; and there seems to have been no *Quellenforschung* except for brief mention of Chaucer's influence upon Part Three and the probable French provenance of Part Two.   Most critics treat it like a spontaneous expression of Scottish civilization, whereas it could be better understood as an expression of Western Civilization as such, one that happened to be written by a Scot in his own tongue.   There is a tendency to study provincial literatures in a vacuum as if they were autochthonic, as if they sprang from their own soil pure and unadulterated by foreign admixture.   This is a false procedure at best, and it is most unfortunate in the case of fifteenth-century Scots, which was not a provincial dialect but a literary language adequately serving both Church and State.   The main stream of Western thought was still in Latin; and Middle Scots served just as well as English, French, or German to tap this unlimited source of knowledge and to disseminate it among the people.

Whether or not *CS* meets our present literary standards,

we should remember that its author accomplished his double mission of instructing and entertaining. That he entertained is proved by the many fond references to his poem in later works. That he instructed may be assumed, even if he made his "sentence" a bit "fantastike" to "feill." Surely the mature wisdom of the Hebrew philosophers was culturally superior to the beliefs and attitudes inherited by his public from their Germanic and Keltic forebears. Like Wittenwiler, our poet was one of the many dedicated souls who helped bring the peoples of Europe into the orbit of Western Civilization, into a civilization now so integrated that Near Easterners make no value distinction between a "Frank" from Scotland and a "Frank" from Switzerland. Without such scholars as cultural intermediaries, Scotland would still lie culturally beyond Hadrian's Wall.

NOTES TO EXPOSITION OF "COLKELBIE SOW"

1. ed. John Small (Edinburgh, 1874), P. 65. Other early references are cited by David Laing in his *Select Remains*, ed. John Small (Edinburgh, 1885), Pp. 234-35.
2. David Irving, *The History of Scottish Poetry*, ed. J. A. Carlyle (Edinburgh, 1861), P. 173.
3. Earl F. Guy, *Some Comic and Burlesque Poems in Two Sixteenth Century Scottish Manuscript Anthologies*, Diss. Edinburgh, 1952, unpublished. P. 53. However, Guy finds the poem "mainly didactic in intent with the 'fantasy' but a humorous vehicle for expression" (P. 63a). On the other hand, Bannatyne must not have thought so when he collected the poem, since he put it in part five of his MS, which consists of "tailis and storeis weill discydit," rather than in part one, which concerns "godis gloir and ouir saluatioun."
4. References are to text in *The Bannatyne MS*, ed. W. T. Ritchie (Edinburgh, 1930), IV, Pp. 279-308. P=Prohemium, I=Part One, II=Part Two, III=Part Three.
5. vv. 333-34: "Aut prodesse volunt aut delectare poetae Aut simul et iucunda et idonea dicere vitae." Wittenwiler wishes to mix *ernstleich sach* with *schimpfes sag* (*Ring*, v. 34) and Robert Henryson, a contemporary and compatriot of the Colkelbie poet, wishes "amang ernist to ming ane merry sport," *The Poems of Robert Henryson*, ed. G. G. Smith (Edinburgh, 1908), STS, 58, II, 3, v. 20. The rime-pair *sport-confort* in CS is like *disport-confort* in similar argument in Prologue to Chaucer's *Canterbury Tales* (*The Poetical Works of Chaucer*, ed. F. N. Robinson, Cambridge, 1933, vv. 775-76).
6. For a concise account of this method, see D. W. Robertson & B. F. Huppé, *Piers Plowman and Scriptural Tradition* (Princeton, 1951), Pp. 1-16.
7. Matth. 25:14-30; Luke 19:12-26.
8. Cf. "He that gadryth to tresorye, Be he never so wys ne slye, These thre sorwes shal he haue, hys tresour for to get and saue: the fyrst, ys trauayle yn the wynniyng; the touther, ys drede to kepe that thyng; the thyrd is the most wo, that tyme that he shall parte tharfro," *Handlyng Synne*, ed. F. J. Furnivall (London, 1903), EETS, 119, vv. 6097-6104. Henryson likewise used this argument: "gottyn with grete laboure, Kepit with dred, and tynt is with doloure" (III, 62, vv. 424-25). This idea had been previously expressed by Guillaume de Nor-

mandie in his *Le Besant de Dieu* (ed. Ernst Martin, Halle, 1869, vv. 953-61): "Ca grant paine a en l'auner E grant peor a bien garder E grant dolor quant hom les pert. Dont poez veeir en apert Que ja a eise ne sera Home qui granz richesces a. Car a grant travail sont conquises E a grant pour sont porsises E au perdre a mult grant dolor." Chaucer uses similar argument, but with a different purpose, in his *Troilus and Criseyde* (Robinson, I, vv. 199-201) when he comments on the labor of winning, the doubt of retaining, and the woe of losing one's love.

9. Eccl. 2:11; 5:10-12; 5:13-17. The origin of this topos in Ecclesiastes is suggested by the *Dicta Salomonis*, a Middle Scots paraphrase of that work: (goods do not profit) "bot with gret syne ar voningè and with gret trawaill are kepit and with grete sorow gais away." *Ratis Raving*, ed. R. Girvan (Edinburgh, 1939), P. 184, vv. 269-70.

10. Cf. *bona tua alienus heres accipiet*, attributed to Socrates. E. Wiessner, *Kommentar zu Heinrich Wittenwilers Ring* (Leipzig, 1935), p. 112, with Eccl. 2:18, "Yea, I hated all my labour which I had taken under the sun: because I should leave it unto the man that shall be after me." It is to be noted that the very next verse in Eccl. is echoed in *CS* (II, 164). In his translation of Boethius' *de Consolatione*, Chaucer says that some men are sad because they will have to leave their riches to the "eyres of straunge folk" (Robinson, II, Prosa 4, v. 98). Sebastian Brant expressed the same idea in his *Ship of Fools*: "Der ist eyn narr der samlet gut Vnd hat dar by kein fryd noch mut Vnd weysz nit wem er solches spart So er zum finstren keller fart" ed. Fr. Zarncke (Leipzig, 1854), III, vv. 1-4.

11. *Ring*, v. 2716: *Ein frömder gast der wirt dich erben*. Henryson (III, 62, v. 419) considers it folly to "spare till othir men of gold an hurd"; and William Dunbar, who gives the same argument as found in *CS*, also warns that others will spend your wealth. *The Poems of William Dunbar*, ed. John Small (Edinburgh, 1893), II, 109, vv. 25-32. In popular epics one of the chief incentives to marriage was the desire for an heir.

12. Aquinas quotes Bede as saying, "But money or silver is the preaching of the Gospel and the word of God," *Catena Aurea*, ed. John H. Parker (London, 1841), III, 636. The figurative meaning of this parable should have been intelligible to the masses too, since it was sometimes explained in popular sermons, e.g. in one by Berchthold of Regensburg (ed. Fr. Pfeiffer, Wien, 1862), I, Pp. 11-28. This interpretation may have been influenced by Ecclesiasticus 20:19, *Sapientia absconsa et thesaurus invisus, que utilitas in utrisque?* This proverb was widespread in the Middle Ages, for example in Freidank's *Bescheidenheit*, ed. H. Bezzenberger (Halle, 1872), 147, vv. 9-10.

13. ed. Robinson, VII, vv. 3438-43.

14. P 26; II 171, 232; III 10, 11, 27, 30, 32, 38, 92.

15. Matth. 21:19; Mark 11:13, 21.

16. St. Augustine explained that the fig tree that had leaves but not fruit represented those who had words but not deeds (verba habent, et facta non habent), Migne, *Patrologia Latina*, 36, Tom. IV, pars. I, 264.

17. Henryson uses *conclude* in this sense (II, 117, v. 1565; III, 24, v. 614), and so does Chaucer in his Canon's Yeman's Tale (Robinson, v. 1472). The word *conclusion* is used in the sense of *moralitas* by Chaucer (e.g., in Cook's Prologue, ed. Robinson, I, A, 4328) and also in King James version of Eccl. 12:13. In *CS* the verb *conclude* is used in the sense of terminate in verse I 409; but in verse III 153 it may have either sense, since the poet has just drawn a "conclusion" or *moralitas* in vv. 145-47.

18. Jude I:12, *arbores autumnales, infructuosae, bis mortuae, eradicatae*. King James version has "trees whose fruit withereth, without fruit, twice dead, plucked up by the roots." Cf. Matth. 3:10, "therefore every tree which bringeth not forth good fruit is hewn down, and cast into the fire." A fruitful tree that does not wither appears as an image in Psalms 1:3.

19. Levit. 11:3, "ye shall not eat of them . . . that divide the hoof." Cf. Deut. 14:7. Deut. 14:9, "all that have fins and scales shall ye eat."

20. Migne, *Patrologia Latina*, 108, II 882-88.
21. Cf. "Vincust be carnale sensualitie," (Henryson, II, 59, v. 776).
22. This theory appeared in the *Secreta Secretorum*, the German transla-
    tion of which ran, "in dem ertrich sint steine / da wechset silber unde
    golt," ed. W. Toischer, *Programm des K. K. Staats-Ober-Gymnasiums*
    (Wiener-Neustadt, 1882), vv. 1998-99.
23. In his *de Consolatione Philosophiae*, which was a popular text through-
    out the Middle Ages, Boethius had preached against the folly of
    wishing fame (II, prose VII), and many medieval moralists followed
    his example.   Dunbar (II, 109, v. 20) says, "For warldly honour
    lestis bot a cry." Such doubts about the eternity of fame may have
    echoed Eccl. 9:5, "quia oblivioni tradita est memoria eorum (of the
    dead)." Wittenwiler states that even fame will not help your soul
    (*Ring*, vv. 4119-23).   On the other hand, poets writing for secular
    patrons often followed the heathen Germanic custom of viewing fame
    as a kind of immortality, for example in "der lop wert sô der lîp
    zergat" in Ulrich von Zatzikhoven's *Lanzelet*, v. 8680.
24. "But the poem, although referring in its allusions (as Dr. Leyden has
    observed) to local and temporary circumstances, which are not ob-
    vious at this distance of time, . ." Laing, p. 235.
25. "Colin . . . is a personal name more or less peculiar to the Camp-
    bells," G. F. Black, *The Surnames of Scotland* (New York, 1946),
    p. 161.
26. Robinson, III, v. 614; V, v. 1474.
27. Cf. "In Sydon, that ryche cuntré, There dar no man abyde nor bee For
    drede of a wylde bare," *The Thornton Romances*, ed. J. O. Halliwell-
    Phillips (London, 1844), 135, vv. 349-51.
28. See *Medium Aevum*, XIX (1950), p. 29, and *Scottish Alliterative
    Poems*, ed. F. J. Amours (Edinburgh, 1897), p. 121, vv. 56.
28a. This tradition seems to derive from St. Paul's epistle to Timothy (I
    Tim. 1:4, 4:7; II Tim. 4:4).
29. The "great red dragon" of Rev. 12:3 ff. was later identified with the
    Anti-Christ. It may be the dragon mentioned by Dunbar (II, 273, v.
    27), which was killed by Christ before it could devour His people.
    Two anonymous poems in the *Bannatyne MS*, in which *CS* appears,
    tell how Christ has killed the dragon Lucifer (II, 88, v. 1; 95, v. 7).
30. *The French Background of Middle Scots Literature* (Edinburgh,
    1934), p. 87.
30a. Robinson, I, A, 1422-48.
31. Henryson (II, 243 ff.) uses the names chanteclere (31), partlot (99),
    sprewtok (113), and coppok (134), all of which appear in *CS*.   He
    probably took the first two names from the Nun's Priest's tale; and
    the third may have developed from Sprotinus, the cock in the Latin
    Reinardus (See ed. Mone, Pp. 145 ff.).   Coppok may have been influ-
    enced by the name Coppen in Caxton's translation of *Reynard the Fox*
    (See ed. A. Arber, London, 1878, p. 9). Henpen has continued to be a
    favorite name for hens in Scotland down to the present.   Several of
    the rooster names seem to reflect moral satire tradition.   If so, this
    would not be surprising, since the entire beast epic, starting with
    Aesop and Physiologus, served primarily as comparisons for human
    behavior. According to DOST, *Crawdoun* means a craven or coward.
    Dunbar (II, 13, v. 50) uses this word in his "Flyting" with Kennedy.
    Perhaps it appears in *CS* because of its similarity with "craw" mean-
    ing to crow.   The name Kekilcrousse suggests DOST *crouse*, "Bold,
    confident, jaunty," and Fekillfaw suggests fickle and faw (parti-
    colored), both of which symbolize inconstancy.   The name Lykouris
    suggests "lecherous"; for Henryson (II, 248, 136) states that his cock
    is "licherouss."   Since the usual Scots spelling is with *ch*, the *k* in *CS*
    may have been influenced by the spelling of the word in Chaucer.
32. Romans 2:12 ff., "For as many as have sinned without the law shall
    also perish without the law; and as many as have sinned in the law
    shall be judged by the law."

33. "Thou shalt not suffer a witch to live" Exodus 22:18; necromancer, Deut. 18:11; scorner, Prov. 9:8 et passim.
34. The prejudice against vagrant entertainers expressed itself in legislation. Miss Mill (p. 37) cites a typical law of 1457 ordering the justices to examine "sonaris bardis maisterfull beggaris or fenyeit fulys" and banish or imprison them. Most of these vagabonds are mentioned in Piers Plowman.
35. In Germany hangmen and torturers (Henker, Scharfrichter) were among the dishonorable professions. Although usury was theoretically forbidden to Christians, it was universally practiced at exhorbitant rates, even by the Church. For Wittenwiler's view about it, see Ring, vv. 4943-46.
36. In the Middle Ages weavers were scorned because of their cowardice and poverty. This was particularly true of linen weavers, who were "dishonorable," having no guilds and working under sweat-shop conditions. Note that Lappenhausen was populated mostly by weavers (Ring, v. 7495). For the status of millers, see G. F. Jones, "Chaucer and the Medieval Miller," Modern Language Quarterly, XVI (March, 1955), Pp. 3-15. The cairtar and cariar may just be a cart-driver and porter, who would be uncouth men often tempted to steal. Chaucer introduces a murderous carter in his Nun's Priest's tale (B 42 49); and one of the herdsmen in CS is named Thoby carior (I 222). On the other hand, considering the company they keep, these worthies may be a card-player (DOST, carter n2) and a jugglr, provided J. B. Murdoch (A Glossary to the Bannatyne MS, Hunterian Club, 1894) is right in glossing caryare that way. The fariar could be a blacksmith; but it is more probably a ferryman (Cf. Ger. Ferge), since ferrymen, like millers, were indispensible and could set their own prices.
37. Cf. "Schäfer und Schinder—Geschwisterkinder." Shepherds were accused of stealing the sheep entrusted to them and blaming it on the wolves.
38. See G. F. Jones, "Christis Kirk, Peblis to the Play, and the German Peasant Brawl," PMLA, 58 (1953), Pp. 1101-25, also Ring Exp. #89 ff.
39. The Torenhofers also carry a cow's tail as a standard (Ring, v. 7975). The Switzers' banner bears a milk-pail (v. 7965), the Lappenhausers have a spool and tailor shears (v. 8582), and the Nissingers have an anvil and skinning knife (v. 8615).
40. CS, I 285. See G. F. Jones, "Wittenwiler's Becki and the Medieval Bagpipe," JEGP, 48 (April, 1949), Pp. 209-28.
41. DOST Bowman, n2 A man having charge of, or a tenant occupying a "bow." Cf. MHG bûman.
42. Black, Pp. 360, 361. However, it should be remembered that hog could refer to the young of various animals, including sheep.
43. See Jones, "Christis Kirk . . ." Pp. 1104-07.
44. Cf. "As foles that gedirs til a somere gamen," in Richard Rolle of Hampole's Psalter, ed. H. R. Bramley (Oxford, 1884), XVI, 12. I can find no satisfactory explanation of muting. Perhaps it is a corruption or variant of "meeting" (Cf. Northumbrian moeta). On the other hand it might be based on a French or Vulgar Latin derivative of mûtus (mute), which would fit the meaning of pantomime.
45. See Jones, "Christis Kirk . . ." Pp. 1108-09 and Ring Exp. #13.
46. Robert Pitcairn believed that the poem "throws much light on the manners and rustic festivities of the Scottish peasantry during a very early period. From the minuteness of its description, it is also highly illustrative of the music, dances, and musical instruments in common use in Scotland in the Fifteenth Century." Cited, apparently with agreement, by Laing, Pp. 235-36. Guy (p. 62) questions this realism.
47. Dunbar, II, p. 117.
48. III 124. This Shrove-Tuesday sport of cockfighting lasted until modern times. British Calendar Customs, Scotland, ed. M. M. Banks (London, 1937), I, 11-13.

CONTROVERSIAL POINTS IN "COLKELBIE SOW"

Since Dr. Guy's glossary largely duplicates mine, this list includes only those points wherein our interpretations differ.

Prohemium

3. DOST *curious*, a.1.d. Careful of one's person; refined.
13. *Ermy deidis* may mean "deeds of arms," since the term "dedes of armys" was a literary commonplace at the time, as in *Sir Eglamour* (v. 10 *et passim*). Possibly the spelling here was influenced by Latin *inermis*. However, *ermy* may have been related to NED *Arm*, miserable, unhappy. Cf. verb *erme*, "grieve, be sad" in Chaucer's Book of the Duchess, v. 80.
21. NED *wit* vb.3, find out, ask. Cf. I 108.
22. DOST *fall* v.3, to become involved in.
28. *recent mind*, loan-trans. from *recentis animi*.
    DOST *e* n³, *to have e*, to have in regard or consideration, to pay heed.
35. *at all* DOST *all*, B.n.c. in all respects, altogether.
41. NED *lack* 2 "Sc. . . . reproach, shame." As in Heryson III, 117 v. 1565; 24 v. 614.
44. *conclude* See note 17 to *CS Exp*.
45. NED *feel* v.8, to perceive mentally, become aware of.

Part One

1. *caiss*. Our author often uses this word, which meant "incident" or "occurrence" (Latin *casus*), in the sense of story or tale. See I 38, 114, 194, 437, 471, 487; II 59, *et passim*.
3. The spellings "cokkelbe" (I 3), "kolkelbe" (I 44), "Cokkelby" (II 51), and "Colkelby" (II 95) suggest that the name could have been a corruption of, or influenced by, the name Rokebye, since *R* and *K* were often written similarly. In a contemporary farce, "The Felon Sow and the Freres of Richmonde," the sow was donated by a certain Raphe of Rokebye, *History of Craven*, ed. T. D. Whitaker (London, 1878), P.568. Otherwise the name "Cokkelbe" may just suggest the word "cuckold." Cf. Cuckow, I 267.
5. NED *ho* Int.²sb.³B. sb. cessation, halt, pause. Cf. *withouten ho*, without stopping.
51. NED *cheer*, sb.6. conc., . . . fare, provisions, viands, food.
53. *perverst*. Before the days of psychoanalysis, "perverted" meant about the opposite of "converted." A favorite word in Proverbs.
56. *milygant*. NED cites this verse, but gives no meaning. Murdoch ventures "a scoundrel, deceiver," but probably through intuition. Guy gives no solution.
63. Guy follows DOST, which glosses *forfarn* from this passage as "undone, like to perish," as in *forfairn*, "wasted" (Dunbar, II, 134 v. 14). Since this does not fit our context, I conjecture a word equivalent to German *herverlaufen* (*Ring*, v. 456) or Middle Scots *forloppin* (Dunbar, II, 139, v. 7), meaning vagrant or vagabond. In 1551 the Scottish Parliament passed a law prohibiting hawkers and hunters from trespassing on their neighbors' fields (note to Dunbar, I, 149 v. 63). Perhaps *forfarn* acquired a new and pejorative *Lehnbedeutung* because its present tense *forfair* resembled French *forfaire*, to commit a fault.
67. *custumar* NED *customer*, 4 b., "a common woman, prostitute." However, it is more probably a tax-collector, publicans having been associated with sinners since the time of Jesus.
71. Guy's emendation to *lour* is unnecessary. These fools first flourished, then bore no fruit. See Prohemium v. 26.
74. *dowble toungit*, loan-translation from *bilinguis*, as in Ecclesiasticus 6:1.
77. NED *tyrant* 4.b. . . . . a ruffian, a desperado; a villain.
81. *lave*. This may be NED *lave* sb¹, "relict, widow," since widows were proverbially more lecherous than lasses. Guy follows Laing in emending to mean lass.

82. NED *lour* sb.² slang. Money. Guy says "lure, that which entices."
100. DOST *dapill*, a. dapple-grey. Perhaps influenced by Prov. 16:31, "The hoary head is a crown of glory, if it be found in the way of righteousness."
113. NED *menseless*, destitute of propriety, decorum, or seemliness.
120. DOST *common* v. 3.b. or 4.
144. NED *ruin* sb.I.1.b. "The act (of a person) falling to the ground." Guy says "ruin."
162. *wrotok*. Related to NED *wroot* s.b. "the snout of a swine," and NED *wroot* vb, "to root like a swine." Cf. the diminutive suffix "ock" in the names of chickens in Part Three.
    writhneb, Twisted Nose. See NED *writhen*. Cf. writhneck and wryneck. NED *neb*, 2. The nose; the snout of an animal.
163. DOST *eb*, n. "the part of the beach left bare at the ebb." Probably an allusion to swine's practise of hunting shell fish on the tidal flats. Cf. I 166. "Being near the Sea-cost, they will feed on all manner of shel-fish." *The Gentleman's Recreation* (London, 1674), P. 36.
164. *hoglyn*. Used by giant as term of endearment for hog killed by Eglamour (v. 458).
166. Baymell, perhaps related to "bayer à la mamelle." See NED *bay* v.³
168. *milhill*, possibly allusion to miller's dishonesty. See *Ring*, Exp. #120.
170. NED *suddle*, a. filthy. Cf. German *besudeln*.
    NED *sordes*, 1. dirt, filth; foul or feculent matter . . .
174. *gorot*. Murdoch gives "grisly," but does not document.
191. DOST *defoul*, 1. trample under foot. Cf. *defoulit* in Matth. 5:13; 7:6 in *New Testament in Scots*, ed. T. G. Law (Edinburgh, 1903), I, P. 28, where King James version has "trodden under foot," "trample under foot."
193. *skerrit*. Could be "separated" from A. S. *scearan*.
201. *seilis*. Professor A. J. Aitken of Edinburgh, who was kind enough to read my proofs and make many valuable suggestions, proposes emendation *feilis*. This would give, "Perceive how the fools behave and look at that accursed company!" which would fit the context better.
204. NED *match*, v. 4. . . . to place in conflict with, to pit against.
205. *kachit*. Guy says "chased," as in DOST *cache*, v.I,1 tr. I prefer, "caught," as in DOST *cache*, v.³, 1 tr.
208. *stock hornis*, "A wind instrument formerly used in Scotland," NED *stock*, s.b.² NED *stoutly*, 5.
214. NED *Lowrie*, 2. crafty person, a "fox"; a hypocrite.
234. NED *Ladrone*, rogue, blackguard (L. latrôn-em).
235. *hundroun*. Roun, "an r-form of Romance -oon, used chiefly in English substantives which indicate despicable individuals." E. Westergaard, *Studies in Prefixes and Suffixes in Middle Scottish*, (Oxford, 1924), P. 100.
242. DOST *doit*, copper coin of small value, to act foolishly, dote.
264. Crumhorne is the name of the cow, not of the standard-bearer as Guy states (p. 226). Cf. the cow with the crumpled horn in "The House that Jack built." Cf. NED *Cromone*. See note 39 to *CS Exp.*
266. *besyd*. The meaning beside is just as good as besides, as proposed by Guy (p. 317).
274. *faw*. Apparently an error for *saw*, a scribal slip caused by *faw* a few lines further down. Guy glosses it as "varigated, variously colored," which would not fit the context.
284. NED *clype*, an ugly ill-shaped fellow.
286. DOST *belly-brace*, 1. a bellyband for a horse.
    DOST *belly*, 5d. glutton.
287. *samyn*. I think this means *same*, as in I 42, II 177, III 99. Guy thinks it is a name.
295. NED *swanky*, sb.1, "a smart, active, strapping young fellow." In spite of this complimentary interpretation in NED, it will be noted that all examples given suggest rustics, including a swineherd.

296. *copyn cull.* Probably a play on "Cope and Cowl," a friar. See DOST *cull* 2.
306. Probably the name of an aubade. Cf. *Ring*, vv. 7100-07.
308. NED *let* v[15], "abandon, forsake." Perhaps an abandoned maiden's complaint.
314. Cf. Simones sonnes of Quhynfell (Dunbar II 193 v. 29). "Whinefell, part of Inglewood Forest, the happy hunting ground of several legendary poachers." (*Ibid.*, I, cclix).
317. *dress* could mean either to dress or to betake oneself. Cf. "The wolf hes drest him to his den" (Dunbar II 138 v. 67) and "to dance he did him dress" (II 120 v. 67).
318. *Orliance*, a dance from Orléans.
319. NED *rusty*, a 4 a, lacking polish or refinement.
   NED lists no example of *bully* as early as *CS*. It originally meant sweetheart or darling, later a swash-buckler.
   bek. It is possible that this is a bagpipe, which would explain why every note is in another's neck. See G. F. Jones, "Wittenwiler's *Becki* and the Medieval Bagpipe," *JEGP*, 48 (1949), Pp. 209-28.
324. *Naverne*, Navarre, but probably influenced by Auvergne.
347. *haryhurlere.* See *CS Exp.* p. 235. Guy believes this a dance.
348. *Custy.* Probably the same as *cust* in v. I 405, which means a "low fellow" (DOST).
350. *knowknois, kynnis.* Murdoch interprets these as "knock knees" and "foundling, bastard," but probably by conjecture. Guy finds no solution.
   DOST *culroun*, "A base person, a rascal." This may be a corruption of "Cullion" (Westergaard, P. 100). See note to v. 235 above.
354. *howis.* See *CS Exp.* P. 234. Guy (P. 367) says, "*houghs*, back part of thigh," but this does not fit context.
370. *yrland.* Probably included Scottish Highlands, since the Lowlanders called the Highlanders "Erschemen." See Dunbar II 121 v. 113; 15 v. 107.
371-81. Guy gives up on *breband, hanyngo, Dittmer, baywer, land, Malestrand,* and *rerall,* which I identify as Brabant, Hainault (German Hennegau), Dittmarsch, Bavaria (Bayern), Lund, Marstrand, and Reval. Since the Hanseatic cities are listed "all thair boindis thame by" (v. 380), it is possible that *Lubwick land* means Lübeck and its adjacent territory, as in the term Baselland. However, *land* is more likely an error for the Swedish city of Lund, where the Hansa kept a depot. The author or the scribe also seemed ignorant of Marstrand and Reval, both of which were important to the Hansa.
385. *muting.* See note 44 to *CS Exp.* Guy gives "noisy debate," which does not fit the context.
398. *practit.* Possibly an error for *practik*, knowledge. See Henryson II 76 v. 1006, *et passim.*
412. NED *samen*, adv. "together." Unless *the* stands for "they," it could be a vestige of an old Germanic form represented by Swedish *tilsamman* and German *zusammen.*
419. *he was heir.* I merely conjecture. Guy suggests emendation.
420. *cheir.* Spirits, courage, as in Henryson II 26 v. 340.
428. DOST *gy*, v. tr. to guide.
433. DOST *be prep.* 3 c.
475. NED *touch*, sb.16, a brief statement or narration.
Part Two
 1. *Off*, for. Cf. "Obey and thank thi god off all" (Henryson III 126 v. 8).
 8. NED *thrall*, sb[2], a space of time, a while.
 18. *carlage.* Either "this rough man" or "this peasant man." In the "Lay of Rig' in the *Poetic Edda*, the husbandman Carl is between the noble Jarl and the serf Thrall.
 29. *honest.* In the fifteenth century the word "honest," like German *ehrlich*, referred more to social position than to personal integrity. See *Ring Exp.* #162 ff.

60. *thre.* As the verse now stands, it means, "I value three poor pennies equally." (See Dost *hald,* v. 15 b). However, since this would be meaningless, I suggest emending *Thre* to *Thir* (these), which would then refer to the second and third pennies, both of which Colkelbie still has (Cf. *thir two,* II 229). For "the same," see note to I 412 above.
80. DOST *copy,* v.1. to note, observe.
93. NED *prevail* 1. to become very strong.
101. *craft.* Possibly "skill," or else "croft." Perhaps no one had a farm for raising grain?
109. *continue,* from Latin *continuare,* a legal term meaning to hand down.
138. I think *heild* is preterite of *haldan.* Guy believes it a variant of *eild.*
257. NED *ken* v¹I,2. to teach one something.

Part Three

11. *spreid,* grow (Henryson II 181 v. 2431).
53. DOST *abuse* v.4. to disuse, discontinue the use of.
60. NED *cast* v.44, intend.
64. NED *guide* v.4.b, manage.
67, 68. mortificat, vivificat. See *CS Exp.* p. 237.
70. NED *surprise* v 3, to do violence, to injure, outrage; to oppress.
72. NED *store* sb.2, livestock. *fie,* not only cattle, but other livestock as well. Cf. *fe,* sheep (Henryson III 90 v. 2).
74. NED *big* a,I,b. "powerful in resources, rich, wealthy." Cf. *big,* "of good standing, full of resources" (Henryson II 203 v. 2733).
102. *detis.* Guy's proposed emendations are unnecessary. See *CS Exp.* p. 241, note 32.
126. NED *bield,* v.2, intr. "to be bold." Guy (p.315) finds no solution.
153. *quhite.* Cf. "flatteraris with pleasand wordis quhyte" (Henryson II 45 v. 593) and "With fenyeit wirdis quhyte" (Dunbar II 118 v. 48). Chaucer also uses "wordes whyte" in this sense. See NED *white,*a, 10, "fair-seeming, specious, plausible." In all these cases the word has a derogatory sense. Perhaps our author was being facetious in saying that he would now submit himself to his hearers' specious correction, whereas in his Prohemium he had submitted to their "discreit correctioun" (v.23). Possibly the word "white' did not have to have a bad connotation. In any case, I do not agree with Guy (p.408) that it means "quite."

CPSIA information can be obtained
at www.ICGtesting.com
Printed in the USA
LVHW031309300621
691479LV00005B/365

9 780807 880180